PROTECTING YOUR FAMILY

WITH LONG TERM CARE INSURANCE

Phyllis Shelton

"We're likely to live longer, but can we afford to live comfortable? The answer is yes—for your parents and yourself—if you plan appropriately. Phyllis Shelton's advice about long term care planning can make all the difference for your entire family."

Terry Savage, Chicago Sun-Times *Financial Columnist and author of* **The Savage Truth on Money**

"With her years of experience and wisdom, Phyllis helps us to understand how health care reform and new economic realities are reshaping the world of long term care while offering sage advice on available options to protect ourselves and our families."

Chris Perna, CEO, Eden Alternative

"The name Phyllis Shelton is synonymous with long-term care education. Who better to guide you through the shoals of LTC planning in this time of rapid change and elevated risk?"

Steve Moses, President, Center for Long-Term Care Reform

"If you think you have taken appropriate measures to protect yourself from the personal and financial tsunamis with regard to long term care or you haven't paid the slightest amount of attention to this issue, 'Murphy' is always waiting around the corner to pull the rug out from under you when you least expect it. Phyllis Shelton may be the person who can protect you from 'Murphy'. But don't take my word for it, read Phyllis Shelton's newest book."

Irwin Cohen, Top of the Table Million Dollar Round Table Member, Illinois

"Medicare, Medicaid, 'stand-alone' long term care insurance, 'hybrids', caregivers, emotion-packed family considerations---if you want to make sense out of consumer chaos before a loved one encounters a long term care event, you need to read Phyllis Shelton's book."

Brian Ashe, Past President, Million Dollar Round Table, Illinois

"Phyllis Shelton is an institution in the field of long-term care insurance. You can count on her new book being accurate, complete, and up to date."

Robert Grella, 50 year insurance veteran and owner of 25 year old financial services firm, Washington

"Phyllis took me from ground zero in knowledge to a place where I am comfortable with my future. She was amazing walking me through the process, answering my many questions, recommending what I needed for my peace of mind."

Chuck Brown, client, Illinois

"Phyllis Shelton made the daunting task of understanding and obtaining LTCI an actual pleasure. Who can ever say that about buying an insurance policy! But what stands out to me most was her willingness to spend the time needed to educate me as thoroughly as I needed and all the while showing patience and the utmost courtesy. She is going to make a real difference in many people's lives down the road."

Liz Bounds, client, Oregon

"Phyllis Shelton is the most informed person I know about long-term care planning and she advocates for her clients to get the best health care possible. I was just involved in a head-on collision and am so glad I listened to her about buying LTC insurance when I was younger."

Blythe Bieging, PhD, RN, client, Maryland

"In 1997, Phyllis Shelton sold us an excellent long term care insurance policy on my wife. She recommended benefits that we had not even thought about. In 2012, we filed a claim with the insurance company and Phyllis was there every step of the way."

Russell Polston, client, Tennessee

PROTECTING YOUR FAMILY

WITH LONG TERM CARE INSURANCE

A Complete Guide to Long Term Care Planning
including traditional and hybrid policies and alternative funding options

PHYLLIS SHELTON

Protecting Your Family with Long-Term Care Insurance

Published by:

LTCi Publishing

108 Rhoades Lane

Hendersonville, TN 37075-8084

www.PhyllisShelton.com

This book is available at special quantity discounts for training, promotion and educational use by contacting the Publisher. For more information contact LTCi Publishing at 888-400-1118.

This book is designed to provide accurate and authoritative information in regard to the subject matter covered and is read with the understanding that the publisher and/ or the author accept no responsibility or liability whatsoever with regard to errors or misinterpretation of the information contained within this book. Readers should not rely on this publication for legal or tax advice and should seek the services or a competent professional for such matters.

ISBN 978-0-615-76752-9

Printed in the United States of America

Dedication and Thanks

"My God shall supply all your need according to His riches in glory by Christ Jesus."

— Philippians 4:19

"Let each of you look out not only for his own interests, but also for the interests of others.

— Philippians 2:4

"Let no one seek his own, but each one the other's well-being."

— I Corinthians 10:24

"He who dwells in the secret place of the Most High shall abide under the shadow of the Almighty. I will say of the Lord, 'He is my refuge and my fortress; my God, in Him I will trust."

— Psalms 91: 1, 2

There wasn't supposed to be another book. This sentence starts the dedication to each new book, but they keep coming out of me. This one is the most precious of all because I see my beloved long-term care insurance industry changing so rapidly and I want to get this information out to help as many people as possible. It is my sincere hope that readers of this book will share it freely with the people they love as the window is inexorably closing on the choices available to plan for long-term care. I believe with all my heart that planning for long-term care is synonymous with retaining dignity and independence as we age. I'd like to thank my husband Bill for not allowing me to rest until I did this book. He is still the wind beneath my wings. Thanks and hugs go to our four-legged children Jackson and Jed Clampett (our hunter) for the endless hours they spent encouraging me with light snoring at my feet. Many kudos go to my wonderful employees Lawrence Vivenzio and Pennye Smith for helping me with the research. Words cannot express how grateful I am to Bob Bubnis who is more of a coach than a layout artist when he produces a book with me. The multi-generational family of Margaret Weaver is displayed beautifully on the cover designed by our graphic artist T.J. Green with the permission of the family and photographer, Thia Konig. Most of all, I thank my God who taught me all things and brought all things to my remembrance as He inspired every word of this publication. (John 14:26)

Other books by Phyllis Shelton

Long-Term Care: Your Financial Planning Guide (15 editions 1991 – 2008)

Phyllis Shelton's WORKSITE Long-Term Care Insurance TOOLBOX (2011)

The ABCs of Long-Term Care Insurance (2011, updated 2012, 2013)

His Harvest, a tribute to Oral Roberts, (2010, Yorkshire Publishing)

TABLE OF CONTENTS

A Special Dedication

My husband Bill, the wind beneath my wings

I also dedicate this book to Suze Orman. We all have a waitress inside of us who dreams of being a world-renowned figure. I'm proud to say I know someone who actually did it. Congratulations Suze, and thanks for inspiring all of us!

PHYLLIS SHELTON

MARCH 1, 2013

INTRODUCTION

Another book about long-term care insurance? Really?

Yes, because it's not just another book. It's the most honest, consumer-oriented book you will ever read on this topic. I've spent a quarter of a century as a national LTC insurance consultant for insurance companies, banks, credit unions, media personalities, attorneys, doctors, home care and nursing facility providers, politicians, state governments and yes, even the federal government, and over 75,000 insurance professionals have gone through my live or web-based training. Along the way, I've talked with thousands of consumers. (That's my favorite thing to do, and some of them you will meet in this book.) The best part about this story is that I don't have a boss. That's right. I don't work for anyone which means no one tells me what I can say or can't say. Get it? Now you know the real reason you want to read this book…to really learn how to take care of your family by planning for long-term care with long-term care insurance.

You're not sure LTC insurance is the best solution for you? No problem. After you read this book, you will know enough to make an informed decision and I will have done my job. However, I caution you to not procrastinate on this decision. The advice in this book has a short shelf life as the long-term care insurance market is changing rapidly. And you, dear friend, could become uninsurable with your next heartbeat. I know this after surviving an automobile accident earlier this year that totaled both cars when a 77 year old lady decided to go 10 mph on the interstate to keep from running out of gas!

But first, we all have to be on the same page…not just this page, but on the issue of long-term care.

A Very Important Preface and What This Book Will Cover

That means don't even think about skipping this section.

Without proper planning, long-term care can be one of the most traumatic experiences a family will ever face and is the one major health expense for which nearly all Americans are uninsured.[1] If you are responsible for someone else 24/7, how do you take care of other family members? How do you take care of yourself? If you can't afford to hire caregivers at $6000+ a month, this is exactly the situation you find yourself in. If historical trends continue, this cost could **quadruple** in the next 30 years.[2] Did your financial planner tell you that in your annual review?

Most people are never in a nursing home. A bright spot. Less than 15% of people who need long-term care receive it in a nursing home.[3] To back this up, the Centers for Disease Control and Prevention reports that only 5% of Medicare enrollees are in a nursing home.[4] The not-so-bright-spot is what happens to the family member who will give up a life to take care of you. Of course, that person could be YOU if you become the caregiver, not the care recipient.

LTC happens to people of all ages. If you are going to argue the point, please guarantee me that you or someone else you know won't be hit by a drunk driver in the next 24 hours.

LTC is not covered by health insurance or Medicare or disability insurance. Health insurance and Medicare pay for short-term care…a few weeks or a couple of months if we're lucky. Disability insurance replaces part of our income if we become disabled so we can pay our bills, plus it ends at age 65. Not a solution.

LTC is covered by Medicaid if you spend most of your money first unless you buy the kind of LTC insurance policy that allows you to keep your assets equal to the benefits paid out – no limit. The Partnership for Long-Term Care is one of the most exciting recent developments in long-term care financing and can save you hundreds of thousands of dollars.

Odds are very high you will need LTC. This statement is especially true for baby boomers who have worked out and really tried to take care of themselves. We are the people who will wear out *v e r y s l o w l y* and need a lot of help getting around in our twilight years.

(Tip: most men aren't killed at age 95 by a jealous husband.)

If you own homeowners insurance, you are not too wealthy to own long-term care insurance. The largest open claims at the end of 2011 were at $1.2 million (male) and $1.7 million (female). "Open" means not closed…**still going.** The largest closed claim to date exceeded $3 million. [5]

Let me lay it out for you. We're talking about something that is:

- very expensive,
- very likely to happen, especially if you are part of a couple; and
- not covered by anything else without spending most of your

money first unless you buy a long-term care insurance (LTCI) policy that protects your assets.

Can you think of any reason you wouldn't want to consider LTC insurance if you could find an affordable way to do so? Just like there are a multitude of ways to get around in this country (ever hear of four-wheel bikes? They're becoming all the rage!), there are many creative and exciting ways to plan for long-term care. Long-term care insurance is one of them, but it comes in many shapes and sizes.

Here are the decisions you need to make to find out what long-term care insurance costs for you:

1. Where would you like to receive care?
2. How much of the bill do you want the insurance company to pay?
3. How do you want to receive the money?
   a. Cash
   b. Hybrid cash/reimbursement
   c. Reimbursement
      i. Traditional LTCI policy
      ii. Combination life/LTC
      iii. Combination annuity/LTC
4. How long do you want to wait before benefits start?
5. What do you want to do about inflation?
6. How long or how much do you want the insurance company to pay?
7. Do you want your premium to be returned to a beneficiary if you die without needing long-term care?

If you are part of a couple, you will need to sit down with your spouse or partner and make these decisions. And don't worry if you don't understand all these terms. I will explain them to you in Chapter Three.

Do you want to explore alternative ways to pay for LTC? Sometimes long-term care insurance isn't the best solution for funding long-term care, or it may be one of several funding sources. You may have an older policy that has not kept up with inflation or doesn't pay enough home care or isn't flexible enough to pay for future services. Or maybe you can't qualify for an insurance policy for medical reasons. Or maybe you need help finding the money to pay the premium. We will discuss each of the following alternate funding mechanisms and how one or more of them may be an appropriate path for you to pursue.

- Continuing Care Retirement Community (CCRC)
- Life settlement (sell your life insurance policy)
- Accelerate the death benefit of a life insurance policy to pay for LTC
- Critical illness insurance
- Reverse mortgage
- VA benefits
- Medicaid

As you can see, this book is designed to give you a myriad of workable ideas based on my first-hand knowledge of how they work. You won't like all of these ideas but hopefully at least one will be helpful, which reminds me of some of the best advice I ever received from my father.

Dad was born in 1928 in East Tennessee and grew up quickly under the stern hand of my grandfather who believed in working the farm from dawn to dusk and running a milk route in the wee hours of the morning. Dad with his down-to-earth mannerisms and full head of glorious white hair was a mixture of Andy Griffith and Buddy Ebsen.

Once when I was scheduled to follow Bob Dole as a main platform speaker for a large insurance organization, I called my dad the night before to tell him how nervous I was about speaking in front of 1200 people the next day.

"Do you know your lesson?" he queried.

"Well, yes Daddy. I do know my lesson."

"And there's supposed to be 1200 people there?"

"That's what they tell me and that's why I'm so scared!"

"Well, if you know your lesson and there's that many people there, there's bound to be at least one person who likes what you have to say."

With that matter-of-fact advice, he went on to talk about something else much more important.

Chapter One:

IT'S NOT ALL ABOUT YOU

People think buying long-term care insurance is a personal decision. It's not. The decision you make to buy or not buy long-term care insurance will impact your family – usually the people you love the most – AND your country.

I don't expect you to accept this at face value, so let's lay the groundwork.

WHAT is Long-Term Care (LTC)?

Long-term care is being expected to need the help of another person for at least three months with at least two basic living activities like bathing, dressing, eating, toileting, continence, or simply moving from a bed to a chair. Care is also considered long-term when someone needs constant supervision due to a cognitive impairment like Alzheimer's or Parkinson's disease. Either situation can wear a caregiver out.

My grandfather was blind, an insulin-dependent diabetic, and my best friend. My mother was a nurse. She worked nights while my father could be with us so she could care for my best friend ten years in our home, with my help. I didn't give him insulin, plan his special diet or bathe or dress him. But I gave him hours of my time. We had to be quiet while she slept, so I read him stories, fetched many glasses of water and led him to the bathroom. Sometimes I just crawled up on his lap to let him make whatever problem I had go away. As I grew older, his room was my first stop when I got home.

My best friend went to a nursing home when I was 12. I knew my mother was struggling between giving him her best and caring for me and my three-year-old brother. She was also working double shifts at the hospital for extra money. When he passed away two years later, I was devastated.

My mother lost a two-year battle with cancer at age 54. I thought about my best friend and finally realized that what was a normal lifestyle for me as a child must have been a tremendous sacrifice for her.

WHY do people need LTC?

- Could people need help with taking a bath, getting dressed and moving from bed to chair after an automobile accident in which they broke both legs and a hip? Could you?
- Could someone need this kind of help after falling on the ice and hitting her head? Could you?
- Could a water skier need this kind of help after hitting a buoy? *(That was my banker...his face had to be wired back together.)* Did you know that Denver, Colorado is one of the top places in the country for rehabilitation facilities, mainly due to snow skiing accidents? Could this be you?
- Could a brain tumor patient need this kind of care? *(That was my friend Sandy who did get better after six months.)* Could you?
- Could someone fall off a horse, become a quadriplegic and need this kind of care for the last ten years of his life? Could you?
- Could a former president of the United States need constant supervision for Alzheimer's the last ten years of his life? Could you?

The reasons for needing help with daily living activities are many. A significant number of Americans need constant caregiving well beyond what health insurance will pay due to vehicle or sporting accidents or disabling conditions like stroke, Lou Gehrig's disease, aneurysm, brain tumor or early onset Alzheimer's or Parkinson's disease.

WHEN do people need it?

The first example above was my 19 year old cousin after an automobile accident. Her mother had to take a six-month leave of absence from her job to get this girl back on her feet.

A third of Americans who are impaired enough to collect benefits from a long-term care insurance policy are under age 65.[1]

A study conducted by the independent non-profit Council for Disability Awareness found that a healthy 35-year-old office worker has a 24% (female) or 21% (male) chance of becoming disabled for 3 months or longer. This article went on to say that "three times as many disabling injuries occur off the job as on the job, and are therefore not covered by workers' compensation".[2]

While strokes still happen more frequently to older people, the stroke rate is rising dramatically among younger Americans. One out of four Americans who have a stroke each year is under age 65.[3] For every 10,000 hospitalizations in 1994-95 compared with 2006-07, strokes increased:[4]

- 51 percent in males 15 to 34 years old
- 17 percent in females 15 to 34

- 47 percent in males 35 to 44
- 36 percent in females 35 to 44

Long-term care needs at younger ages are on the rise... especially strokes... perhaps influenced by lifestyle choices that lead to diabetes, obesity and even depression.

> Allison, a nurse who coordinates stroke care at Forsyth Medical Center in Winston-Salem, North Carolina said her hospital also is seeing more strokes in younger people with risk factors such as smoking, obesity, high blood pressure, alcohol overuse and diabetes. "I'd say at least half of our population (of stroke patients) is in their 40s or early 50s," she said, "and devastating strokes, too." [5]

Lifestyle Choices

As much as we like to think that we have healthier lifestyles, obesity is rampant in America. The Centers for Disease Control and Prevention reports that one third of Americans are overweight and one third obese. (People are considered obese if they have a body mass index (BMI) of 30 or higher, roughly 30 or more pounds over a healthy weight.)[6] If that weren't bad enough, the report "F as in Fat" projects that half of Americans will be obese by 2030![7] The risk of stroke is exacerbated when obesity is combined with one or more health problems such as high blood pressure or high cholesterol or lifestyle choices such as smoking or lack of exercise.

Diabetes affects nearly 26 million Americans of all ages and 79 million people have what doctors call "prediabetes". A Society of Actuaries report says diabetes is costing $116 billion annually in direct medical expenses, and the most prevalent reason for so many people developing it is weight gain. [8] The report says that excess weight and obesity together are costing the nation $300 billion annually. [9] A long-term care need can easily develop due to impaired mobility caused by excess weight overloading weight-bearing joints like knees and hips.

Then sometimes, things just happen for no good reason.

A 49 year old Blue Cross Blue Shield of Tennessee employee called me to help her file a long-term care insurance claim. She said she had broken her ankle and two weeks after getting the bone set, she suffered a pulmonary embolism, with a blood clot in each lung. She almost died. She spent several weeks in a skilled nursing facility, then began having home health care. She collected $3000 from the long-term care insurance carrier for her care in the fourth month, during which she recovered.

WHERE do people need it?

Most people are never in a nursing home as you read in the "not to be skipped" preface of this book. Claims experience collected from the major insurance carriers shows that only 20 percent of home care claims evolve into an assisted living facility or a nursing home. [10]

One carrier with over 30 years claims paying experience that pays out $3.4 million a day reports these characteristics: [11]

- 67% of claims from 2007-2009 were for home care; 20% assisted living; only 13% nursing home care

- the youngest claimant being age 32 and the oldest 103
- Largest single claim $1 million
- Top three diagnoses for claims that last more than a year: dementia, cardiovascular and musculoskeletal
- Average duration of claim that lasts more than a year: 3.8 years

Data like this supports the two main messages of the long-term care insurance story:

- a. care can be needed at any age; and
- b. very little care is in a nursing home.

In fact, **long-term care insurance may be the only thing that keeps people out of a nursing home** or certainly makes it the care option of last resort.

HOW much does it cost?

Long-term care is very expensive. Ten hours of home care or semi-private care in a nursing facility averages: [12]

- $222 a day
- $6,750 a month
- $81,000 a year

The chart below shows how long $500,000 would last with only one person needing care at $75,000 a year, assuming a 4% investment yield on savings after tax:

Year	Assets at Start of Year	Income Needs	LTC Expense	Investment Yield	Assets at End of Year
1	$500,000	$60,000	$75,000	$20,000	$385,000
2	$385,000	$61,800	$78,800	$15,400	$259,800
3	$259,800	$63,700	$82,700	$10,400	$123,800
4	$123,800	$65,600	$86,700	$5,000	($23,700)
5	($23,700)	$67,500	$91,200	(0)	($182,400)

Note: "Income Needs" is the portion of household income needs that the assets had been relied upon to provide and assumes annual inflation of 3%. "LTC Expense" is based on a typical annual cost and is subject to 5% annual inflation.

Having around the clock care at double the cost would eliminate the $500,000 in less than two years!

Inflation Trend

The cost of care has more than tripled in the last 25 years (the average cost of care in 1987 was $56 a day).[13] Don't you think it will do the same in the next 25 years considering the demand created by the baby boomers and the national shortage of caregivers? At that rate, $6,750 will grow to $30,000 a year in 30 years at which time a four year period of care for one person could easily reach $1,300,000!

WHAT pays for long-term care?

Apparently Americans are beginning to understand how expensive long-term care is.

AARP published a survey of the 50-plus labor force which clearly reports that the 50+ population is more worried about paying for long-term care than health care in retirement.[14]

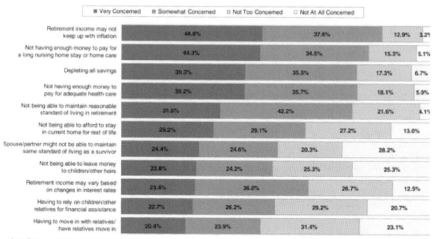

Q111. Please indicate how concerned you are about each of the following [if out of the labor force: in retirement]: Are you very concerned, somewhat concerned, not too concerned, or not at all concerned? Base: Total (n = 5,027).

Yet only 3% of Americans over age 18 have long-term care insurance.[15]

When the same AARP survey asked the 50-plus labor force what they plan to do about health care expenditures, only one in four said they have purchased long-term care insurance or plan to.[16]

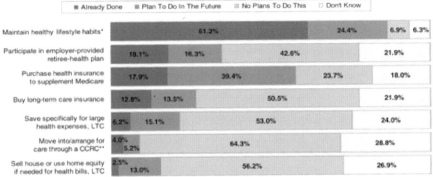

Dealing With Health Expenditures

■ Already Done   ■ Plan To Do In The Future   ▨ No Plans To Do This   ☐ Don't Know

	Already Done	Plan To Do In The Future	No Plans To Do This	Don't Know
Maintain healthy lifestyle habits*	61.2%		24.4%	6.9% / 6.3%
Participate in employer-provided retiree-health plan	18.1%	16.3%	42.6%	21.9%
Purchase health insurance to supplement Medicare	17.9%	39.4%	23.7%	18.0%
Buy long-term care insurance	12.8%	13.5%	50.5%	21.9%
Save specifically for large health expenses, LTC	6.2%	15.1%	53.0%	24.0%
Move into/arrange for care through a CCRC**	4.0% / 5.2%	64.3%		28.8%
Sell house or use home equity if needed for health bills, LTC	2.5%	13.0%	56.2%	26.9%

*Such as a proper diet, regular exercise, and preventive care.

**Continuing care retirement community.

Q113. Now we are going to ask specifically about things some people do to protect themselves financially when it comes to health expenses. To protect yourself financially, have you or do you plan to...? Base: Total (n = 5,027).

What gives? Ignorance. It is astounding to me that almost every year some think tank conducts a survey to ask Americans how they think long-term care is paid for, and the answer remains the same. A 2011 Prudential survey reported that only one out of four responders listed long-term care insurance as a source of payment because a third think Medicare or health insurance will pay or that they can self-insure.[17]

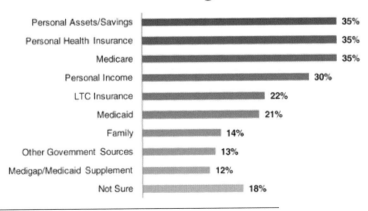

Consumer Perceptions of Funding Sources for Long-Term Care

Personal Assets/Savings	35%
Personal Health Insurance	35%
Medicare	35%
Personal Income	30%
LTC Insurance	22%
Medicaid	21%
Family	14%
Other Government Sources	13%
Medigap/Medicaid Supplement	12%
Not Sure	18%

** multiple responses were allowed

Health insurance, including individual and group health insurance for people under 65 or retiree health plans, restricts coverage to SKILLED CARE—and that's why conventional health insurance does not pay for long-term care. Health Maintenance Organizations (HMOs), the managed care programs for people of all ages, are even more restrictive than regular health insurance and pay very little for home health and nursing home care.

What is meant by skilled care? *Skilled care has nothing to do with how sick you are.* A person can be totally paralyzed or in a coma and still not be receiving skilled care, in which case private insurance will not pay. Skilled care is care to get you better—IVs, dressing bedsores, providing physical and speech therapy after a stroke, etc. Once progress stops, however, the care is "chronic" or "maintenance" and is no longer skilled. Daily cleaning of a colostomy drain or a catheter, or even oxygen or respiratory therapy needed regularly for an emphysema patient in a nursing home, are examples of care that is not skilled.

Medicare can approve up to 100 days in a nursing home per benefit period but patients usually collect less. Why? Because Medicare pays only for *skilled care*, and the majority of nursing home care is not skilled. In fact, the average number of days that patients collect from Medicare for nursing home care is only about 27 days, because most people don't have many days that qualify as skilled care under Medicare guidelines.[18] Medicare pays nothing for eight-hour shifts at home and only pays home health care visits, when some skilled care is being provided. An Alzheimer's patient is a classic example of someone who needs little or no skilled care and would likely not benefit from Medicare. Medicare supplements and Medicare Advantage plans won't pay for this type of care unless Medicare approves it, so they don't help.

Due to recent legislation to promote cost containment in the Medicare program, restricted access to Medicare payments for home health care and nursing home care is expected to continue, which just serves to shift care back to the family.

Now look back at the chart from the Prudential survey. Only 21% listed Medicaid as a payer, and yet Medicaid, the federal and state welfare program for the poor, pays two-thirds of the nation's long-term care bill.[19]

Why is this such a big deal?

It should come as no surprise when I tell you that states have just experienced their deepest fiscal crisis in more than 50 years.[20]

The exploding Medicaid program has gutted many state budgets. Few realize that Medicaid expenses consume approximately 24% of most state budgets today and the figure is projected to grow to more than a third in 20 years.[21] In fact, the National Association of State Budget Officers reports that Medicaid is second only to K-12 as the largest expenditure of state funds and is the #1 expenditure in some states in total funds, which is the combination of state and federal dollars. [22]

While long-term care (LTC) consumes about 30% of Medicaid budgets today, it's easy to see why that number is expected to grow to a whopping 50% by 2030, since the nation's 80 million baby boomers began turning age 65 in 2011.[23]

Thirty-one states faced budget deficits for fiscal year 2013 and closed them with spending cuts on top of prior years' deep cuts in education, health care and human services.[24] Over 30 states have raised taxes in addition to cutting state services.[25]

According to the Center on Budget and Policy Priorities, these cuts will delay the nation's economic recovery and undermine efforts to create jobs.[26] Now consider that we have 155 million employees in the country vs. 62 million people accessing Medicaid today.[27, 28] This low ratio of 2.5 taxpayers compared to every person on Medicaid creates an untenable situation as demand for Medicaid dollars continues to grow.

> *Every dollar of long-term care insurance benefits is a dollar that didn't decrease the state budget and cause higher tuition costs, fewer scholarships and higher property, sales and state income tax dollars.*

Cost-cutting legislation for federal and state programs makes long-term care insurance much more meaningful and underlines the need for financial professionals to educate care providers, consumer, legislative officials and other centers of influence that private LTC insurance is the best funding vehicle for long-term care services and supports. Yes, it provides more care choices for consumers but it also makes the most sense for the state and federal economy.

Revenue to support the increasing demand for state services has dropped. High unemployment has played a role in decreasing revenue as unemployed people pay less state income tax and don't buy as much which lowers sales tax receipts. Unemployment has also led to young families having to rely on Medicaid for health insurance as most states allow low-income adults with dependent children to turn to Medicaid for health insurance.

On top of everything else, The Patient Protection and Affordable Care Act (PPACA) is adding more pressure on an already staggering payment system by requiring states to cover more home and community care such as assisted living facilities and adult day care in addition to nursing homes.

The straw that threatens to break the back of the state is that beginning in 2014, PPACA requires states to use Medicaid to provide free health insurance to everyone with an income up to 133% of the federal poverty level.[29] Generally, this will be childless adults as typically states only provide Medicaid to adults today if they are low-income with dependent children. Here is what that looks like in today's dollars:

2013 Income at 133% of Federal Poverty Level	Monthly Income
Individual	$1,240
Couple	$1,680
Family of four	$2,555

Unlike the federal government, states are required to balance their budget each year. Read this March 1, 2011 excerpt from *The Washington Post*:

Utah Gov. Gary R. Herbert complained that by prohibiting states from limiting who is eligible for Medicaid, the law has locked them into unsustainable spending at a time of fiscal crisis.

"Worst of all," added Herbert, is the law's mandatory expansion of Medicaid to cover a larger share of the poor beginning in 2014

"Medicaid is poised to wreak havoc on the state's budget for years to come," he said, "threatening our ability to fund critical services, such as

transportation and education." Aizenman, N.C. "Republicans Shift Focus to Medicaid Complaints" The Washington Post, March 1, 2011

Utah was one of 26 states that sued the Federal government in an effort to challenge the constitutionality of being forced to accept this Medicaid expansion in addition to PPACA's requirement that every American must have health insurance. The other states were Alabama, Alaska, Arizona, Colorado, Florida, Georgia, Idaho, Indiana, Iowa, Kansas, Louisiana, Maine, Michigan, Mississippi, Nebraska, Nevada, North Dakota, Ohio, Pennsylvania, South Carolina, South Dakota, Texas, Washington, Wisconsin, and Wyoming. [30]

The Supreme Court ruled on June 28, 2012 that the federal government could expand Medicaid as long as it didn't threaten states with the withdrawal of federal funding for existing Medicaid programs.[31] Before the ruling, the federal government could threaten to withdraw Medicaid funding from the states if they didn't play ball with this new plan. Now states are deciding one by one whether or not to participate in this Medicaid expansion to younger adults.

> *Fortunately, there is a solution that we can implement NOW to head off this perfect storm.*

It is a public-private partnership that allows special state-approved insurance policies to pay first, instead of Medicaid, which takes the burden off state budgets and provides maximum consumer choice for care. Then Medicaid is still available if the insurance dollars aren't enough, assuming the person needs the level of care that meets the state's functional or cognitive eligibility trigger. The best part is that the insurance policyholders are allowed to protect assets equal to the benefits paid out when they apply for Medicaid…no limit. Further, the asset protection carries over to estate recovery which will prevent families from losing homes and farms that have been in the family for generations. This program is called The Long-Term Care Partnership and it is in 40 states so far:

Alabama	**Arizona**	**Arkansas**
California	**Colorado**	**Connecticut**
Florida	**Georgia**	**Idaho**
Indiana	**Iowa**	**Kansas**
Kentucky	**Louisiana**	**Maine**
Maryland	**Minnesota**	**Missouri**
Montana	**Nebraska**	**Nevada**
New Hampshire	**New Jersey**	**New York**
North Carolina	**North Dakota**	**Ohio**
Oklahoma	**Oregon**	**Pennsylvania**
Rhode Island	**South Carolina**	**South Dakota**
Tennessee	**Texas**	**Virginia**
Washington	**West Virginia**	**Wisconsin**
	Wyoming	

Now let me connect some dots for you that no one else seems to be connecting.

The Long-Term Care Partnership satisfies the #1 reason cited in the 2005 and 2010 Long-Term Care Insurance Buyer/Non-Buyer Survey by consumers who made the decision not to buy that could persuade them to buy.

> *Twenty-nine percent of the Non-Buyers said they would consider long-term care insurance "if government paid for care when benefits cease".[32]*

We will talk more about this in Chapters 3 and 7 in this book when we discuss long-term care insurance and Medicaid in more detail, but for now, just know that **this is exactly what the Long-Term Care Partnership does.**

> *Do you ever watch the news and feel overwhelmed by the nation's economic problems? And think "What can I do about it? I'm only one person."*

Educating your community about this one point may be one of the most meaningful contributions you can ever make. In order to maximize the impact of long-term care insurance being able to take the burden off the Medicaid budget and save jobs and services, it's important to reach as many people as quickly as possible. The fastest way that can happen is if **employers offer long-term care insurance to employees ages 18+ so that almost all employees and spouses can qualify with good health at younger ages.** Most employer offerings provide a one-time opportunity for the employees to qualify for long-term care insurance with limited health questions and some extend that one-time opportunity to working spouses.

With proper employee education, many extended family members can also purchase while they are still insurable. Employers don't have to contribute anything, but if they pay some or all of the employee premium, dollars are freed up for employees to cover their spouses. Otherwise, if the spouse needs care, the employee has to miss work or ultimately leave the workforce. It's much less costly for employers to contribute to employee premium than to sustain the inevitable productivity dive when spouses of baby boomer employees begin to experience long-term care events in large numbers in the next 20-30 years.

This solution sounds promising, right? There's just one problem. There's a disconnect in our society between planning for long-term care and long-term care insurance and it needs to be addressed NOW.

We have 80 million baby boomers that started to turn 65 years old in 2011 and we have the largest shortage of paid caregivers in the history of our nation. To meet this demand, one report said we need 1.1 million **NEW** paid caregivers in the next decade![33]

"The United States is in the midst of a significant and growing caregiving crisis."[35]

The number of people with Alzheimer's is expected to grow 50% in the next 20 years![33] An Ameriprise survey said that "boomers are literally caught in middle age, providing financial support to their elderly parents and to their grown children."[36]

In a little over 200 years, life expectancy has doubled in this nation. "Eighty percent of the growth in the American population is taking place in people over 50," says Ken Dychtwald, one of the nation's leading gerontologists.[37] The Social Security Administration expects women to live another 20 years from age 65 and men to live another 17.8 years.[38]

Here's where we are:[39]

Today	one in six adults are 65+
2020	21% will be 65+ (more than one in five)
2030	26% (more than one in four)

But get this. There are at least 70,000 people alive today over 100 years old, and that number is expected to grow eight times by 2050!![40] (I don't know about you, but I think they're all driving!)

Popular movies like *Hope Springs* chronicle the lifestyle changes of the baby boomers as Meryl Streep and Tommy Lee Jones seek to put a spark back into their 40 year marriage. The baby boomers, people born between 1946-1964, continue to leave an indelible mark on our society as the largest generation ever to influence our culture. Celebrities like Sally Field, Denzel Washington, Harrison Ford, Kevin Costner and Richard Gere grace the cover of the AARP magazine. Paul McCartney, Tina Turner, The Rolling Stones and Cher are still rocking audiences around the world. And Rod Stewart? Well, you might have caught his interview in *Smiler* magazine, entitled "Do You Think I'm Sixty?"[41]

Mature Services, Inc., a successful employment agency specializing in workers in their 50s, 60s and 70s, provides paid training to adults 55+ to help them return to the workforce.[42] It's a win-win: Older workers tend to already have a pension and Medicare, so working part-time without benefits creates a low-maintenance, highly trained labor pool for grateful employers.

Ray Crist, a chemist who helped produce the atomic bomb as part of the Manhattan Project, was honored as the World's Oldest Worker at age 102 by Experience Works, another nonprofit organization that provides training and employment services for mature workers. He retired from teaching environmental science at Messiah College in Carlisle, Pennsylvania at the mature age of 104. He continued to live to age 105 when he passed away on July 30, 2005.[43]

Nola Ochs entered the Guinness Book of World Records on May 12, 2007 as the oldest person to be awarded an earned college degree at age 95. In an interview on Graduation Day, she said "Truthfully, I just don't dwell on my age. That might limit what I can do. As long as I have my mind and health, age is just a number." When asked what she planned to do next, she said she would like to be a storyteller on a cruise ship. Sure enough, after graduation, Princess Cruises hired her as a guest lecturer on a nine-day Caribbean cruise. But she wasn't finished. In 2009, she graduated with a Master's Degree in Liberal Studies with a concentration in history. November 22, 2011 found her turning 100 and pursuing a full master's degree in history and having just completed a Graduate Teaching Assistant for the History department the preceding spring.[44]

Could there be a more experienced expert on aging than Emma Shulman? A gerontologist at N.Y.U. Langone Medical Center, she was, from 1981 to 2005, a senior social worker and research associate at what is now its Center for Excellence on Brain Aging and Dementia, and she is currently a consultant. She did some of the first research on how to care for Alzheimer's patients and co-wrote a training manual about it. She lectures widely on memory retention. Oh, and did we mention that she is 96?[45]

These three individuals are exemplary examples of healthy aging. They won awards and were featured in the news because they were so unusual. Most people aren't so lucky.

The number of workers in the 55 years and older age group is projected to grow by 38 percent by 2020, over five times the 6.8 percent growth projected for the labor force overall. This group is projected to increase by 12 million and make up nearly one-quarter of the labor force in 2020.[46] Why is this significant? In a May 1, 2012 National Public Radio interview, Cheryl Matheis, AARP Senior Vice President, tells us exactly why:

In 20 years, we're going to have twice as many people over 65 as we have now. So the average worker is going to end up being a caregiver. [47]

This is a direct message to women, because two-thirds of the caregivers are women, and women make up 47 percent of the workforce in the United States. [48, 49]

When a spouse, parent or even an adult child has a disabling accident or illness, the working caregiver has to take time away from work to find caregivers if she can afford them at $18+ an hour, or if she can't afford that, she may have to go part-time or even leave the workforce in order to be a full-time caregiver. [50]

Just when women have finally broken through into executive positions and millions have become business owners themselves, this caregiving tidal wave could be the greatest threat to everything women have accomplished in the workplace!

If there is any possibility you will be a caregiver, please investigate long-term care insurance for yourself and your family members before it's too late, while health is good and insuring as an option. Being able to afford to hire paid caregivers cam mean the difference between being able to preserve the lifestyle that you've worked so hard for vs. being responsible 24/7 for someone else's care without the financial means to spend time with your children, pay for their education, live where you want to live, take vacations, or even meet day-to-day financial obligations. You get the picture. Without the means to pay caregivers, the quality of life can suffer greatly for you and your family.

A Story of Two Women

Kathy and her husband Jim had it all. They had a successful insurance agency in Wisconsin and had every kind of insurance protection on themselves – except long-term care insurance. They were too young for that, they thought. At age 41, Jim was diagnosed with Parkinson's disease. Kathy had to learn the insurance business and take over his practice to care for him and provide for their family, especially their children's education. By the time Jim died, Kathy had spent almost everything, including their retirement savings. Today she dedicates her time to getting the word out about how long-term care insurance can protect families.[51]

The second story has a different ending.

Kim M. and her husband were in their late 30's when they attended one of my long-term care insurance training seminars. She went straight home and purchased LTC insurance on herself and her husband. They had a son, an only child, and Kim didn't want him to have the emotional and financial burden for either one of them. Three days after her husband's 45th birthday he had a grand-mal seizure at work and the diagnosis turned out to be a brain tumor. They couldn't have been more shocked as he had always been strong and enjoyed good health, which was essential for his physically demanding job working offshore in the merchant marine. After eight years, he is now tumor-free yet remains right-side impaired. Kim is so grateful for that decision at a young age to plan ahead for long-term care as her husband is uninsurable today for long-term care insurance.[52]

These stories blow apart the myth that long-term care is only needed by older people.

Bill Jones, President of MedAmerica, an insurance company that has specialized in long-term care insurance since 1987, says "An event with terrible consequences requiring long-term care can happen at any age. The chances simply increase with age." [53]

Americans ARE concerned. A March 2010 Age Wave/Harris Interactive survey said that when asked their greatest fear about having a long-term illness, people are over five times more worried about being a burden on their family than dying, and that the greatest worry of becoming a caregiver is the emotional strain – even more than the financial costs.[54]

I find that most families feel that way. So consider this chapter a lifeline that I'm throwing to you so you can see that it's possible to protect yourself and your family from the ravages of caregiving IF you plan ahead.

The Ostrich Plan Doesn't Work

To do this, you must talk about this as a family! You need to sit down with your spouse and your adult children and talk about the type of care you would want, the role of each family member in the situation and most importantly, how the care will be paid for. The same Age Wave survey referenced above said that:

- 92% of people haven't discussed all three topics with their spouse
- 95% of parents haven't discussed them with their adult children and
- 96% of adult children haven't discussed them with their parents.

Don't wait. I hear from people every week who want to get their mother with Parkinson's disease or their dad with "slight memory problems" a long-term care insurance policy. It doesn't work like that. Does "the house is already on fire" ring a bell?

The younger the applicant, the better chance he or she has to qualify for a policy. **No amount of money will purchase long-term care insurance once someone is uninsurable due to a significant physical or mental health problem.**

For this reason, please don't listen to anyone who advises you (or your parents) to wait to age 60 to apply for long-term care insurance. That advice is about 15 years old. Today's policies cost more and are hard to get from an underwriting standpoint because the insurance companies have learned the hard way how much it costs to pay expensive long-term care claims. Policies are available from 18-85, but the younger you are when you apply, the better. You will pay longer (unless you have a claim at a younger age) but you will pay less than if you wait. This happens because the longer you wait, the larger the benefit you will have to buy due to how fast the cost of care is going up.

"My Best Friend" on my 5th birthday

Chapter Two:

SO YOU THINK YOU CAN SELF-INSURE LTC?

———∞∞∞———

People from East Tennessee can be extremely persistent and focused. That's a nice way of saying "stubborn". I am one of those people when it comes to talking to people about the need to plan for long-term care. For example, if you happen to be in the seat next to me on an airplane, you can bet I'll speak to you about your plan to protect your family in the event of a long-term care need. Sometimes I get it into the conversation on the hotel shuttle. I really do have an elevator speech about planning for long-term care:

"I help people plan for extended episodes of health care that would cause them to have to rely on their children or other family members for care."

If they want to know more, I helpfully volunteer this information: "Hopefully our elevator won't fall. I have a friend who is a dentist who broke her hip and leg in an elevator fall and needed help getting around for six months. Fortunately she and her husband already had their long-term care insurance policies because she sure couldn't get one today."

When they ask how much it costs, I can ask for an appointment so I can ask questions and customize a plan for them.

Another famous East Tennessean who feels strongly about what she does for a living is Dolly Parton, whom we all admire and respect immensely. People often compare our laugh or sometimes our accent. We were born 30 miles apart so that's not surprising. Sometimes I have big hair because I love it too. That's about the end of the comparisons, which reminds me of my first national speech about planning for long-term care. It put me on the map, in more ways than one.

It was for the Million Dollar Round Table, the largest and most prestigious insurance organization with about 5,000 members from all over the world. The year was 1992 and the location was Chicago. I loved the Million Dollar Round Table immediately because most of the attendees were male. This meant I could go to the bathroom whenever I wanted and it was so much fun to sail past the hundreds of men standing in line for the men's room on each break.

I had hardly ever been out of Tennessee so I could barely breathe with excitement over the entire experience. I was so excited in fact that I forgot to pack the "killer" suit that I had purchased for this occasion which I was sure would turn out to be the highlight of my life. Fortunately, I pieced together another outfit that worked nicely with another pair of very high heels I had brought. However, a shopping trip became necessary as I wasn't prepared for the weather. Even though it was June, I quickly learned how the Windy City got its name. After being completely intimidated by the prices in a couple of stores, I happily bought a pair of Black Hawk kid's sweatpants in the gift shop of the hotel in order to attend the first event which was in Millennium Park on Lake Michigan..

To this day, MDRT is the most inspirational and exciting meeting I've ever attended, but in 1992, I felt like I had been invited to speak at the White House.

I was assigned a bodyguard when I arrived at the Hyatt Regency in downtown Chicago, a very nice gentleman from Washington state who immediately saw that without his help, I would probably not survive the entire experience. My sense of direction alone would probably ensure that I never reached the assigned room for my presentation. He took his duties so seriously that he even offered to introduce me to the audience of about 400 attendees, mostly male.

I had a few notes at the podium as during the formal rehearsal, I was instructed to deliver my information in a certain way. I don't do well with notes but was prepared to try. The stage was very high and my face was already flushed from nerves and the bright lights. It was destined to stay that way. My wonderful new friend the bodyguard began my introduction. He too had a few notes. I listened carefully to hear him begin:

"I'm very honored to introduce Phyllis Shelton to deliver her presentation "Long-Term Care: Is Your Family Protected?" This is her first time at MDRT so please make her welcome. (Applause). To tell you a little about her, Phyllis is from East Tennessee and she tells me she was born about 30 miles from where Dolly Parton was born. They both love country music, and that's where the resemblance stops."

I have no idea where he was going with that as the noise from 400 men falling out of their seats with laughter made it impossible for him to finish. I literally watched the red creep from his chin to his hairline while he was standing there. The only good thing about the moment was that my notes swept themselves supernaturally off the podium and wafted gracefully into the dark abyss at my feet as I tried to regain my composure. I did much better without them.

In this chapter, I want to address those of you who are of the mind that you can self-insure for long-term care. What if you pay premiums for many years and drop dead with a heart attack and never need care? Haven't you wasted your money? Maybe. Let me ask you another question.

Did you lie awake last night and worry that you haven't had a house fire and gotten your money's worth out of your homeowner's insurance premium? Or are you worried because you haven't had enough automobile accidents this year to justify what you've paid in car insurance premium? If you are in fact worried about that, let me know so I can send someone to back into your vehicle tonight! We kinda don't worry about those things, do we? We pay the premium year in and year out and hope and pray we never have a house fire or car wreck. (That's the proper terminology south of the Mason-Dixon line, and we drive "vee-hicles".) Or when's the last time you thought to yourself, "If I just had a brain tumor, I'd feel like I'm getting something back for all these health insurance premiums…"

With those unusual thoughts in your mind, let's look at this one more way. If you buy long-term care insurance and never need long-term care, could it be that you made a little mistake…maybe a $250 month or $5,000 a year mistake or however much your LTC insurance premium is? But if you don't buy long-term care insurance and you do need care, would it be fair to say you have then made a really BIG mistake…maybe a $30,000 a month or a $360,000 a year mistake, as that's what the cost for care is projected to be in 30 years?[1] And much higher in some parts of the country!

I kinda like the idea of buying long-term care insurance and never needing it. But that's just me.

My concern is not so much about people who have made a conscious, well-informed decision to self-insure for long-term care as the people who are self-insuring by default…mainly because they've never thought about it or worse, their financial advisor hasn't made them think about it.

For example, here's a large disconnect. A Nationwide/Harris Interactive survey published in February 2012 said that only one in five respondents had discussed health care costs in retirement not covered by Medicare with a financial advisor.[2] Why is this a disconnect? Because Medicare does not cover long-term care, the cost of which has the potential to dwarf acute-care costs. For example, almost half of the survey respondents said they expect health care to be their biggest expense throughout retirement and they estimate spending an average of $5,621 a year.[3]

However, Fidelity Consulting Services just said a couple of years earlier that a 65 year old couple retiring and living for 20 years will see an estimated $250,000 to $430,000 in health care costs…more like $10,750 a year in out-of-pocket health expenses.[4] "Well, the larger number probably includes long-term care costs so if I don't need long-term care, that won't apply to me." WRONG. Those estimates do NOT include paying for long-term care which will be out of YOUR pocket if you don't plan ahead.

Besides just plain old being in denial about needing long-term care, the other huge disconnect I see every day is people (and their financial advisors) failing to account properly for inflation of long-term care costs when they so carefully construct a retirement plan that will keep them from outliving their money. Such a plan has to be very well constructed as you know and you definitely don't want any bumps in the road.

News flash folks. Long-term care is not a bump. It's an earthquake…and few financial plans survive it.

I can give you a very simple formula to apply to your financial plan to determine how much money you may need to build toward for long-term care. I urge you to show this to your financial advisor at the earliest opportunity.

1. Start with the cost of care in your community for 10 hours of home care or care in a nursing facility (it's about the same).

2. If you are age 60 or younger or have extreme longevity in your family such as people living into their 90s, project what it will be in 30 years using 5% compound. This is very easy because at 5% compound, a number doubles every 15 years. So just double your starting number twice.

3. Multiply that amount X four years as this time frame is currently covering about 85% of the claims.[5] (If you really want to be exact, you have to bump up years 2, 3, and 4 by 5% compound)

4. Decide if you are comfortable paying that much out of your assets and if not, how much of that would you like to transfer to an insurance company? Half, two-thirds, 80%?

5. If you are part of a couple, even though it isn't likely both of you will need at least four years of care, it does happen so to plan thoroughly, you will double the answer for Step 2.

So let's say you started with $6000 a month ($200 a day) for your area. Doubling that twice, in 30 years you are looking at $24,000 a month ($800 a day). That's $288,000 a year x four years = $1,125,000 x 2 (if you are part of a couple) and you're at $2.3 million. It will be a little more than that as I explained because each year the cost will continue to increase. If you live in a higher cost area like New York City, Boston, parts of California, that amount could be 1 ½ or double, so over $4 million. If you want more than 10 hours of home care a day, make it bigger! Or one person could need ten years of care or longer like my cousin Carolyn.

My cousin Carolyn was beautiful. She was my favorite baby sitter when I was four. She could play the piano by ear and I remember watching her with awe on our black and white television when she played "Down Yonder" on a local television station when I was five. She was in high school and went to all the dances -- she could jitter-bug like nobody's business. I loved to watch her get dressed for a dance in her pretty dance dresses of all colors with huge crinoline petticoats under them. My favorite one was the red dress. With her raven black hair and sparkling brown eyes, it made her look gorgeous. Maybe I loved her so much because every day when she combed my long hair after my nap, she made me feel pretty, too.

Carolyn suffered a massive stroke at age 61. She has been in a nursing home 11 years and can do nothing for herself. She is tube-fed, paralyzed on one side of her body, and can't speak intelligibly..

A really sad part to this story is that her husband assured me years ago that he bought the group long-term care insurance plan offered through his employer. When Carolyn had the stroke and I rushed to the hospital to be with them and their three children, I said "Aren't you so glad you bought that long-term care insurance, Lester? Now she can be taken care of and you won't have to worry."

Instead of the expression of relief that I expected, his answer astonished me. "We didn't get it," he said in a flat tone. He had just told me that several years ago to stop me from bringing it up. Carolyn is in a nursing home today as a Medicaid patient in a room with two other people, occasionally three. But when I visit her, her eyes speak volumes of love so I know my favorite cousin is still here.

But whatever. You are saying to me that you are comfortable self-insuring a few million dollars.

There is a third huge disconnect I see about self-insuring for long-term care and that is that people (and their financial advisors) don't add in the lost investment opportunity when the money to pay for long-term care is taken out of the investment portfolio. When that happens, the decision to self-insure is made with incomplete information. Let me show you what I mean:

Self-Insure Vs LTC Insurance: Estate Shrinkage Using 6% Lost Investment Opportunity[6]	

• Couple ages 56 & 43
• $6,000 month current cost at 5% inflation
• Assume 56 year old has 4 years of care in 25 years $1,000,840
• Premium Paid = $142,741
• Benefits: $942,788
• Out-of-Pocket: $58,052
• $6,000 MB, 6 year Benefit Period, 90 day, preferred annual premium = $4,610
	Estate shrinkage using 6% investment opportunity and a 40 year planning Period:
	
	  ▫ No insurance $2,326,365
	  ▫ With insurance: $448,609
	  ▫ Out-of-pocket: $58,052
	
	Investing the premium to equal the benefits paid out would require an annual 13.4% after tax rate of return.

What this illustration is telling you is that the true cost of self-insuring means adding what you will pay at the future cost of care to what you would have earned on that money if it had stayed in your investment portfolio. In the above example, the four years of care in 25 years only cost $1 million. Losing 6% on that money from the first day it started to go for care through his wife's 83rd birthday (a 40 year planning period) added $1,325,525 to the loss for a total of $2,326,365. The point is, once the money goes out to pay for care, it never returns to the investment portfolio. Does this make sense?

Conversely, paying LTC insurance premium then calculating a 6% lost investment opportunity on money spent to pay LTC insurance premium over that time period and to pay the 90 day deductible at future cost drops the estate shrinkage to only $448,609.

Further, investing the premium paid over the 40 year planning period ($142,741 in this example) to equal the insurance benefits paid would have required an annual after tax rate of return of 13.4%.

This makes a huge difference, doesn't it?

Let me position the decision of self-insuring for LTC another way.

Remember the pain you felt in September 2008 when the stock market plunged and kept going over that cliff? Did you change some of your investments to more conservative instruments to avoid experiencing that kind of pain again?

I have two thoughts for you:

1. Paying for LTC out of your assets at $25,000 to $50,000 a month depending on where you live (and more if you and your spouse

or partner need care at the same time) can give you that same sick feeling in the pit of your stomach…especially if you are purchasing care for a condition like Alzheimer's which can last from 4-20 years according to the Alzheimer's Association.

2. If you did go into more conservative investments, you won't have nearly as much money to pay for long-term care as your investments will likely not grow as fast as the cost of LTC.

You're looking for a great economic recovery after the 2012 presidential election so your money will start growing quickly again? I sure hope you're right, but not being an investment expert, my opinion on that topic doesn't matter. I can however tell you that you are at odds with people like Suze Orman and Warren Buffett who believe low interest rates will continue a long time. I'm listening to Suze and Warren about investments.

If you are still comfortable with self-insuring for LTC after this discussion, that's fine. That's what I love so much about our wonderful country. People have the freedom to make decisions for themselves. You probably believe so strongly that you won't need long-term care and you just don't want to pay premium for something you will never use. If you are in this group, I have two more thoughts for you:

1. Rather than pay 100% of your LTC costs, I really wish you would insure for LTC and use the savings for scholarships to give more kids a chance in this difficult world, or give to other charitable causes like the Alzheimer's Association to find a cure for Alzheimer's or to fight ALS, MS, cancer…you get the picture.

2. You can actually have your cake and eat it too by simply repositioning a portion of your assets into a policy that either combines life insurance with LTCI or an annuity with LTCI. In both situations, you can pull the money out tax-free for qualified long-term care expenses (see "Claims" in Chapter Four) and if you don't need care, the death benefit or annuity account value goes to the beneficiary of your choice. There's even a joint policy that has a second-to-die payout so the money stays in the pot for your spouse or partner after you depart this world. When I say "reposition", I simply mean you could do a 1035 exchange with no tax consequences from an existing life insurance or annuity into a combo LTC product, or you can move money from taxable accounts like CDs, money market or savings accounts. Or you could sell real estate you no longer need and use that money. Either way, these assets are working harder for you as they are covering an LTC need just in case the improbable happens and you or your spouse or partner wind up needing care. Here are three advantages to this approach:

    a. the premiums are guaranteed and you don't have to worry about rate increases in the future;
    b. you can get your money back at any time if you change your mind; and
    c. you get rid of the "use it or lose it" objection.

You do have to plan carefully for inflation with a combo product. Unfortunately many are bought with no inflation benefit and will wind up paying maybe 20% of the cost of care in 30 years. That doesn't have to happen to you if you will use the formula I gave you earlier in this chapter to figure out how much money you need to set aside for long-term care.

To summarize, there are two types of combination policies for you to consider:

- A combination life insurance/long-term care insurance policy (life/LTC)
- A combination annuity/long-term care insurance policy (annuity/LTC)

Both plans have an option to continue benefits if you need care after:

- The long-term care coverage leveraged by the death benefit has been paid out on a combination life/LTC policy; or
- The long-term care coverage leveraged by the annuity account value has been paid out on a combination annuity/LTC policy.

Two important laws made this type of long-term care planning possible:

1. **The Health Insurance Portability and Accountability Act of 1996 (HIPAA)** made withdrawals for qualified long-term care expenses from life insurance contracts tax-free and not subject to the 10% early withdrawal penalty. The tax-free cap ($320 in 2013) has no bearing as long as the combo life/LTC product is a reimbursement product that won't pay more than the actual charge for qualified long-term care expenses. HIPAA is Public Law 104-191.

2. **The Pension Protection Act of 2006 (PPA)** hit the other three bases for a home run, effective January 1, 2010. The PPA is Public Law 109-280.

- o The PPA made withdrawals from cash value in life insurance contracts tax-free to pay the premium for qualified long-term care insurance benefits in the contract.
- o The PPA made withdrawals from **non-qualified** annuities issued after 12/31/96 used to pay for qualified long-term care expenses tax-free, regardless of cost basis.
- o The PPA allows tax-free exchanges of one life insurance or annuity contract for a combination life/LTC or annuity/LTC contract or a standalone LTC contract. [Public Law 109-280, Sec. 844 (b) and 6050U (g) (1) and (2)]

The exchange opportunity follows the IRC Sec. 1035 exchange rules:

- Life insurance to life insurance
- Life insurance to annuity
- Annuity to annuity
- Life insurance to standalone long-term care insurance contract
- Annuity to standalone long-term care insurance contract
- Annuity can't be exchanged into a life insurance contract

The really exciting opportunity is the potential to exchange old non-qualified annuities with gain for a combination annuity/LTC policy and take the gain out tax-free if it is used for qualified long-term care expenses.

The term "qualified" as it relates to long-term care insurance means the benefits are paid to someone who meets the definition of "chronically ill" as defined by the HIPAA and this is also true for combination LTC policies:[7]

- an expectation of needing help with at least two activities of daily living for at least 90 days; or
- needing help with a severe cognitive impairment that makes one a threat to self or others.

These laws open up new planning opportunities for funding long-term care. Combination life or annuity/LTC products are good for people who:

- plan to self-insure because they don't want to pay insurance premium for care they may never need; or
- can make up the difference (co-insure) if there is a significant shortfall between the monthly benefit and the actual cost of care; or
- have a traditional long-term care insurance policy but want more coverage, as this plan can be a good wraparound for the benefits they already own; or
- aren't concerned about leaving a significant death benefit or account value to a beneficiary in the event they need long-term care and drain the policy.

To clarify, a true combination product provides an option to extend the payout beyond the death benefit of the life insurance policy or the account value of the annuity. Many life insurance contracts allow the death benefit to be accelerated for chronically or terminally ill individuals as that is what HIPAA allows, but there is no opportunity for the benefits to continue if the insured still needs care.

Common Types of Life/Long Term Care Products

Whole Life + LTC Insurance (State Life, owned by OneAmerica)

Issue age for single individuals generally begins at 35, and joint policies for two people (e.g., mother and daughter, as well as spouses) can be purchased, if the average age of the two people falls within certain parameters. Asset-Care I is a second-to-die policy and the only joint combination life/LTC available. Age 80 is typically the maximum issue age, although there is no age limit for the benefit payments once a policy is issued. The single premium deposit can be made with cash, CDs, money market accounts, non-qualified and qualified annuities, or IRAs and Keogh plans. It is also possible to fund this policy with another life insurance policy with no adverse tax consequences as long as it is a "like-for-like" exchange which means the owner and the insured must be exactly the same for both policies. Issue ages can vary based on the source of the premium (i.e., older issue ages of 59 ½ are required for transfers from qualified annuities, IRAs and Keoghs to avoid the early distribution penalty).

The idea of this policy is that whatever amount you deposit purchases a death benefit like any other life insurance policy. At the time of purchase, the client chooses how the death benefit will be paid out for a long-term care event. The policy could pay as much as 50 months of benefits at 2% per month of the long-term care amount, three years of benefits at 3% per month or two years at 4% per month. While minimum deposits can be in the $10,000-$20,000 range, a meaningful benefit based on today's costs requires somewhere in the $115,000 range for a 61-year-old couple. A $115,000 deposit provides a death benefit of approximately $260,000 and a monthly benefit for 50 months of approximately $5,200 each, if both spouses need long-term care. If they need care at the same time, they would each receive benefits for 25 months. This payout example doesn't have the optional inflation factor on this base plan, because it is not approved in all states. It is simply a whole life policy with a minimum interest rate of 4%.

For additional GUARANTEED premium in any state, you can add an inflation rider that makes the LTC account grow, not the death benefit. For guaranteed 5% simple inflation on the monthly LTC benefit, the 61 year old couple could pay another $37,000 single premium or $2,700 annual premium. (5% compound inflation would cost $53,000 single premium or $5,100 annual premium.) If this 61-year-old couple wanted a 50 month extension, they could pay an additional $24,000 single premium or $2,650 for ten years or $1,065 annual continuous premium. A lifetime (unlimited) extension with 5% compound inflation would cost an additional $38,000 single premium, $4,200 as 10-pay or $1,725 annually. If they don't buy the inflation benefit on the base plan (or if their state hasn't approved it), they should select the 4% factor to accelerate the initial death benefit as quickly as possible; i.e. 24 months, so that they hit the extended benefit period quickly and tap into the monthly benefit that has been growing at 5% compound each year. (The lifetime benefit period is not available if you do this.) With Asset-Care IV, you can pay either annually or pay the premium over 10-20 years to make it more affordable. **Premium is still guaranteed to never increase.**

An important feature is that you can take back the premium for the whole life insurance at any point with no penalty. The premium used to buy the inflation or the extension of benefits is considered pure insurance premium and is not returnable. For that reason, it is advisable to pay annual premium for those features instead of single or 10-pay, especially since it is guaranteed never to increase.

As with other life insurance policies, you can take out a certain amount of accumulated interest with no surrender charge. But if you need to access more, the amount taken out will generate a surrender penalty. On this product, surrender penalties are graded downward each year until they disappear in ten years. Of course, you don't want to purchase this type of policy with the intention of making withdrawals, because that would lower both the death benefit and the amount available for long-term care.

A special version of this policy called Asset Care III is the only combination product that allows qualified money as a funding source. "Qualified" means tax-deferred funds such as money you have saved in an IRA or 401(k). The qualified money is transferred into a qualified deferred annuity which pays for a 20-pay whole life insurance policy. Long-term care benefits paid after the life insurance is paid up are tax-free. If long-term care is needed during the 20 year period, part of the monthly benefit will be provided by the annuity and part from the LTC pool of the whole life policy. Funds coming out of the annuity either to pay the life insurance premium or to pay a long-term care benefit are subject to the normal exclusion ratio for tax purposes.

Universal Life + LTC Insurance (Lincoln National Life's *MoneyGuard* Reserve Plus and Genworth's Total Living Care)

There are other single-premium life insurance/long-term care policies using universal life insurance. Typically, they will accelerate the death benefit 24, 36 or 48 months then offer an extension of 24 or 48 months or even unlimited.

The monthly benefit and premium may or may not be guaranteed. What they all have in common though is that **neither the distributions from the death benefit for qualified long-term care expenses nor the distributions from the cash value to pay the LTC premium are taxable income.**[8]

The following examples will show you how the LTC benefits on the Lincoln product vary greatly with a $100,000 single premium for a 65 year old female based on the selection of an inflation factor and/or an extension, but they are guaranteed to never increase.

No inflation and no extension:

- $7,898 monthly benefit paid for two years
- $189,550 death benefit and total LTC benefit ($7,898 x 24 months)

Adding 5% compound inflation and no extension:

- $5,188 **initial** monthly benefit paid for two years
- $124,500 death benefit and total **initial** LTC benefit ($5,188 x 24 months)

Adding 3% compound inflation with a two year extension:

- $4,340 **initial** monthly benefit paid out at 2 years base + 2 years extension (4 years)
- $208,364 and total **initial** LTC benefit ($4,340 x 48 months)
- At age 85: $7,612 monthly benefit x 48 months = $365,368 total LTC benefit

Adding a four year extension without inflation:

- $6,255 monthly benefit paid out at 2 years base + 4 years extension (6 years)
- $150,121 death benefit
- $450,363 total LTC benefit ($6,255 x 72 months)

The last selection is common and can fall significantly short at claim time the longer the 65 year old female lives. If the single premium is too steep for you to buy the amount of coverage you want, these products may allow you to spread the premiums out over three, five, seven or ten years. All amounts are guaranteed.

The Genworth Total Living Care (TLC) policy is the type that allows the monthly benefit to fluctuate with interest rates or policy charges. To compensate, the policy can be fixed to adjust the benefits downward to prevent lapse, then to notify the insured if an additional deposit is needed. As of this writing, a $100,000 deposit for a 65 year old female non-smoker in standard health buys:

Example A

- $5,859 monthly benefit paid out at 2 years + 2 years extension (4 years)
- $140,600 death benefit
- $281,225 total LTC benefit ($5,859 x 48 months)

However, Genworth says that 42% of their applicants for this product qualify for a preferred health discount and 80% qualify for a couples' discount, which means both you and your spouse are issued a Genworth TLC policy. This changes the coverage to:

Example B

- $7,313 monthly benefit paid out at 2 years + 2 years extension (4 years)
- $175,500 death benefit
- $351,000 total LTC benefit ($7,313 x 48 months)

Further, the company says that 80% of their applicants purchase a four year extension to the two year base plan, so here are the coverage amounts with a couples' discount:

Example C

- $7,109 monthly benefit paid out at 2 years + 4 years extension (6 years)
- $170,615 death benefit
- $511,845 total LTC benefit ($7,109 x 72 months)

This same plan with 3% compound inflation looks like this:

Example D

- $4,539 initial monthly benefit paid out at 2 years + 4 years extension (6 years)
- $108,940 initial death benefit
- $326,820 total initial LTC benefit ($4,539 x 72 months)
- At age 84: $7,959 monthly benefit x 72 = $573,081 total LTC benefit

You can see that adding an inflation benefit reduces the starting benefits significantly, so most buyers leave it off and take the higher starting benefits as in Example D.

Some people are nervous about running out of benefits after four or six years in the above examples. It is important to note that benefits could actually last longer than four or six years because this is a reimbursement product. This means if eligible expenses are less than the monthly benefit, the difference stays in the benefit pool, extending the payout beyond the stated time period above.

Return of premium

On the universal life policies, the ability to take the money back (guaranteed surrender value) may be built in as in the Lincoln plan or may be available for additional premium as in the Genworth plan. The return will be the greater of the initial premium or the cash surrender value. Most people never exercise this clause because they intend to leave the coverage in place for long-term care, and also because there may be tax implications that increase the longer the policy has been held. It's nice to know it's there, however.

Waiting Periods/Elimination Periods range from zero for home care or for all benefits to 60 or 90 days for facility care. If there is an elimination period on a combo product, it's a real deductible which means you have to incur eligible expenses for that many days before benefits become payable. (This is in contrast to a calendar day waiting period on a traditional long-term care insurance product which just requires you to wait a certain number of days before benefits are available, with no charges required.)

International benefits are typically available only for facility care at 50% or 75% for either the base plan only or for a maximum of four years.

Spouse and preferred health discounts may be available.

Inflation riders are typically 5% simple or 3% or 5% compound and may apply to both the base plan and the extension; however some states don't allow an inflation rider on the base plan. If an inflation rider is available on the base plan, it is better to pay for it with annual premium if that is an option instead of with a lump sum when the policy is initially purchased. Why? Because putting a lump sum toward the inflation benefit takes it away from the death benefit and reduces the initial death benefit dramatically. One product however that can include the inflation benefit on the entire policy seamlessly is Pacific Life's PremierCare.

Home care benefits on the Genworth plan may include **informal caregivers** as long as the caregiver isn't an immediate family member unless the benefit is paid to an organization that employs the family member.

A Different Approach – Mass Mutual's LTC Access Rider Combined with Standalone Coverage

Mass Mutual has approached the combination life insurance/LTC product a little differently. For a minimal charge, one can purchase a whole life policy and designate up to 90% of the death benefit to be available for long-term care. The monthly benefit is determined by choosing a time period over which the benefit can be paid, which is also known as a benefit period. The choices are 2, 3, 4, 5, 6 or 10 years. Here's an example:

Assume you purchase a policy with a $1,000,000 death benefit:

1. You elect to make the maximum amount of $900,000 (90%) available for accelerated for long-term care. The remaining $100,000 will be paid to your beneficiary at your death and therefore is not available for LTC.

2. You choose a 5-year benefit period.

3. Your initial monthly benefit will be $15,000 which is $900,000 ÷ 60 months.

You can grow your benefits in two ways:

1. You can allow the dividends to purchase more death benefit so this will increase your benefit pool which in turn increases your monthly benefit.

2. You can purchase an option that makes your monthly benefit start growing at 4% of the original amount at age 61 and allows it to grow for 25 years, which happens to be how long it will take to double at this growth rate. This doesn't grow your benefit pool. It just allows you to access your benefit pool faster than the 5 years in this example. Also note that it is growing at simple interest, not compound. Applying it to the $15,000 monthly benefit in this example means it will grow at $600 annually for 25 years until it reaches $30,000.

Practical Application: A 40 year old may need a significant amount of life insurance which doesn't leave enough room in the budget to buy long-term care insurance. Buying life insurance with this long-term care rider can make it possible to buy a traditional long-term care insurance policy with a smaller benefit, say at age 50, as it will be supplementing the benefit from the LTC rider. Let's see how this would work with Robert and Jane.

Robert and Jane are 40 and 35 years old with three children. After meeting with a financial planner, they know they need life insurance but Jane is also concerned about a long-term care need as both of Robert's parents have suffered with Alzheimer's. The cost of care in their area is $7,500 a month which is expected to be $30,000 a month in 30 years. They would like to insure four years of the long-term care risk at 80% of the cost at that time, so they would ultimately like a $24,000 monthly benefit. However their budget won't accommodate both premiums at this time. Their financial planner came up with this solution:

They would both purchase a $1,000,000 term life policy with a child rider and Robert would purchase a $400,000 whole life policy that would allow access to 90% of the death benefit ($360,000) for long-term care, payable at $7,500 per month over 48 months. His annual premium is $5,849 which includes only $183.18 for the LTC rider which includes the option that makes the monthly benefit grow at $300 (4% simple interest) annually beginning at age 61 for 25 years until it doubles to $15,000. In 30 years when Robert is age 70, the monthly benefit has had nine years to grow at $300 annually, so it is at $10,200, which will be $13,800 short of the $24,000 target.

In ten years at age 50, Robert can purchase a smaller standalone long-term care insurance policy with a $170 daily benefit to supplement the LTC rider from the whole life policy. This policy has a 5% compound inflation rider so it will grow to $$451 a day by the time he is age 70 which is $13,200 a month. That plus the $10,200 gets him very close to the $24,000 target. His premium for that policy would be $2,252 a year.

What really works in this plan is that the standalone policy will continue to grow at 5% compounded annually for the rest of his life as long as he hasn't used all the benefits, and the LTC rider on his life insurance policy will continue to grow until it reaches $15,000 a month. Assuming the cost of long-term care continues to grow about 5% a year, here is where he will be at age 85.

Monthly Benefit	LTC Access Rider	Signature 500 5% compound $170 DB	Total	80% Target Cost of Care	Projected Cost of Care
30 years (Age70)	$10,200	$13,720 ($451/day)	$24,000	$24,000	$30,000
40 years (Age 80)	$13,200	$22,350 ($735/day)	$35,000	$34,000	$43,000
45 years (Age 85)	$15,000	$28,500 ($937/day)	$44,000	$44,000	$55,000

Assuming Robert has a stroke at age 85 and needs four years of care before passing away, here is what his benefits from both policies could look like:

Year	Daily Benefit Stand-alone	Duration	Total Standalone	Monthly Benefit LTC life insurance rider	Total LTC life insurance rider	Total Both Polices
Year 1	$937.72	365 days	$314,136	$15,000	$180,000	$494,136
Year 2	$984.60	365 days	$359,379	$15,000	$180,000	$539,379
Year 3	$1,033.83	365 days	$377,347	$15,000	$180,000	$557,347
Year 4	$1,085.52	365 days	$396,214	$15,000	$180,000	$576,214
			$1,447,076		$720,000	$2,167,076

Robert had also selected the feature to allow his death benefit to grow with dividends, so at the time of his death, the LTC benefits paid at $180,000 for four years equaled $720,000. However, his family received $570,388 in unused death benefit. So total benefits between the two policies and the remaining death benefit actually totaled $2,737,464.

$1,447,076 – **Standalone**
$ 720,000 – **Life insurance Rider**
$ 570,388 – **Death Benefit**

 $2,737,464

What really sold Robert on this plan initially was when his financial planner showed him the premium for his long-term care coverage over 40 years would only be $97,407, which is $183.18 for the LTC life insurance rider + $2,252 for the standalone policy = $2,435.18 x 40 years). While the premium for the LTC life insurance rider was guaranteed, his financial planner was careful to tell him there could be a class rate increase on the standalone policy. Even so, Robert understood the concept of paying a little to get a lot. Even if he never needed care, the death benefit from the life insurance policy would pay his estate back for the standalone policy premium several times over.

And Jane? Robert made sure to buy a bigger standalone policy on her at the same time he bought his so they could both receive the significant couples' discount. Together their premium equaled $5,534 which included $55 to waive the premium on both of them if only one of them had a claim. Her plan had a $250 daily benefit with a four year benefit period which was enough to pay 80% of the projected charge at that time and would also grow at 5% compound. At that rate it will double every 15 years, which would give her $1000 daily benefit by age 90. She likes that as longevity runs in her family.

The "hole" in this plan is that Robert and Jane were gambling that both of them would be insurable for the standalone coverage in 10 years but they accepted this risk with full disclosure from their financial planner.

Underwriting

Don't expect combination life/LTC products to be easier to get from an underwriting standpoint than a traditional long-term care insurance policy. A tip, however, is that the decline rate is a little higher on a combination product that bases the underwriting decision on a short application and an underwriting phone call vs. obtaining your medical records from your doctor and looking at you more thoroughly. For example, someone who is taking Sinemet for restless leg syndrome would likely result in a decline from a company that does quick underwriting, as Sinemet is also a popular drug for Parkinson's disease. Full underwriting might approve the case and may even award a preferred health discount.

Important Tax Information

At this point, some of you may be smiling at the idea that a single premium may constitute a large tax deduction. Only the premium for the pure insurance options can be treated like long-term care insurance premium. This would be premium for an inflation rider or extension that enables the contract to pay more than the death benefit or annuity account value, and even that premium is deductible only if it is paid outside of the initial deposit into the combo product. If it is taken out of the cash value, it isn't deductible due to **Sec. 844(e)(2) Denial of Deduction Under Section 213** of the PPA which says:

> *No deduction shall be allowed under section 213(a) for any payment made for coverage under a qualified long-term care insurance contract if such payment is made as a charge against the cash surrender value of a life insurance contract or the cash value of an annuity contract. [Public Law 109-280, Sec. 844 (c) (e) (2)]*

If the premium is deductible, it would be the age-based amount of premium unless it is deducted at 100% by a C-Corporation for the owner. For example, a group of doctors may be set up as a PC (Professional Corporation) that elected C Corporation status. Also, any type of business could deduct it at 100% if the company is paying the premium for an employee. In these examples, annual or 10-pay premium paid separately for the inflation rider and extension may be deductible at 100%, but deducting single pay rider premium would be a definite gray area, just like it is for a traditional single pay LTCI contract. However, you should check with a professional tax advisor for a final determination.

Gift-Tax Exclusion

There is also a misunderstanding that 100% of long-term care insurance premium is eligible for the annual gift-tax exclusion per IRC Sec. 2503(e), as long as the premium is paid directly to the insurance company. This would be nice, especially with the single premium combination products, wouldn't it? Not true, however. IRC Sec. 2503(e) specifies medical care as defined in Section 213(d), which says: "In the case of a qualified long-term care insurance contract (as defined in section 7702B(b), only eligible long-term care premiums as defined in paragraph (10) shall be taken into account." Paragraph (10) sets the age-based premium limitations. Therefore, the amount of long-term care insurance premium that qualifies for the gift tax exclusion is equal to an age-based amount which we will cover later in this chapter.

Common Types of Annuity/Long-Term Care Products

An annuity/LTC product can also provide a place where "self-insure" money can work harder.

Tax Treatment of Annuity/LTC Products

With any product design, there is an opportunity to reduce taxable gain. Like the combo life/LTC product, however, the withdrawal of the account value each year to fund the LTC insurance premium reduces the cost basis. Here's a simple example of how that works:

- $50,000 cost basis
- $50,000 gain
- $1,000 LTC insurance charges each year
- After 10 years, the cost basis is reduced to $40,000
- At surrender or death, the beneficiary pays tax on $60,000, not $50,000
- If the annuitant needs long-term care, the gain is reduced and the tax bill is reduced

The potential exists to eliminate the gain and tax liability entirely if the annuitant needs a significant amount of long-term care.

Annuity/LTC Underwriting

There's a misconception that all of these products are underwritten almost as extensively as traditional long-term care insurance plans, or that at least the life/LTC and annuity/LTC plans are underwritten the same. Not so. Depending on how the insurance company views the risk, an annuity/LTC product can play a significant role in helping people who cannot qualify for long-term care insurance due to age or health problems. With the life/LTC product, the client's money is leveraged from day one as a larger death benefit, which can be equal to the LTC insurance benefits. With the annuity/LTC product, the death benefit is simply the client's cash value. A carrier that views these products this way will apply less extensive underwriting to the annuity/LTC product, because mortality concerns are reviewed more critically on the life product due to the larger death benefit.

This type of carrier will say that the medical qualification process is not nearly as stringent as it is for standard long-term care insurance products and ask only a few broad health questions on the application. The questions deal with major conditions like dementia, Parkinson's disease, multiple sclerosis, Lou Gehrig's disease, and whether or not the client is dependent on a walker or wheelchair or are bedridden. Being in a nursing home in the past two years would disqualify someone, but having a couple of weeks of home health care in that same time frame would not. This annuity/LTC product is available to age 85, which is older than today's typical standalone LTCI product.

The State Life/OneAmerica LTC annuity ("Annuity Care") is attractive for these reasons:

1. It has a separate LTC account with a higher interest rate.
2. It provides an option to continue paying benefits for long-term care after the annuity account value is exhausted at increments of 36 months or unlimited.
3. It provides a 5% compound inflation option for the portion that pays after the annuity account value is paid out.
4. Benefits can begin as soon as seven days of eligible charges have been incurred after the insured's doctor verifies that for a tax-qualified policy benefit trigger is met; i.e. needing help with at least two ADLs for at least 90 days or severe cognitive impairment.
5. It is a little easier to qualify for medically than the life/LTC combo products.

6. All premiums are guaranteed, so no worries about rate increases in the future.

Product Design

The original version of this product uses an annuity with two funds. One fund, which is for long-term care expenses, grows at a higher interest rate with a five-year rate guarantee. The five-year jumpstart on the long-term care fund ensures a higher amount available for long-term care. At the end of the fifth year, the insured decides if he or she wants the strategy of growing the LTC fund at a higher rate to continue, or if the desire is to equalize the growth rate between the two funds. (The funds are automatically equalized in 20 years.) The interest rate as of March 2013 is 1.20%, which is equal to 1.71% in a taxable fund for someone in a combined 30% tax bracket. The other fund, which is just the regular cash fund in an annuity, grows at a guaranteed rate of 1.05%.

The benefit is reimbursement, not indemnity, which means it will pay no more than actual expenses up to the monthly limit for a minimum of 36 months (18 months if a joint policy and both annuitants are receiving care at the same time). Benefits are available after incurring eligible charges for seven days. The monthly benefit is determined by dividing the annuity account value by 34.5 as in this example:

Example of how LTC withdrawals will be calculated	
$200,000	LTC fund balance at time of claim
34.5	Factor to ensure a minimum of 36 months of coverage
$5,797	Monthly benefit available for actual expenses

If the money is not used for long-term care, any amount remaining in the cash fund will be passed to a beneficiary outside of probate at the insured's death, or the death of the surviving annuitant (second-to-die) if it is a joint contract.

An additional premium outside of the single premium can be paid to extend benefits for another 36 months or to add a 5% compound inflation factor. This extra premium is guaranteed to never increase and can be paid with a single or 10-pay premium, or paid annually. Since the extension and/or inflation factor is true insurance, it is in the client's best interest to pay this additional premium annually as it is not returnable. The down side of the inflation factor, however, is that it only applies to the benefit extension. The base plan (i.e. the annuity account value) grows at current interest rates, except the initial interest rate is guaranteed for five years.

A variation of this product ("Annuity Care II") requires the policyholder to incur eligible charges for 90 days before benefits can start. The premium for the benefit extension and 5% compound inflation option is built into the product as a percentage of cash value instead of being paid separately. This means the purchaser can pay a single premium for the entire contract. If long-term care is needed, the money accumulated from the initial deposit would last a minimum of 24 months for a single person and 30 months for a couple. You have to decide when you buy this plan if you want the benefits to pay longer than that. The extension options are:

- 3 years (available ages 40 to 80)
- 6 years (available ages 40 to 75)
- 9 years (available ages 40 to 70)

There was formerly an option to make the benefit indemnity instead of reimbursement. This was withdrawn in August, 2012 as it was rarely purchased.

Both plans allow withdrawals up to 10% each year with no surrender charge. If more is withdrawn, there is a decreasing surrender charge that starts at less than 10% in the first year and goes away after 9 years.

Annuity/LTC "Leverage" model: The most popular product like this determines the total LTC benefit by multiplying the original deposit x 3 and allowing that amount to pay for long-term care for a minimum period of six years. I say minimum because it reimburses you for eligible LTC expenses so any day that you didn't use the entire daily benefit, the difference would stay in the pool and make it last longer than six years. The daily benefit on this plan is determined by dividing the total amount by 2,190 days. Here's how it works:

Initial deposit of $200,000 x 3 = $600,000 LTC benefit ÷ 2,190 days = $274 daily benefit

There is a one-time 90 day deductible before benefits are available after the policyholder is approved for LTC benefits. You have to incur 90 days of eligible charges to meet it, but you can do that over a period of 270 days. Guaranty Income Life Insurance Company (GILICO) offers a product like this.

Don't be misled. Many companies are advertising long-term care benefits but on closer inspection, they are only advancing the annuity account value to pay LTC. Once it is paid out, LTC benefits end. I'm sure new products will come out to meet the demand of the baby boomers, so just ask the financial professional approaching you if benefits are available after the annuity account value is paid out and if it is possible to add an inflation benefit. That leads me to my final comment about combo products.

Both life/LTC and annuity/LTC products provide a place for "self-insure" money to work harder and the prevailing thought has been that these products are mainly for clients with investable assets of $300,000+ (not counting their home). Accordingly, emphasis may be placed more on the leveraging factor vs. the actual daily or monthly benefit payout at claim time. Beware of any financial professional who just says "Give me $100,000 and I'll give you several hundred thousand for long-term care" without explaining what the policy will pay on a daily or monthly basis when a claim is filed.

If you are expecting the combo product to function as a robust long-term care insurance policy, you will want to make sure it is funded sufficiently to accommodate inflation needs. Project the average cost for care in your area at a compounded annual growth rate of at least five percent for the time frame in which you think you may need to access the LTC benefit, which will be largely determined by your age (10, 15, 20 years, etc.), then decide how much of that cost you are willing to self-insure. Here is an example of how that could work:

Ramona is a 60 year old single woman who owns 2500 acres in Tennessee. Her financial advisor has told her she can self-insure for long-term care, but she is concerned about leaving an inheritance to certain individuals. She is somewhat interested in long-term *care insurance, but not crazy about the "use it or lose it" aspect of traditional LTCI. If she does buy long-term care insurance, she is interested in a plan that will pretty much handle the entire cost in her area, which is $200/day ($6000 a month). In 25 years, this amount is expected to grow to about $25,000 a month, if historical inflation rates for long-term care costs continue.[9] Ideally, she would like an unlimited benefit period so she won't have to worry about running out of benefits. When presented with the Annuity/LTC combo, she became much more interested, especially when she learned the benefits would be tax-free due to legislation effective January 1, 2010.[10] Let's look at how the different versions of this product can help her:*

Annuity/LTC Combo with two funds – original version: The LTC fund is guaranteed to grow tax-deferred at 1.20% for the first five years and the general fund is guaranteed not to fall below 1.05%. (It will automatically change to an equalized interest rate in 20 years.)

- **Initial deposit required to generate a $6000 monthly benefit in the first year:** $207,000
- **Benefit Period:** 36 months plus annual premium of $2,415 which means her benefits can continue indefinitely after the money accumulated from her initial deposit has been used up, as long as she remains physically or mentally eligible for benefits
- **Inflation:** The extension benefits will grow at 5% compounded annually for the rest of her life
- **Deductible:** Seven days, once benefit eligibility is established.

What she likes about this plan:

1. If she dies without using it, the amount in the general fund (not the LTC fund) will go to a beneficiary. Since there would be no surrender charges at death, her beneficiary would receive more than her initial deposit even if she died in the first year as it would have grown some.

2. She only has to incur eligible charges for seven days for benefits to start after she is certified as being eligible for benefits.

3. There is no waiting period for the coverage to be effective; i.e. she could file a claim immediately if she was unfortunate enough to experience a long-term care event right after she bought the policy.

4. She only has to answer five health questions.

What she doesn't like about this plan:

1. Additional premium required for the rest of her life to extend the benefits beyond the initial 36 months. Even though this premium is guaranteed, she isn't crazy about being required to pay the additional $2,415 annually for an unlimited benefit period with 5% compound inflation.

2. The 5% compound inflation factor only applies to the extension. Her initial $207,000 deposit will only grow at the current interest rate which is guaranteed for 5 years not to be less than 1.20%. She has to use up this account over a 36 month period if she needs long-term care before she tap into the extended benefit pool which grows at 5% compounded annually from the first day she owns the plan.

At that point, her financial professional showed her the newer version of this product which allows her to pay one premium and be done with it. The LTC fund has a slightly lower interest rate which is guaranteed not to fall below 1.15% for the first five years and the general fund is guaranteed not to fall below 1.05%. Using the same $207,000 deposit that she had planned to put into the original version of this product, here is the coverage she will have:

- **Monthly benefit in the first year:** $6,641
- **Benefit Period:** 24 months plus about $48,000 of her $207,000 goes to purchase the maximum extension of 108 months = 132 months (11 years)
- **Deductible:** 90 days, once benefit eligibility is established.

What she likes about this plan:

1. She pays a single premium and doesn't have to worry about future premiums and setting up a mechanism for the time when she may not be physically or cognitively able to be sure they are paid
2. If she dies without using it, the amount in the general fund (not the LTC fund) will go to a beneficiary. Since there would be no surrender charges at death, her beneficiary would receive more than her initial deposit even if she died in the first year as it would have grown some.
3. There is no waiting period for the coverage to be effective; i.e. she could file a claim immediately if she was unfortunate enough to experience a long-term care event right after she bought the policy.

What she doesn't like about this plan:

1. It doesn't give her the unlimited benefit period like the original version of the product does.

2. The 5% compound inflation factor only applies to the extension. However, the extension account is now bundled with her original deposit, so together they average a compounded annual growth of about 4%. For example:

End of Policy Year	Age	Total LTC Balance	Monthly Benefit (Total LTC Balance ÷ 132 months)
1	61	$875,756	$6,641
15	75	$1,564,201	$11,850
25	85	$2,447,189	$18,539

If the cost in Ramona's area does reach $25,000 a month in 25 years, her LTC benefit will fund about 75%, and she is happy with that. She also thinks this solution to the inflation problem outweighs her wish for an unlimited benefit period, especially when her financial professional informs her that less than ten percent of long-term care insurance claims last longer than five years.[11]

Once her financial professional understood how she felt, he showed her the "Leverage" model that would provide three times her $207,000 deposit available for long-term care, divided over 2,190 days (six years). The benefits on this plan are expressed as daily, not monthly. This plan pays the actual charge up to the daily benefit so benefits could last longer than six years if she doesn't use the entire daily benefit every single day. At the guaranteed interest rate of 1%, here is how much coverage she would have:

Annuity "Leverage" Model:

End of Policy Year	Age	Total LTC Balance	Daily Benefit (Total LTC Balance ÷ six years)
1	61	$635,505	$290 ($8,826 monthly)
15	75	$871,166	$397 ($12,100 mo.)
25	85	$1,091,302	$498 ($15,157 mo.)

What About "Qualified" Money?

Many people have their savings mostly in savings accounts funded with pre-tax dollars. This is called "qualified" money and you have to pay income on it when you start taking it out. If you take it out prior to age 59 ½, in most instances you will have to pay an additional tax of 10% as a penalty for early withdrawal. Both of the products above will allow you to spread the amount you deposit into the annuity over four or five years without going through underwriting more than once. For example, Ramona could withdraw enough from her qualified account each year for five years to pay tax on that money, then deposit $41,400 into her new LTC annuity, for a total of $207,000 by the end of the 5th year. That way she can spread the tax burden over five years.

A Different Use for an LTC Annuity

Before we leave this topic, however, let's explore how a combo product could be used with a non-affluent client to lower the cost of a traditional long-term care insurance plan. Here is the story of a retired school teacher who had a small sum that would go quickly if she used it for care.

Using a Combination Annuity/LTC
to Lower the Cost of Traditional LTCI

Mrs. Teacher retired from a long teaching career in June 2010 and wants LTCI. She is age 61 and her husband is 66. They have less than $250,000 in assets and their house isn't paid off. The most LTCI they can afford comfortably is a two year benefit period with 5% simple inflation, and Mrs. Teacher expressed a monthly budget of $250. The advisor showed them a product with first day coverage for a 40% cash alternative benefit in lieu of the entire benefit, but if they need to tap the full benefit, they can't afford a long deductible. The premium for that plan with a 60 day elimination period (no charges required) is about $310. Using the following strategy gets it down to the $250 monthly budget:

The school system gave Mrs. Teacher a $37,000 403(b) plan when she retired as a culmination of unused sick days and other benefits. She appreciated that but was not happy about losing her life insurance when she retired. Exchanging the qualified annuity for a combo life/LTC especially designed for qualified money resulted in a death benefit of about $60,000, which will be paid out at 2% to 50 months for a long-term care need. We structured it with 5% simple inflation to assure growth. If they just happen to both need care at the same time, it will pay the full monthly benefit for each of them, and would pay out 25 months instead of 50. That's ok as their traditional plan is also a two year benefit period. Here's the magic: The resulting $1200 monthly benefit from the combo plan enabled her to buy a $4000 monthly benefit on a traditional plan instead of $5000. There's a good chance she won't use the entire 50 months and if she doesn't, she is comforted that her children may receive a small death benefit. (Note: this plan is designed for qualified money because exchanging an annuity for life insurance isn't allowed. Therefore, the $37,000 is exchanged for an annuity within the combo product which will pay out over 20 years to buy a life insurance policy that is paid up in 20 years. This is a combo life/LTC policy that allows the death benefit to be paid out tax-free for qualified LTC.).

A taxable amount of $2,415 is withdrawn from the annuity each year to pay the life insurance premium, but spreading it over 20 years minimizes the tax impact. Plus, it is more than enough to satisfy the Required Minimum Distribution for her at age 70½. It also helps that she is older than 59½ so there is no concern about the 10% early distribution penalty. The death benefit is a combination of the life insurance death benefit and the annuity account value. This will shift over the 20 years until the death benefit is all in the life insurance policy with a LTC benefit balance double the death benefit. The life insurance has a guaranteed minimum interest rate of 4% and the annuity has a guaranteed minimum of 3%. Both can increase but can't go lower than the minimum. The insurance charges are guaranteed not to ever increase, as at this time the guaranteed and non-guaranteed numbers are the same. This means the worst case scenario with maximum charges is already illustrated. Last but not least, if Mrs. Teacher changes her mind, she can get the single premium back anytime less the amount that went for the 5% simple inflation rider.

Combo sales have enjoyed double digit growth since 2009.[12] This section has demonstrated many uses for them, and with forward thinking and innovation, many more uses can be discovered to make it easier to plan for long-term care.

Good News for Consumers: New Producer Training Requirement for Sellers of Annuities

Most states are adopting a new training requirement set forth by the National Association of Insurance Commissioners (NAIC). As a result, producers selling LTC/annuity combination products should be able to do a better job for you as they have two new training requirements to sell annuity/LTC products as this regulation is passed in their state:

1. company/product specific training; and
2. a four hour annuity continuing education course.

No More "Use It or Lose It"

The best part about any combination LTC product is if you never need care, your family or any designated beneficiary can receive the life insurance death benefit or annuity account value. Some life insurance policies will still pay a residual death benefit of perhaps 10% to your beneficiary, even if the entire death benefit is consumed by a long-term care event.

A really cool idea along these lines is that you can use a combo product to create a return of premium for a standalone product. Just as you saw in the Mass Mutual example in this chapter, you can buy enough death benefit or annuity account value to pay your estate back for the premium you spend on a standalone long-term care insurance policy. So if you have an existing standalone policy and want more coverage, you could supplement with a combo plan which will increase your long-term care insurance benefits, plus pay your estate back for that premium if you never need care.

A Parting Word

Please be sure that the long-term care insurance benefits are intended to be tax-free in any combination product that you consider. There are two ways this can be done:

1. The combo product is intended to be a tax-qualified long-term care insurance policy as that is what makes it possible for the LTC insurance premium to come out of the account value tax-free and the benefits to paid out tax-free up to a federally established daily benefit which we will cover in the next section. You can know it is by the disclosure language on the illustration your financial professional provides, which will look something like this:

The long term care riders are intended to be federally tax-qualified. LTC benefit payments made under the terms of a contract federally tax-qualified under section 7702B(b) are not subject to federal income tax.

2. A life insurance rider as in the Mass Mutual whole life policy may have this wording:

The benefits provided by the LTCAccess Rider are intended to be excludable from federal gross income underSection 101(g) of the IRC. However to receive tax-free treatment, IRC section 101(g) requires that the payment of benefits be for costs incurred by the payee for covered Long Term Care Services.

Tax Incentives for Long-Term Care Insurance

OK, you are circling the boat on buying long-term care insurance. Could I reel you in if the government paid a hefty amount of your LTCI premium? If you own a C-Corporation as many medical professionals or business executives do, that could very well happen as 100% of long-term care insurance premium is deductible just like health insurance. Even if you are self-employed as a sole proprietor, Partnership, Subchapter S-Corporation or Limited Liability Corporation (LLC), you can still deduct part of your long-term care insurance premium in addition to your self-employed health insurance premium deduction on Line 29 of Form 1040. Or, if you are simply Mr. and Mrs. Smith, you can deduct an age-based amount of your premium as an IRS-approved medical expense which can be a significant reduction in your older years when you are likely to incur medical expenses above the required threshold of adjusted gross income for deductibility. Last but not least, Health Savings Account owners can pay that same age-based amount of premium with pre-tax dollars, which means getting a discount on your premium equal to whatever tax bracket you are in.

This section will explain all of these avenues to have Uncle Sam either wholly or partially fund your long-term care insurance premium. But let me cut to the chase on a quick tip just in case you don't feel like wading through the tax deduction verbiage.

The best deal on the table right now is for owners of C-Corporations as they can deduct 100% of a limited pay LTCI plan for themselves and their spouse and even for dependent children 18+. This means they will accelerate the premium at today's rates and pay it off in a minimum of 10 years. The fabulous thing about this is these lucky policy owners are not subject to future rate increases after the plan is paid up as the insurance company can never ask for more premium after that date. If the C-Corporation owner was also smart enough to buy the kind of inflation benefit that makes the benefits grow automatically each year, the benefits will continue to grow annually even after no premium is being paid. So two thoughts for you here:

1. Several insurance companies have eliminated limited pay plans altogether so if you want one, now is the time to get it, whether you are a business owner or not.

2. The best inflation benefit (5% compound for life) has proven to be very expensive for the insurance companies with people living so long. A limited pay plan with this feature is the ultimate plan

for long-term care insurance coverage, and I guarantee you this deal will not be on the table much longer.

Now, here is the full scoop on long-term care insurance tax deductibility:

To encourage Americans to plan for their own long-term care needs and to ensure that long-term care insurance has great value for the future, the federal government provided tax incentives for long-term care insurance policies issued on and after January 1, 1997 as part of the Health Insurance Portability and Accountability Act of 1996 (HIPAA). Policies issued prior to that were grandfathered to receive the same favorable tax treatment as long as they do not sustain a "material change". A material change would be a benefit increase such as adding an inflation rider, lengthening the benefit period, increasing the daily benefit, or reducing the elimination period.

The intent of this law was also to standardize the benefits somewhat to offer the best value for the consumer. This legislation can be found in IRC Section 7702B which defines long-term care insurance as an accident and health benefit. For "tax-qualified" policies that meet these criteria, the following apply for 2013:

- Benefits will not be taxable income, as long as benefit payments above $320 per day (or the monthly equivalent) do not exceed the actual cost of care. Conversely, benefit payments in excess of $320 per day that do exceed the actual cost of care will be taxed as income.
- A portion of a long-term care insurance premium based on the age of the policyholder counts as a medical expense per IRC Sec. 213(d)(10)(A). Since medical expenses in excess of 10% (7.5% for people age 65 through 2016) of adjusted gross income are tax

deductible, this means that a portion of long-term care insurance premium may help clients reach that threshold and may even put them over it to receive a tax deduction. Here are the amounts that count in 2013, and they are allowed to increase each year based on the medical Consumer Price Index:

Attained age before the close of the taxable year:	Amount that counts as a medical expense:
40 or less	$360
41 – 50	$680
51 – 60	$1,360
61 - 70	$3,640
71 and older	$4,550

While younger people generally don't have enough medical expenses to gain a tax deduction from long-term care insurance premiums, this provision may make it worthwhile for older Americans to itemize. Remember you can add co-payments, deductibles plus premium for Medicare supplemental coverage and Medicare Part B. Here's a quick example:

Mary and Bob are 65 and 67 with an annual adjusted gross income of $50,000. Medical expenses in excess of $3,750 are tax-deductible. Their long-term care insurance premium is $5,000 a year and they have an additional $3,500 in medical expenses as Bob takes some fairly expensive medications. They should ask their accountant if they would be better off itemizing on their tax return vs. taking the standard deduction.

Tax Incentives for Self-Employed

- The allowable percentage of an LTC insurance premium is now treated like health insurance premium for the self-employed tax deduction, which provides a first-dollar tax deduction of 100% on Line 29 of IRS Form 1040. "First-dollar" means a self-employed taxpayer can claim this deduction whether he or she chooses to itemize or claim the standard deduction. The self-employed tax deduction lowers adjusted gross income.

- A person is self-employed if he or she is treated as an employee under IRC Section 401(c)(1). IRC Section 162(1) permits a self-employed individual to deduct insurance premiums for "medical care for the taxpayer, his spouse and dependents". "Self-employed" means sole proprietors, general partners in a partnership, and members of a Limited Liability Corporation (LLC) that is taxed as a partnership.

S-Corporations: IRS Notice 2008-1 says that greater than 2% shareholder/employees of an S-corporation are also entitled to this deduction if the premium is paid by the S-Corporation and added to the shareholder/employee's gross income. The premium payments are included in wages for income-tax withholding on W-2 but are generally not subject to Social Security and Medicare taxes. The net result is the LTC insurance premium amount lowers adjusted gross income on the first page of IRS Form 1040, then is included as W-2 salary. Some greater than 2% shareholders of S-corporations do this as they want the business to pay the premium for cash-flow purposes, rather than pay it out of their personal checking account.

Rule of Spousal Attribution: Some think if the greater than 2% shareholder's spouse is an employee of the S-Corporation and doesn't own any shares, 100% of all eligible health insurance including 100% of the LTC insurance premium (not the age-based amount) can be deducted on

Schedule C as a business expense. This is not true. IRC Section 1372(b) treats the spouse of a more than 2% shareholder as also owning the shares owned by the more than 2% shareholder spouse. In other words, both spouses are treated as a greater than 2% shareholder even if all the shares are directly owned by only one spouse.

However, an individual who is both self-employed and an employee eligible to participate in a subsidized plan maintained by his employer or his spouse's employer cannot take the deduction. [Code Sec. 7702B(c), 7702B(b), Code Sec. 162(l)(2)(B)]

Important: all potential health insurance deductions, including long-term care insurance, can't exceed the taxpayer's earned income from the business that is paying the premium. [IRC Section 162(1) (2)(A)]

Mary owns an S-Corporation, so she is considered self-employed by the IRS. Her health insurance premium is $2,500 per year and her long-term care insurance is $1,000 per year. Based on her age of 48, she is allowed to add $680 of her long-term care insurance premium to her $2,500 health insurance premium for a total premium of $3,180, which she will receive as a first-dollar tax deduction for tax year 2013. Therefore, her adjusted gross income for 2013 will be lowered by that amount.

Tax Incentives for Any Type of Corporation

- Any type of corporation can deduct any portion of the long-term care insurance premiums paid for employees as a business expense. The deduction is not limited to the age-based amount. Employers who are defined as a C-corporation will receive this deduction on the owners as well as the employees. Premium paid for employees does not count as income for the employees, and the benefits are still tax-free to the employee. This 100% deduction extends to spouses just as in health insurance. It also includes limited pay plans as short as ten years. [IRC 7702B(a)(3) and Sec. 162] The consensus in the industry is that a single premium would not be deductible in a single year. If a return of premium rider is deducted by a corporation, it will likely be taxable income to the beneficiary. However, you should consult a tax professional for that question and any others related to information in this section, as this course in no way intends to give professional tax advice.

- Employers can select by class (e.g. tenure, job title, salary) as long as it is not a self-insured LTC plan, which is rare in the marketplace; e.g. CalPERS (California Public Employee's Retirement System). Additional rules prohibiting discrimination on the basis of salary were adopted for **insured** health plans in section 1001 of the Patient Protection and Affordability Act, in a new section 2716 as part of the Public Health Services Act. An employer violating the new rules in plan years on or after September 23, 2010 could be subject to an excise tax of $100 per day, per insured employee. However, the Public Health Services Act contains an exception the new section doesn't apply to benefits that aren't integrated into the health insurance plan. It further says benefits not subject to these requirements if offered separately include benefits for long-term care, nursing home care, home health care, community-based care, or any combination thereof. Therefore, long-term care insurance does not fall under this requirement as long as it is offered as a separate policy that is not part of the health insurance plan. [Citations: United States Code (USC) 42 §300gg-21(d)(1) and 42 §300gg-91(c)(2)]

- LTC insurance cannot be included in a cafeteria plan under Section 125, nor can LTC services be reimbursed by a Flexible Spending Account. The tax code specifically excludes any product which is advertised, marketed, or offered as long-term care insurance from the definition of qualified benefits that can be offered through a Section 125 plan. [IRC § 7702B(a)(1). IRC § 125(f)] (The only exception to this is if LTCI premium is paid out of a health savings account that was funded through a Section 125 plan.)

- The purchase of a qualified long-term care insurance policy cannot be financed through a salary reduction arrangement for the same reason it can't be funded with pre-tax dollars from a Section 125 cafeteria plan.

- Premium contributions made by all types of employers are not taxable income to employees. [IRC. Sec. 106(a)]

Health Savings Accounts

- The age-based long-term care insurance premiums are an acceptable medical expense under Health Savings Accounts (HSA's). **This means that Americans who own an HSA can pay the age-based amount of LTCI premium with pre-tax dollars.** Here's a general description of how they work in 2013 (the dollar amounts cited below generally increase each January but were the same for 2012-2013):

Section 1201 of the Medicare Drug Bill, Public Law No. 108-173, added Section 223 to the Internal Revenue Code to permit eligible individuals to establish Health Savings Accounts (HSA's) for taxable years beginning with 2004. Health Savings Accounts are available to anyone with a deductible of at least $1,250 with a maximum contribution of $3,250 for an individual plan with annual out-of-pocket expenses (deductibles, co-payments, not premiums) not exceeding $6,250 (Family plans: at least a $2,500 deductible with a maximum contribution of $6,450 and out-of-pocket max of $12,500). An additional contribution of $1,000 is allowed for age 55+. As of 2007, the month-to-month accumulation is gone; i.e. if one is eligible in December, he/she can contribute the entire allowed amount for the entire year.

Any unused amounts at the end of the year in HSA's are allowed to grow tax-deferred, which is much better than the "use it or lose it" feature of a flexible spending account.

Americans who have high-deductible health insurance plans (HDHPs) in the amounts specified above may deposit up to the maximum contribution above in a pre-tax account and may use that money to pay for any IRS-approved medical expense, plus three types of insurance premium: COBRA premium, health insurance premium only if the applicant is receiving unemployment, and "qualified" long-term care insurance premium, which means the age-based amounts. Prior to age 65, a 20% penalty is imposed for distributions after 12/31/10 not used for qualified medical expenses. [IRC Section 223 (f)(4)(A)]. At age 65, funds used at age 65 for other than qualified medical expenses are included in taxable income but there is no penalty.

Qualified medical expenses for individuals over 65 may include premiums for Medicare Part A, B, D, Medicare Advantage, premium for employer-sponsored health insurance (including retiree health insurance), but not Medicare supplement premiums. (Note: Americans who are eligible for Medicare can't set up a Health Savings Account, but if they set one up prior to becoming eligible for Medicare, they can keep it – they just can't make new contributions after becoming Medicare-eligible.)

Premiums are typically 30%-50% lower than managed care or traditional health insurance plans. HSA's are available to individual high-deductible health plan policyholders and to employees through employer-sponsored health insurance plans. (Some employers pay the high-deductible health plan premium and also make a contribution into each employee's HSA account.)

- Qualified long-term care insurance premiums are eligible expenses in a Section 105 Medical Reimbursement Plan, which is available to small businesses and farms to deduct family health insurance premiums and medical, vision and dental expenses not covered by insurance. To be eligible, a sole proprietor must be married and be legitimately able to employ his/her spouse.

- The age-based LTC insurance premiums are an acceptable medical expense under a Health Reimbursement Arrangement, the employer-provided medical care expense plan in which reimbursements for medical care expenses made from the plan are excludable from employee gross income. (Rev. Rule. 2002-41)

- Unreimbursed expenses for "qualified" long-term care **services** — the cost of long-term care itself, not LTC insurance premiums — will count toward the itemized medical deduction if paid on behalf of yourself, your spouse or your dependents.

"Wages and certain taxes for nursing services for chronically ill people" qualify as IRS-approved medical expenses. (The taxes you can deduct are Social Security, Medicare tax, Federal Unemployment Tax [FUTA] and state employment tax.)

This means unreimbursed "qualified" care, as well as long-term care insurance premiums that you pay for a parent, will count as long as you contribute more than 50% of your parent's support. The allowable portion of long-term care insurance premiums that count is based on the parent's age, not yours. Sometimes children form a "multiple support agreement," which means collectively they provide more than 50% of a parent's support. In this case, one child each year can take the tax deduction as long as that child individually provides at least 10% of the parent's support.

- "Qualified" services means the care recipient must be certified by a licensed health care practitioner (doctor, registered nurse or licensed social worker) as being expected to need help with at least two Activities of Daily Living (bathing, dressing, transferring, toileting, continence, eating) for at least 90 days and/or have a severe cognitive impairment that makes him/her a threat to self or others.

Long-Term Care Insurance Tax Deduction for Retired Public Safety Officers

Effective January 1, 2007, up to $3,000 in any taxable year is excluded from gross income for retired public safety officers who elect to have premiums for qualified health insurance premiums deducted from their

"Eligible Government Plan" for themselves, spouse and/or dependents and **paid directly to the insurance company.**

The term "public safety officer" means anyone who separates from service either at normal retirement age or due to a disability and has served in an official capacity with or without compensation as a:

- law enforcement officer;
- firefighter;
- Chaplain; or
- member of an ambulance or rescue squad crew.

An Eligible Government Plan is either a 401(a), 403(a), 403(b), or 457(b) plan as defined in Section 414(d) of the Internal Revenue Code of 1986. The employer sponsoring the Eligible Government Plan is not required to offer this election.

This deduction applies to qualified health insurance premium which includes premium for a qualified long-term care insurance plan for the eligible retired public safety officer and his or her spouse and dependents. "Qualified" as you know means a tax-qualified long-term care insurance plan, but the exciting news about this provision is that the entire premium is excluded from gross income, not the age-based amounts.

The tax-free distribution is only available to the retired public safety officer not to a surviving spouse or dependents. However, it is available for any benefits accrued from holding other jobs with the employer offering the pension plan, as long as the individual separated from service as a retired public safety officer at normal retirement age or due to a disability.

If you wish to research this tax deduction further, the citation is IRC Sec. 845(a) from the Pension Protection Act of 2006 that amends Sec. 402(l).

Gift-Tax Exclusion

Since HIPAA clarifies that LTC insurance is treated as health insurance, the premium is included in qualifying medical expenses for the annual gift tax exclusion per IRC Sec. 2503(e), as long as the premium is paid directly to the insurance company. The policy must be a QUALIFIED (based on the HIPAA definition) LTC policy, and IRC Sec 2503(e)(2)(B) specifies medical care as defined in Section 213(d).

Section 213(d) says: "In the case of a qualified long-term care insurance contract (as defined in section 7702B(b), only eligible long-term care premiums (as defined in paragraph (10) shall be taken into account." Paragraph (10) sets the age-based premium limitations above. Therefore, the amount of the premium that qualifies for the gift tax exclusion is equal to the HIPAA allowed amounts based on age. Qualifying expenses also include QUALIFIED LTC services as long as payments go directly to the provider of care and not to a family member.

People often ask me why we don't all have a first-dollar tax deduction for long-term care insurance since it would take such a significant burden off Medicaid if more people had it, especially the baby boomers. The reason we don't is because under our current budget method, any new tax incentive has to be introduced with a corresponding savings (cut) elsewhere in the budget to offset it. This process doesn't work with long-term care insurance as the savings will be down the road when people use the policy first and rely on Medicaid last, if at all. Most people who buy long-term care insurance with an appropriate inflation benefit have not had to turn to Medicaid at all, as we will learn in Chapter Seven when we discuss Medicaid long-term care benefits.

Here I am with my children Jackson and Jed (Clampett).

Chapter Three:

THE INS AND OUTS OF LONG-TERM CARE INSURANCE

———⚬⚬⚬———

This chapter deals with how long-term care insurance actually works to help families and is largely the reason I felt so compelled to write this book at this time as dramatic changes are occurring **right now** that consumers need to know about. Due to the recent economy in particular, insurance carriers are having to withdraw some of the better benefits in order to keep rates as stable as possible. I am in a unique position to have this knowledge and not be constrained by a home office or compliance attorney about what I can tell you. I describe myself as a consumer advocate for long-term care insurance, and I hope you will understand that by the time you finish reading this chapter. Every time you see this symbol ✳ ***CONSUMER ALERT***, you will know I'm giving you this type of valuable information.

Most long-term care insurance carriers have reported growth in the last couple of years in both the number of policies sold and the premium these sales brought in, but the market penetration is still single digit. Can you believe that less than 10 million Americans have long-term care insurance when we have 240 million people in this country over age 18??? [1]

My concern is with all the upheaval in the Medicaid program, it is highly questionable as to how many Medicaid dollars will be there for LTC in the future. In 20-30 years, people who need long-term care will be sharply divided between haves and have-nots. **Many people who elected to self-insure will be squarely in the middle of the have-not bucket as the cost of care soars to $1000 a day in 30 years.**[2]

Money buys choices.

Without long-term care insurance, most families simply won't have the money to buy care and their worst nightmare will happen as the burden for their care falls on their children and grandchildren.

Evaluating Long-Term Care Insurance

So if you decide to consider long-term care insurance, what do you need to know? How do you evaluate plans? We will discuss insurance company evaluation and plan design in this chapter.

Insurance Company Evaluation

First, you should evaluate the company as you want it to be there to pay your claims in the future. There are four major rating services you can consult.

- **A.M. Best** provides a financial and operating performance rating on virtually all life and health insurance companies.
- **Standard & Poor's** provides financial strength ratings for those insurers who request a rating. S&P also provides financial strength ratings from public information for other insurers.
- **Moody's** and **Fitch** provide ratings for those insurers who request a rating. Therefore, ratings from these two services are not available for all insurance companies.*

---

* I am not a believer in the Weiss rating system for reasons I don't care to discuss in this book, so I am not directing you to that organization for rating information.

My advice is to stay within the top three rating categories when you choose a long-term care insurance carrier as follows:

Ranking	A.M. Best	Standard & Poors	Moody's	Fitch
#1	A++, A+ Superior	AAA Extremely Strong	Aaa Exceptional	AAA Exceptionally Strong
#2	A, A- Excellent	AA Very Strong	Aa Excellent	AA Very Strong
#3	B++ Very Good B+ Good	A Strong	A Good	A Strong

To get ratings on selected companies at no cost:

- A.M. Best / 908-439-2200

  www3.ambest.com/consumers

- Standard & Poor's / 877-772-5436 options 3, 1

  www.standardandpoors.com/ratings

- Moody's / 212-553-1658

  www.moodys.com/page/lookuparating.aspx

- Fitch / 800-853-4824 / 212-908-0500

  www.fitchratings.com

The A. M. Best rating can also be obtained by visiting the reference section of your local library. Ask for the most recent Best's book, because it is published annually. Please know that for some of the websites, a free registration may be required.

Ratings are important but that's only the beginning of evaluating a carrier in my opinion. Size is important. The A.M. Best book also shows the total assets of a company or companies if it is part of a group. I like companies with billions in assets, not millions!

A good point of reference is to find out if there have been complaints filed by policyholders. The National Association of Insurance Commissions (NAIC) keeps up with this at https://eapps.naic.org/cis/. If a company has had issues with paying claims, you will see that on this site.

But let's look at another very important area for evaluating a company.

Experience and commitment: How long has the carrier been in the long-term care insurance market? How many rate increases has it had? Is long-term care insurance really a commitment or is it offered merely as a convenience to the carrier's career agents?

Plan Design

Let's start with answering the questions I posed in the Preface to this book that you read and did not skip. As there were less than 20 carriers selling new policies in the long-term care insurance market nationally in early 2013, I will occasionally mention specific insurance companies that offer various features but this isn't an exhaustive list. Your financial professional may introduce you to other carriers that offer similar benefits. Just ask to see the benefit in an outline of coverage or sample policy to know for sure.

1. Where would you like to receive care?

Most people's first reaction to this question is "at home". But think through this with me. Someone living alone has to manage medications as well as personal care like bathing and dressing, cook meals and maintain a home.

Hiring 24-hour caregivers can be cost prohibitive as high as $400 a day or more, which is much higher than nursing home care in most areas.

Fortunately, there are three types of products available in most states.

Comprehensive: Long-term care insurance plans that pay for care in four main settings:

- At home
- Adult day care center
- Assisted living facility
- Nursing facility (aka nursing home)

Facilities-Only: plans that pay for assisted living or nursing facility but not at home or in adult day care (premium savings of 20% - 40%)

Community-Only: plans that pay at home or in an adult day care center but not in a facility (premium savings of 15%-20%)

If you live alone and your state allows it, you may be better off buying a facilities-only policy with "Cadillac" benefit levels; i.e. a monthly benefit high enough to get into the nicest assisted living facility in the area, 5% compound inflation for life, a longer benefit period, and the like.

The premium difference between a comprehensive policy with home care benefits and a facilities-only policy that covers assisted living and nursing home care is significant at 30%-40%. (If home care is not optional, you can ask your agent if a lower home care benefit, such as 50%, is available to reduce the premium.)

If you considering an option for little or no home care benefits either for affordability or because you live alone, remember that this type of policy will still make nursing home care the last resort by providing coverage for the beautiful assisted living facilities that are going up everywhere.

If there is a significant age difference between spouses or partners, the younger one may also find a facilities-only policy an interesting idea.

When would you consider a plan that pays only at home; i.e. the community-only policy? *Don't buy this plan because you are certain you will never be in a nursing home.* If you walk through any nursing home and ask the patients how many of them planned to be there, I doubt that you would find many who say "Yes". The people who are a candidate for the community-only plan are generally people who bought older policies with limited home care benefits and they really want home care benefits. A community-only plan makes a great supplement to the older policy as it will pay in addition to any other benefits. This is especially helpful if the community-only plan is an all cash policy as it can give you the ability to pay family members and other informal caregivers, no questions asked.

✻ CONSUMER ALERT: Most companies have stopped selling anything except comprehensive policies. If you want a facilities-only or community-only plan, you need to buy it now.

2. How much of the bill do you want the insurance company to pay?

You will be asked to choose a daily or monthly benefit. Choices today are $50 - $500 per day or $1,500 - $16,000 per month. Here is the formula for determining the right amount for you:

- Look at the average cost in your area for 8-10 hours of home care (or where you plan to move to when you retire), and decide if you want a plan that provides full coverage or if you are willing to pay part of the cost.
- If you are planning on self-insuring part of the cost, you can ask for an insurance quote that would pay 2/3 or 80%. For example, if the cost of a home health aide is $20 an hour ($200 for ten hours), and you are willing to pay 20% of that, you could ask for the closest benefit to 80% of $200, so $160 per day or $4800 a month. Long-term care insurance policies are sold in increments of $10 for daily benefits and monthly benefits are usually rounded off to the nearest $500. So you would ask for a quote for $160 per day or $5000 a month.
- To find out the cost of care in your area, your insurance professional can help you, and most insurance carriers that offer long-term care insurance have a cost of care survey on their website by state.

Tip: A monthly benefit is more flexible for home care. If you need more care some days than others, you can max out a daily benefit.

3. How long do you want to wait before benefits start?

Most people choose a waiting period (deductible) of 90 or 100 days for four reasons:

- this is a one-time event in today's policies no matter how many times they have a claim;
- they aren't worried about needing care for three months, they're worried about needing care for three years;

- many plans have made this a calendar day waiting period with no charges required or some have even waived it for home care; or
- they bought the policy at work and 90 days was the only choice available.

Some states allow insurance companies to offer longer waiting periods as long as 180 or 365 days but the premium savings don't justify these. There are shorter waiting periods as well like 20, 30 or 60 days. The premium difference between 20 and 100 days with most companies is about 20 percent, so you have to contrast that with self-insuring the cost for an additional 80 days - not just at today's costs but at future costs. On the other hand, there may be an option to waive the waiting period entirely for home care benefits or a few products like Genworth and Transamerica do that for no additional premium. The Mutual of Omaha/United of Omaha products waive it for home care any month you use the alternative cash benefit (see #5 "How Do You Want to Receive the Money?")

You will also see this feature referred to as an elimination period. I don't use that term as it makes me think of the Mafia!

4. What do you want to do about inflation?

This is the factor that you choose to make your benefits grow each year and can likely be the most important decision you make about your long-term care insurance coverage next to the carrier you choose. It's easy to get caught up in the size of the benefit pool available to pay benefits, but please don't lose sight of the actual daily or monthly benefit the policy can pay out at claim time. Without the appropriate inflation factor, you can wind up with a policy that you thought would pay 80%, only to find it will only pay 30%. Then the people who love you have to find the other 70%, which is the last thing you wanted to happen. I continue to hear from consumers just like this one:

> *My mother has a long-term care insurance policy with a $60 daily benefit. We need to file a claim. How can I get more coverage for her as this won't even pay half the bill?*

The answer is, she can't. Her mother is uninsurable now that she needs to use her policy. All we can do is encourage the daughter to buy a good policy on herself so her children aren't struggling with inadequate resources to care for her someday.

✸ *CONSUMER ALERT:* **BUY INFLATION COVERAGE.** *Would you buy health insurance that only pays hospital room rates at what they cost today?*

Here are common inflation options and how long it takes the benefit to double so you can see how fast they grow:

5% compound	15 years
4% compound	18 years
3% compound	24 years
5% simple	20 years
4% simple	25 years
3% simple	33 years

The cost of nursing home care has almost quadrupled in the 25 years since 1987 ($56 a day to $222 a day in 2012).[3] That's an average annual growth rate of 5.66%. But don't take my word for this. Here's a great calculator that you can use to see for yourself. Just enter the current amount and the starting amount with the number of years inbetween and it will compute the average annual growth for you: http://tinyurl.com/auypm74

Home care and assisted living has grown much slower but the demands of the baby boomers may accelerate the growth rate.

The 5% compound for life inflation factor

The 5% compound inflation factor that grows until you have used all your benefits has been the most popular inflation factor since it was introduced back in 1990. However, premiums for this benefit have increased dramatically in the last five years as the insurance companies see that people are living much longer which means their benefits can grow to extremely high amounts with this inflation option. Since it causes the benefits to double every 15 years, a 40 year old buying a $200 daily benefit could see her daily benefit quadruple to $800 by the time she is 70 and double again to $1600 by the time she is 85!!

The benefit account also grows as you will learn in #6 of this section *"How long or how much do you want the insurance company to pay in your life?"* The caveat here is that with most policies, it is affected by whether or not you are on claim. If you are receiving benefits, the benefit account grows at 5% each year, less claims paid out.

✸ *CONSUMER ALERT:* If you own an older Genworth, MedAmerica, New York Life, Prudential or Transamerica policy, you likely have the kind of inflation benefit that grows the benefit maximum each year as though no claims had been paid, then subtracts any claims paid out in the preceding year. Do not let this plan go. It is rare.

Alternatives to the 5% compound for life inflation factor

To address this issue yet provide ways for applicants to buy inflation coverage, the long-term care insurance industry has come up with a variety of alternatives to the 5% compound for life using either lower factors for compound or by using simple interest which makes the benefit grow at 3% or 5% of the original amount.

Again, if you're like me, you need to see what I'm talking about. Take a look at the chart on the next page that shows the growth of a $200 daily benefit over 30 years, using the various inflation factors on the market today. The last two columns show a 3% and 5% compound step-rated. This means that the benefit **and** the premium grow each year, which may not be a bad thing. This idea especially helps the younger buyer who wants the 5% compound inflation factor but can't afford it due to competing financial responsibilities. I'll show you a sample premium for a 40 year old with this approach when we look at premiums later in this chapter.

	3% Compound for life	3.5% Compound for life	4% Compound for life	4.5% Compound for life	5% Compound for life	5% Compound (20 year)	5% Compound (2x)	5% Compound (3x)	5% compound (4x)	5% simple for life	3% simple for life	3% Compound for life step rated	5% Compound for life step rated
Initial benefit	$200.00	$200.00	$200.00	$200.00	$200.00	$200.00	$200.00	$200.00	$200.00	$200.00	$200.00	$200.00	$200.00
Year 1	$206.00	$207.00	$208.00	$209.00	$210.00	$210.00	$210.00	$210.00	$210.00	$210.00	$206.00	$200.00	$200.00
Year 2	$212.18	$214.25	$216.32	$218.41	$220.50	$220.50	$220.50	$220.50	$220.50	$220.00	$212.00	$200.00	$200.00
Year 3	$218.55	$221.74	$224.97	$228.23	$231.53	$231.53	$231.53	$231.53	$231.53	$230.00	$218.00	$200.00	$200.00
Year 4	$225.10	$229.50	$233.97	$238.50	$243.10	$243.10	$243.10	$243.10	$243.10	$240.00	$224.00	$200.00	$200.00
Year 5	$231.85	$237.54	$243.33	$249.24	$255.26	$255.26	$255.26	$255.26	$255.26	$250.00	$230.00	$232.00	$256.00
Year 6	$238.81	$245.85	$253.06	$260.45	$268.02	$268.02	$268.02	$268.02	$268.02	$260.00	$236.00	$232.00	$256.00
Year 7	$245.97	$254.46	$263.19	$272.17	$281.42	$281.42	$281.42	$281.42	$281.42	$270.00	$242.00	$232.00	$256.00
Year 8	$253.35	$263.36	$273.71	$284.42	$295.49	$295.49	$295.49	$295.49	$295.49	$280.00	$248.00	$232.00	$256.00
Year 9	$260.95	$272.58	$284.66	$297.22	$310.27	$310.27	$310.27	$310.27	$310.27	$290.00	$254.00	$232.00	$256.00
Year 10	$268.78	$282.12	$296.05	$310.59	$325.78	$325.78	$325.78	$325.78	$325.78	$300.00	$260.00	$269.00	$326.00
Year 11	$276.85	$291.99	$307.89	$324.57	$342.07	$342.07	$342.07	$342.07	$342.07	$310.00	$266.00	$269.00	$326.00
Year 12	$285.15	$302.21	$320.21	$339.18	$359.17	$359.17	$359.17	$359.17	$359.17	$320.00	$272.00	$269.00	$326.00
Year 13	$293.71	$312.79	$333.01	$354.44	$377.13	$377.13	$377.13	$377.13	$377.13	$330.00	$278.00	$269.00	$326.00
Year 14	$302.52	$323.74	$346.34	$370.39	$395.99	$395.99	$395.99	$395.99	$395.99	$340.00	$284.00	$269.00	$326.00
Year 15	$311.59	$335.07	$360.19	$387.06	$415.79	$415.79	$400.00	$415.79	$415.79	$350.00	$290.00	$362.00	$416.00
Year 16	$320.94	$346.80	$374.60	$404.47	$436.57	$436.57	$400.00	$436.57	$436.57	$360.00	$296.00	$362.00	$416.00
Year 17	$330.57	$358.94	$389.58	$422.68	$458.40	$458.40	$400.00	$458.40	$458.40	$370.00	$302.00	$362.00	$416.00
Year 18	$340.49	$371.50	$405.16	$441.70	$481.32	$481.32	$400.00	$481.32	$481.32	$380.00	$308.00	$362.00	$416.00

Year 19	$350.70	$384.50	$421.37	$461.57	$505.39	$505.39	$400.00	$505.39	$505.39	$390.00	$314.00	$362.00	$416.00
Year 20	$361.22	$397.96	$438.22	$482.34	$530.66	$505.39	$400.00	$530.66	$530.66	$400.00	$320.00	$419.00	$531.00
Year 21	$372.06	$411.89	$455.75	$504.05	$557.19	$505.39	$400.00	$557.19	$557.19	$410.00	$326.00	$419.00	$531.00
Year 22	$383.22	$426.30	$473.98	$526.73	$585.05	$505.39	$400.00	$585.05	$585.05	$420.00	$332.00	$419.00	$531.00
Year 23	$394.72	$441.22	$492.94	$550.43	$614.30	$505.39	$400.00	$600.00	$614.30	$430.00	$338.00	$419.00	$531.00
Year 24	$406.56	$456.67	$512.66	$575.20	$645.02	$505.39	$400.00	$600.00	$645.02	$440.00	$344.00	$419.00	$531.00
Year 25	$418.76	$472.65	$533.17	$601.09	$677.27	$505.39	$400.00	$600.00	$677.27	$450.00	$350.00	$486.00	$678.00
Year 26	$431.32	$489.19	$554.49	$628.14	$711.13	$505.39	$400.00	$600.00	$711.13	$460.00	$356.00	$486.00	$678.00
Year 27	$444.26	$506.31	$576.67	$656.40	$746.69	$505.39	$400.00	$600.00	$746.69	$470.00	$362.00	$486.00	$678.00
Year 28	$457.59	$524.03	$599.74	$685.94	$784.03	$505.39	$400.00	$600.00	$784.03	$480.00	$368.00	$486.00	$678.00
Year 29	$471.31	$542.38	$623.73	$716.81	$823.23	$505.39	$400.00	$600.00	$800.00	$490.00	$374.00	$486.00	$678.00
Year 30	$485.45	$561.36	$648.68	$749.06	$864.39	$505.39	$400.00	$600.00	$800.00	$500.00	$380.00	$563.00	$865.00

Another popular approach has been the CPI inflation factor. This makes the daily or monthly benefit grow each year based on the consumer price index. According to the Bureau of Labor Statistics, the consumer price index has averaged about 3.5% since 1913.[4]

✳ *CONSUMER ALERT:* This 5% compound for life with a level premium except for class rate increases will be off the table soon!

MY ADVICE: THERE ARE STILL A FEW SOLID CARRIERS THAT HAVEN'T MADE THIS TYPE OF INFLATION EXTREMELY COSTLY, SO IF YOU WANT IT, NOW IS AN EXCELLENT TIME TO GET IT.

However, there are other ways to do this, especially if that factor isn't affordable by the time you read this book. The simple formula is this:

- Look at the current cost of care in your area or the area in which you plan to retire.

- Project that cost at 5% for the number of years until you are 80-85, depending on longevity in your family.

- Multiply that by the percentage of the cost of care you want the insurance to pay, remembering that you should have other income or assets to put with it.

- Choose the daily or monthly benefit combined with the inflation factor that will grow it to that amount.

You can do this. It's not rocket science. A great compound interest calculator for the second step is at www.moneychimp.com/calculator. Here is what it shows for $222 (national average today for 10 hours of home care or semi-private care in a nursing facility per the 2012 MetLife Market Survey of Long-Term Care Costs) x 30 years:

Inputs		
Current Principal:	$	222
Annual Addition:	$	
Years to grow:		30
Interest Rate:		5 %
Compound interest 1 time(s) annually		
Make additions at start end of each compounding period		
Results		
Future Value:	$	959.47

So knowing that the cost of care is likely to be in the $1000 a day range in 30 years, if you want to insure two-thirds of that, you would select a daily or monthly benefit with an inflation factor that would grow to $700 a day ($21,000 a month) in 30 years. Using the same calculator, you can see that these combinations would get you there:

- a daily benefit of $160 or a monthly benefit of $5000 at 5%

- a daily benefit of $210 or a monthly benefit of $6500 at 4%

- a daily benefit of $250 or a monthly benefit of $7500 at 3.5%

- a daily benefit of $280 or a monthly benefit of $8500 at 3%

- a daily benefit of $280 or a monthly benefit of $8500 at 5% simple

Remember, simple interest is calculated at 5% of the **original** amount, so the $280 daily benefit will grow at $14 a year for 30 years until it reaches $700 in 30 years. If you used the 3% simple inflation factor, you would have to start with a daily benefit of $370 since it would grow $11.10 each year until it reached $703 in 30 years.

There are other options in the marketplace such as 5% compound 2X, 3X or 4X. In other words, the benefit will either double, triple or quadruple then stop growing. There are combination compound/simple riders. Insurance carriers are working hard to develop creative inflation factors to keep long-term care insurance affordable. These can make sense for older Americans unless you have extreme longevity in your genes.

In summary, if you use an inflation factor lower than 5% compound for life, just choose a higher daily or monthly benefit to offset slower or capped growth. Ask your financial professional to include the page in the illustration that compares the various inflation options so you can make an informed decision.

Well, that was exhausting, especially for an English major ☺ But now you get the idea and can do it yourself.

Important: To get the asset protection equal to benefits paid by your long-term care insurance policy in those states that offer Long-Term Care Partnership policies, you have to buy a compound inflation benefit if you are under age 61 when you apply for coverage. We will talk more about this at the end of Chapter Seven.

Different Approaches to Managing Inflation

Three insurance companies have thought totally outside the box to help consumers plan for inflation with lower premiums at younger ages when many other financial needs compete for their dollars. Let's take this sample plan and compare how it would work with all three for a 40 year old with a spouse or partner also being accepted for coverage. That means you would get a couples' discount, which can range from 20% to 40%.

Daily/Monthly Benefit:	$150/$4500
Waiting Period:	90 days
Benefit Period:	three years
Benefit Account:	$164,250 ($150 x 1095 days) or $162,000 for monthly benefit ($4500 x 36 months)
Home Care:	100%
Inflation:	5% compound for life (benefits double every 15 years)
Health:	Standard, without preferred health discount

United of Omaha Flex-to-Age-85

United of Omaha (part of Mutual of Omaha) will allow applicants 18-60 to start paying at either 70%, 80% or 90% of the normal premium.* The premium increases gradually each year at a factor based on the age of purchase until it levels at age 65 then is paid up at age 85. The coverage will continue after age 85 with no premium due. The factors for the 70% plan are below on the Assured Solutions Gold product.

*not available in Florida, New York, Maryland and Texas

Regular premium:	$1,659
Initial Premium for this plan:	$1,161
Premium at age 65:	$2,498, based on the 3.7% factor on the chart below
Total premium paid with regular premium by age 85:	$74,655
Total premium paid with Flex-Pay by age 85:	$104,600
Benefits at age 85:	$1.3 million ($36,000 monthly benefit x 36 months)

The benefits at age 85 with either premium paying method wind up the same, as they double every 15 years.

The picture would look even better if the applicant qualified for the 15% preferred health discount which would start the premium at $987 instead of $1,161, and you would pay in 15% less over the life of the policy.

Here I am telling the story of my Grandpa John A., my best friend when I was little.

Applicant Age	Flex 70% Factor	Flex 70% 3.7% increase to 65	
		Age	Premium
35	3.4%	40	$1,161.51
36	3.4%	41	$1,204.79
37	3.5%	42	$1,249.68
38	3.6%	43	$1,296.24
39	3.6%	44	$1,344.54
40	3.7%	45	$1,394.64
41	3.8%	46	$1,446.60
42	3.9%	47	$1,500.50
43	4.0%	48	$1,556.41
44	4.1%	49	$1,614.40
45	4.3%	50	$1,674.55
46	4.4%	51	$1,736.94
47	4.6%	52	$1,801.66
48	4.8%	53	$1,868.79
49	5.0%	54	$1,938.42
50	5.2%	55	$2,010.65
51	5.5%	56	$2,085.57
52	5.7%	57	$2,163.28
53	6.1%	58	$2,243.88
54	6.5%	59	$2,327.49
55	7.0%	60	$2,414.21
56	7.6%	61	$2,504.16
57	8.3%	62	$2,597.47
58	8.6%	63	$2,694.25
59	9.0%	64	$2,794.64
60	9.5%	65 - 84	$2,898.77
		85+	$0.00
			$104,600.67

Transamerica TransCare II Step-Rated

Premiums begin lower and increase by 3% or 5% of the current year's premium as the benefit increases by 3% or 5% of the current benefit amount of the policy less claims already paid. Using the same plan with the 5% compound we just did with the above United of Omaha example, here's what it means:

Regular premium:	$1,806
Initial Premium for this plan:	$763
Premium at age 65:	$6,872
Total premium paid with regular premium by age 85:	$81,270
Total premium paid with 5% step-rated by age 85:	$117,347
Benefits at age 85:	$1.4 million ($1,348 daily benefit x 1,095 days)

The picture would look even better if the applicant qualified for the 10% preferred health discount which would start the premium at $686 instead of $763. **That's only $62 a month!**

John Hancock Benefit Builder

The new John Hancock product called Benefit Builder has a very different approach to inflation. In a nutshell, it says that the only way the benefit will grow is if the reserve fund grows at least 3%. The footnote at the bottom of the page says "Any future excess earnings credits will be offset to make up for any prior excess earnings credits that are less than zero."

Here is the explanation:

*This means that if the portfolio rate of return is 2% in a given year, after you subtract 3%, you would be left with a negative 1% (therefore **less than zero**) so there would be a negative excess earnings credit that year, yet the policyholder's benefits would remain the same as it was the previous year. If in the following year, if the portfolio rate of return is 5%, we would subtract the 3% leaving 2% and then after that we would multiply that by the allocated reserve value, and then adjust for the negative excess earning credit carried forward from the previous year.*

Each time I read it, I am speechless for about 30 seconds as I ponder the explanation. The premium is about a fourth of what other carriers are charging for comparable plans so I predict that it will be very popular with insurance agents and consumers. However you interpret the above paragraph, I think you will agree that the chances of the benefit growing consistently are small. To be fair, however, I do want to add that this product also includes the opportunity to increase the benefit by 10% at your attained age with no health questions every 3 years through age 75 as long as this opportunity isn't declined twice in a row under age 65 and not declined at all age 65 and up.

Really?

Let's cut to the chase on this. **IF** the reserve fund grew at least 3% every single year and **IF** you bought the additional 10% in benefit every three years at your new age, you could start at an annual premium of $483 for the sample plan above and wind up with an annual premium of $3,324 at age 75, having paid a total of $80,650 in premium by age 85. Your daily benefit will have grown from $150 to $428 and your benefit pool from $164,250 to $528,885. This benefit pool is significantly lower than the United of Omaha and Transamerica plans because you aren't allowed to buy additional benefit past age 75 which means the daily benefit is frozen at that point.

To reiterate, if you bought the same plan with 5% compound inflation at the average premium today of $1,878,[5] you would pay about $84,500 by age 85. Your benefits would double every 15 years and be about $1300 per day ($36,500 per month) and your benefit pool would be about $1.4 million.

The illustration for the John Hancock Benefit Builder product that you get from an insurance professional shows a hypothetical rate of return for the reserve fund of 5%, 6% and 7% in addition to 3%. I used 3% in my example because you have to make up the loss for any year it dips below 3%.

You may decide a premium that is less than a third of the prevailing market premium is worth having the lower benefit at claim time. Just don't make the mistake of thinking you can invest the difference in this example of $1,121 a year and make up the difference.

> $1,121 a year at 6% for 45 years = $253,915 before taxes and investment fees vs. a benefit pool of $1.3 million

All of these plans are subject to class rate increases. One could argue that the John Hancock approach will result in fewer rate increases since the benefits are limited which means John Hancock will pay out less in claims. The Benefit Builder plan is also paid up at age 95.

Guaranteed Purchase Options (Future Purchase Options)

The opportunity to start with a low premium and buy more coverage as you get older with no health questions is called Guaranteed Purchase Options (GPO) or Future Purchase Option (FPO), depending on the carrier. It simply means you can buy more as you get older but it is priced at the age at which you decide to buy more, like term life insurance. The inherent problem with this method is that the older you get, the less likely you are to exercise this option as the premium at older ages becomes very steep. If this is the only inflation option you can afford, then I encourage you to buy the highest benefit you can afford and lock that amount in at your current age. (You will learn in Chapter Seven that even these plans do not qualify for the asset protection under The Long-Term Care Partnership for purchasers under age 76.)

A few plans like United of Omaha (part of the Mutual of Omaha group) allow you to purchase a lower compound inflation factor and buy up to a higher one before age 85. Choices include 3%, 3.5%, 4%, 4.5% and 5%. Or, you can purchase no inflation and buy a 3% or 5% compound rider in the next five years.

Transamerica TransCare II Deferred Benefit Increase Option

Transamerica has taken the inflation alternative one step further by allowing the applicant to start with no inflation but add it within 90 days prior to the first, the third and the fifth anniversary date of the policy, as long as the policyholder hasn't become eligible to receive benefits. The additional premium for this benefit will be based on the age you add the inflation rider and the benefits begin increasing at that time, not when you first bought the policy. Using the above example, the annual premium would start at $519 instead of $763, and only $467 with the preferred health discount.

With all of the future purchase options, you can't be eligible to receive benefits when you accept an offer, and the inflation rider is priced at the age you are at that time. These are good options to have, however, if you can't start with a 5% compound rider.

5. How do you want to receive the money?

- *Cash* — you receive a check each month and you can use the money however you need it, which means you can use it to pay informal caregivers like family, friends, neighbors or sitters and companions provided by a caregiving agency. You don't have to account for how you spend it, except you or the person responsible for you will have to certify periodically that you still qualify for benefits and are following the plan of care laid out for you when you first met the qualifications to receive benefits and any subsequent changes.

Pro: Cash can be especially helpful in rural areas when licensed caregivers can be difficult to find. It can also be helpful to pay for new services that aren't covered by current long-term care insurance policies (i.e. robots) and also to pay caregivers with whom your loved one is comfortable. The only company that sells an all-cash product is MedAmerica Insurance Company (www.medamericaltc.com).

Con: if you hire your own informal caregivers, you will likely be responsible for the employer's contribution of the caregiver's Social Security, Medicare and state unemployment taxes. You may have to enlist the services of a bookkeeping service or accountant to help you with that, or a company like Hire Family that can help people manage their care by using informal caregivers. Their fee is small and it comes out of your long-term care insurance daily or monthly benefit, not out of your pocket. You can learn more about this valuable service at www.hirefamily.com.

- *Reimbursement* – you use licensed care providers as defined in the contract and file claims for their charges. The actual charge is paid up to the daily or monthly benefit. If you don't use it all, you don't lose it. The difference stays in your benefit pool to be used later. To collect benefits, you must provide proof of services from qualified caregivers. These are usually licensed caregivers such as a home health aide licensed as a certified nurse assistant (CNA), not unlicensed caregivers such as sitters or companions. This method of payment is utilized in most traditional LTCI policies and in most combination life/LTC and combination annuity/LTC plans.

  o *Hybrid cash/reimbursement* — For no additional premium, this type of policy that allows you to take 30%-40% of the home care benefit any month you like in cash and use however you need it **in lieu of** the entire monthly benefit. You don't lose the rest of the benefit that month. It stays in your benefit pool and makes your benefits last longer. For a little more premium, you can even bump the home care benefit up to 50% so the cash amount is larger. Here's an example:

    Home care benefit of $4,500 @ 40% = $1,800 cash benefit
    Home care benefit of $4,500 @ 50% = $2,250 cash benefit

Companies that offer this benefit are MedAmerica's FlexCare, Mutual of Omaha, Transamerica and United of Omaha.

- **_Flexible benefit_** — You can use up to half of any unused benefit to pay informal caregivers such as friends or neighbors or even immediate family members living with you. For example, if a third of your monthly benefit is being used for licensed caregivers, you can use half of the remaining benefit to pay informal caregivers. If you are receiving all of your care through informal caregivers, you can use the entire 50% of your monthly benefit this way. It's still a reimbursement policy because the insurance company reimburses the informal caregiver at the going rate in the area for the number of hours of home care you need as determined by your plan of care (see "How to Get a Claim Paid" in the next chapter.) Unlike the hybrid cash/reimbursement plan above, you can use part of your benefit to pay licensed caregivers and part of it can be flexible to pay for unlicensed care and services, all in the same month. The company that does it this way is LifeSecure, a subsidiary of Blue Cross Blue Shield of Michigan.

  Indemnity — you receive the daily or monthly benefit regardless of what the charge is. Unlike a cash plan, you still have to provide proof of services from qualified caregivers to receive benefits. The difference is you can keep any difference between the charge and your daily or monthly benefit vs. receiving a benefit no more than the actual charge which is what happens in a reimbursement policy.

With all types of policies, the benefits are tax-free up to $320 per day/$9700 in 2013, and beyond if you can justify that you spent the money on qualified long-term care. "Qualified long-term care" means you need help with at least two activities of daily living for longer than 90 days or have a severe cognitive impairment that makes you a threat to yourself or others. This is the same criteria that you have to meet to qualify for long-term care insurance benefits to be paid as you will see in the claims section of this chapter.

6. How long or how much do you want the insurance company to pay in your life?

This choice, which is called the "benefit period" or "benefit maximum" or "lifetime maximum", should be made after all of the above choices have been made. This is not how long you can be covered, by the way. You can be covered until you're 104 if you live that long. In today's policies, it's really how much the insurance company will pay out when you become impaired enough to qualify for benefits instead of how long. Choices are one, two, three, four, five, six, eight, ten years, but you should think of the number of years merely as a factor that determine the total benefits available when you have a claim when multiplied by the daily or monthly benefit you choose. For this reason, you can also think of it as your benefit account. Here are some examples:

> Three year benefit period with a $150 daily benefit:
> $150 x 3 x 365 = $164,250
> Three year benefit period with a $4500 monthly benefit:
> $4500 x 36 months = $162,000
> Five year benefit period with a $200 daily benefit:
> $200 x 5 x 365 = $365,000
> Five year benefit period with a $6000 monthly benefit:
> $6000 x 60 months = $360,000

The benefit maximum choices range from $18,250 to $1,000,000. The length of time is determined by the monthly benefit you choose. Here are some examples:

$200,000 ÷ $4500 monthly benefit = 44.4 months (3.7 years)

$300,000 ÷ $4500 monthly benefit = 66.6 months (5.5 years)

$500,000 ÷ $6000 monthly benefit = 83.3 months (6.9 years)

All will grow with inflation coverage, of course. Usually all benefits grow at the same rate. It's rare, but the benefit account might have a lower inflation factor like 3%, when the daily benefit is growing at 5%.

How much coverage should you purchase?

The answer is, as much as you can afford, without being uncomfortable with the premium. You are probably wondering how long claims typically last.

The Society of Actuaries looks at this question. Claims experience from 1984 – 2007 was published in 2011 with the results below.

HOW LONG ARE PEOPLE USING THEIR LTCI BENEFITS?

All Claims	Claims Lasting Longer Than a Year (a different story)
Half are less than a year	
Two-thirds < 2 years	One-third < 2 years
Three-fourths < 3 years	Half < 3 years
85% < 4 years	Three-fourths < 4 years
90% < 5 years	80% < 5 years
Average duration: 2 years	Average Duration: 3.5 years

The left side of the chart is the information that was published but that didn't interest me all that much. I wanted to know how long the claims lasted that lasted longer than a year as that to me is true long-term care. Fortunately, I was able to get that information and you see it on the right side of the chart.[6] With an average duration of 3.5 years, it's easy to see that a four year benefit period takes care of most people.

Who is at risk for longer periods? Four major categories:

1. People who take really good care of themselves may be the very people who need long episodes of long-term care. They are less likely to suffer a major heart attack or massive stroke, and instead, they just wear out! The healthier they are, the longer that can take—four years, six years, ten years! The fix? If you live in the South, you can visit Hardees or Cracker Barrel every day and alternate sausage biscuits with biscuits and gravy for breakfast. Yum! If you don't live in the South? I don't know. I live in the South, so you tell me ☺

2. Alzheimer's patients –the Alzheimer's Association says caregiving time can be four to 20 years.[7]

3. A younger person with a head or spinal cord injury

4. People with longevity in the family – is it common for relatives to live past age 90?

As the average purchasing age for long-term care insurance declines, insurance companies are uncomfortable with the risk of younger people incurring injuries or health conditions that can cause them to need many years of long-term care.

✳ **CONSUMER ALERT:** A few companies still offer an unlimited benefit period but this is almost a thing of the past. If this is really important to you (e.g. if you have a family history of Alzheimer's), my advice is to buy a policy with an unlimited benefit period now while it's still available. Once you have it, no one can take it away from you as long as the insurance company is in business. Country Financial and the Federal Long-Term Care Insurance Program have a reasonably priced unlimited benefit period.

My Advice: If an unlimited benefit period is really important to you and you can't find one, you can build a very long benefit period by combining a high daily or monthly benefit with a long benefit period or large benefit maximum.

$1,000,000 = $12,000 monthly benefit = 83.3 months (6.9 years)

This second plan greatly overfunds today's cost of care unless you are trying to build an insurance plan that pays for 24/7 home care.

Using a current cost of $6750 a month, $12,000 a month is almost double that, so you are really building a plan that could last almost 14 years instead of almost seven years in the above example.

It's also really important to remember that any day or month you don't use your entire benefit, the difference stays in your benefit pool and makes it last longer. So when you hear "three year benefit period", you should think "that's the MINIMUM amount of time the plan will pay". The only way your benefits will end in three years is if you use the entire daily or monthly benefit every single day or month.

- What if you are having home care five days a week and not seven?
- What if you are in an assisted living facility that costs 75% of your daily or monthly benefit?

You get the picture.

Now I'm going to show you how to truly maximize your benefit period/benefit maximum with two benefit options that most long-term care insurance plans offer.

Restoration of benefits – if you no longer need qualified long-term care (i.e. help with at least two basic activities of daily living like bathing and dressing) for at least 180 consecutive days, the benefits paid out will all be restored to your benefit pool and you get to start all over if you have a second claim. This feature typically costs 2%-4% and is a no-brainer especially for younger people. Anyone can have an accident or even a moderate stroke then ultimately recover after receiving a few months of benefits. Just don't count on this feature to restore your benefits after receiving them for as long as a year. People don't typically recover after receiving care that long.

Shared care – I love this benefit. As carriers started eliminating the unlimited benefit period, this benefit was introduced to make the coverage more attractive and affordable for couples. It basically says "we don't think both of us will need care for a really long time, but we don't know which one of us might." With shared care, you don't have to know as you have access to each other's benefits if one needs more care than a single benefit period can pay for. Or, if one dies without needing care, the surviving spouse inherits the unused benefits. Three versions of this idea exist in current policy selections:

- The lowest cost version allows spouses to share a single benefit period at a lower premium than two separate benefit periods would cost. If one spouse dies without using all the benefits, the surviving spouse is entitled to the remainder of the benefit period.

- Another version has separate benefit periods, but for a little more premium it allows spouses to access each other's benefit period. For example, each spouse has a six-year benefit period. If one spouse uses only one year of benefits then passes away, the other spouse would have eleven years of benefits left. Or if one spouse needs eight years of care, that spouse would use two years from the other's benefit period, leaving the healthier spouse with four years. Some companies require the healthy spouse to retain a minimum of one or two years of benefits to protect that spouse from having no benefits if he or she needs care at some point.

- A third version provides separate benefit periods of the same length for each spouse, then allows the couple to purchase an additional benefit equal to the primary benefit period to share first come, first served. For example, if the spouses each purchased a three-year benefit period, the insurance company would allow them to purchase a third three-year benefit period that both could access as needed.

Spouses or partners don't have to buy the same benefits, but to get this feature, they do. Also, a few companies won't offer it to couples with a wide age difference such as more than 15 years.

A Comforting Thought

Here's a comforting thought if you are concerned about how long you could need care and want to buy a long benefit period: If you purchase a longer benefit period, such as lifetime (unlimited) or build one by buying a large daily or monthly benefit combined with a longer benefit period or larger benefit maximum and you decide later that it's too much premium, there's an out. You can always reduce your premium by reducing your benefits, and that's fine with the insurance company. If you start out with a shorter benefit period or small benefit account and decide later you want to increase it, the insurance company will require you to start over with new medical questions, and you will have to pay premium for the larger benefit at your new age. It's in your best interest to start out with the largest benefit you think you might want, because you can always come down. Increasing benefits later is more expensive, and if you have developed a progressive health problem, you will likely be ineligible for a benefit increase.

The Most Important Point

The important point here is that you should never sacrifice inflation coverage for a longer benefit period or a larger benefit account. Why? Because if you can't make up the difference at claim time, you may have to apply for Medicaid and lose your private pay choices sooner rather than later. Even if you bought a Partnership policy, it won't help you because the asset protection feature is based on how much the policy has paid out when you apply for Medicaid.

So buy as many years as you can afford and if it's only two years, that's two years of private pay choices that you might not otherwise have.

7. Do you want your premium to be returned to a beneficiary if you die without needing long-term care?

This is a very seductive thought, isn't it? This is called nonforfeiture as it means if you never need care, someone benefits from the premium you paid for long-term care insurance. Actually some products like the United of Omaha *Cash-First* automatically return your premium to your beneficiary if you die without needing care before age 65 (age 67 for Transamerica's TransCare II) and you don't have to pay extra for this.

Many products provide a return of premium option that will return the premium at any age less claims paid out. MedAmerica and United of Omaha even offer a full return of premium that will return the premium whether or not you ever received benefits. Yes, these options are very pricey – perhaps an additional 30%-50% in premium. (The full return of premium is most utilized when a C-Corporation is buying long-term care insurance on executives as the entire premium is 100% tax deductible as an employee benefit. Whether or not the executive ever needs care, the premium flows back into the corporation at the death of the employee as taxable income since it was deducted.)

Shortened Benefit Period — This is a nonforfeiture benefit that the National Association of Insurance Commissioners (NAIC) tried to make mandatory. I was one of many who breathed a huge sigh of relief when that didn't happen. Companies have to offer it but you don't have to buy it. It can add about 15% to your premium. It means that if you've had your policy at least three years, you can cancel it for any reason and the insurance company has to pay a claim equal to the premium you put in at any point in your life even though your policy is no longer in force. Sounds great, doesn't it? Let's play that out.

Let's assume you paid $3,000 a year in premium which amounts to $9,000 after three years. You cancel your policy and in 30 years you need care. If the historical trend continues that we discussed earlier, the cost of care will be around $30,000 a month at that point, so your $9,000 would pay for about ten days. Better than a sharp stick in the eye but is it worth the additional 15% in premium that you could have spent on better inflation coverage? If you are over age 75, you could spend the additional premium on a higher daily or monthly benefit if you want to build in some immediate inflation protection. I say over age 75 because Long-Term Care Partnership plans don't require applicants above that age to buy an inflation factor.

The good news about this benefit and another reason not to pay extra for it is that it is required to be in today's policies in the form of "contingent non-forfeiture" which means you get it if premium increases above a certain percentage based on issue age. Here is the table:

Contingent Nonforfeiture	
Cumulative Premium increase Over Initial Premium that Qualifies for Contingent Nonforfeiture Percentage increase is cumulative from date of original issue. It does NOT represent a one-time increase.	
Issue Age	**Percent Increase Over Initial Premium**
29 and under	200%
30-34	190%
35-39	170%
40-44	150%
45-49	130%
50-54	110%
55-59	90%
60	70%
61	66%
62	62%
63	58%
64	54%
65	50%
66	48%
67	46%
68	44%
69	42%
70	40%
71	38%
72	36%
73	34%
74	32%
75	30%
76	28%
77	26%
78	24%
79	22%
80	20%
81	19%
82	18%
83	17%
84	16%
85	15%
86	14%
87	13%
88	12%
89	11%
90 and over	10%

Miscellaneous Benefits

We have now covered the main decisions that you need to make in order to choose a long-term care insurance plan. There are many additional benefits included in today's policies however that make long-term care insurance such a great value.

Alternate Plan of Care—If your doctor and the insurance company agree that you can be taken care of at home adequately, most policies allow money taken from your benefits to provide enhancements to your home, such as handrails, wheelchair ramps, shower stall improvements, etc., or even an emergency response system to make it easier for you to stay home. This benefit is also used to pay for new long-term care services as they are developed. This is a great feature, because without it, the insurance company would have to amend your policy to pay for new services, a process that can take a long time.

Caution: Beware of anyone who tells you the alternate plan of care benefit means it is not necessary to purchase home health coverage when you buy your policy. You may be able to get some home care assistance under the alternate plan of care provision, but it is by no means a defined benefit for home care, assisted living or adult day care. If you want home care benefits, make sure that the "comprehensive" block is checked on the application, and that your policy specifically states that you have benefits for home care, assisted living and adult day care. (The real intent of the alternate plan of care provision is to find ways to provide care that is less expensive than nursing home care.)

Stay-at-Home benefit—also called a transition benefit with some policies, this is a very meaningful benefit that provides money during the waiting period before your benefits start that can be used to pay for things like caregiver training, durable medical equipment, medical alert system, and home modifications. A typical benefit is two times the monthly home care benefit.

Double home care benefit: at no additional charge you can receive 2X the monthly home care benefit if the need for care is due to an accidental injury or if you need the services of a professional at home such as a Registered Nurse, physical therapist, speech therapist, or respiratory therapist. This is especially meaningful as professional home care is very expensive and with this double benefit, you wouldn't have to give up the day to day caregiver helping with bathing and dressing, etc. in order to pay for the professional home care.

Why would someone need professional home care? Two great examples would be if you had a bad accident or had a severe stroke. With so much emphasis placed on managed care in health care reform, health insurance or Medicare may stop paying for physical or speech therapy at some point in your recuperation, saying you aren't improving enough to justify it. Your family may disagree and say you are certainly still getting better, just slowly. Wouldn't it be great to have the money to continue the professional services on your own? United of Omaha's Cash-First product offers these double home care benefits.

Hospice—Most long-term care insurance policies cover hospice, which is care for terminally ill people to keep them as comfortable as possible and provide respite care to family members. Most health insurance policies also cover hospice and Medicare has a virtually unlimited benefit for hospice. Tax-qualified policies are not allowed to duplicate Medicare payments, so when would the long-term care insurance policy pay? Medicare's inpatient respite care benefit for hospice is only five days per stay and the family may need a longer period of respite care. Medicare's home care benefit for hospice won't pay eight-hour shifts except in a crisis situation. Long-term care insurance will pay eight-hour shifts indefinitely as long as benefit triggers are met and benefit maximums are not exhausted.

Respite Care—a specific benefit to give the primary caregiver a break. The break could be a few hours off to go shopping or a week or two for a vacation. This benefit is usually paid at home but the better policies pay also in a nursing home or assisted living facility to cover the 24-hour care that will be needed if the caregiver needs to be away several days. Benefit triggers (Activities of Daily Living or cognitive impairment) usually must be met to access the respite care benefit, but the elimination period often does not have to be satisfied.

Homemaker Services—a benefit that pays for personal caregiving services such as cooking, cleaning, laundry, shopping, telephoning and transportation when a benefit trigger is met. Some policies will pay homemaker services only when you are receiving other home care services, such as care provided by a home health aide, nurse or therapist.

Alternate Payer Designation (Third Party Notification)—The policy-holder has the opportunity to designate someone else to get a copy of a lapse notice in case the policyholder doesn't pay the premium. Take advantage of this opportunity because this feature protects against policies lapsing if policyholders develop a mental or physical problem that makes them unable to pay the premium.

Impairment Reinstatement—If the policyholder allows the policy to lapse due to a cognitive or physical impairment, the insurance company will reinstate the policy with appropriate premium payment within a specific time period, such as five, six, or nine months. Without this provision in the policy, an insurance company is under no obligation to reinstate your policy if you miss the grace period by even one day. Tax-qualified policies are required to have a minimum reinstatement period of five months.

Bed Reservation—If you have to go to a hospital during a nursing home stay, this benefit will pay to hold your bed at the nursing home. Without this benefit, your family would have to pay or the nursing home could give the bed to someone else. Some nursing homes have waiting lists. Without a bed hold payment, you would have to find another nursing home if you lost your bed to someone else and the nursing home was full. Newer policies provide the bed-reservation benefit when the patient leaves the nursing home for any reason, such as for short visits with family and friends, and policies also pay to hold your bed if you have to go to the hospital while you are in an assisted living facility. Another significant advantage to this benefit is for patients with dementia who get very upset over changes in their environment. If your mother has Alzheimer's and has to return from a hospital stay to a bed by a wall instead of a window, that could be very traumatic for her.

Care Coordination—This benefit pays a licensed medical professional, usually a Registered Nurse, to manage your care and report regularly to your family, although some companies require you to use care coordinators affiliated with the insurance company. The care coordinator would perform services like helping you get approved for benefits initially and developing the initial plan of care to determine the best place for you to receive care, i.e., at home, in an assisted living facility, adult day care or a nursing home. Ongoing, the care coordinator monitors your care and helps make sure you are getting the best care possible.

A care coordinator is especially helpful when children or other family members don't live nearby, because the care coordinator can give care reports regularly to the family members. Some companies want policyholders to use this benefit so much that they don't reduce the benefit maximum whenever you use it, which makes it a free benefit. They feel this way because they know a care coordinator will help you get the most out of your long-term care insurance policy by using your benefits most effectively and efficiently. Some companies require the use of care coordinators before paying benefits at all, but you may have the option to purchase a benefit that pays a private care coordinator if for whatever reason you don't wish to use the free care coordinator provided by the insurance company. Transamerica's TransCare II product has this option.

The Federal Long-Term Care Insurance Program makes care coordinators available to the immediate family members of the policyholder even though the family members don't have an insurance policy. Some carriers like Genworth and John Hancock have continued that effort which is very helpful, especially with taking care of parents who didn't or couldn't buy long-term care insurance.

Worldwide Coverage—Most long-term care insurance policies will not pay outside the United States and Canada, but a few will pay worldwide, or in a list of specified countries, especially if you live in the U.S. at least six months of the year. Payment is usually made to you in U.S. currency and benefits may be reduced to compensate for the additional administration required to process claims with international complexities. If this is important to you, ask if there are any benefit reductions for worldwide coverage. If this is really important to you, you might want to consider a cash plan that gives a monthly benefit check that you can use anyway you like without proving services. That way you will have total freedom to purchase whatever services are available in the other country.

Wellness — You are hearing about wellness programs everywhere in an effort to fight the escalating obesity epidemic in our country, so why not in long-term care insurance? Carriers like Genworth are forging alliances with health organizations like the Mayo Clinic to promote health care assessments and online health coaching in an effort to keep policyholders healthier and defer claims filing.

OK. That concludes the benefits section. Now let's take a close look at what's happening with long-term care insurance today.

Chapter Four:

WHERE THE RUBBER HITS THE ROAD: PREMIUM, UNDERWRITING AND CLAIMS

———∞∞∞———

Let's kick this chapter off with the top two trends in the long-term care insurance industry as they both directly affect consumers.

#1 – Higher premium for new applicants, aka the "Rate Refresh"

It's not unusual for insurance companies to introduce new products that cost more. However, a more recent trend is instead of bringing out a new policy that is priced higher, carriers are drawing a line in the sand and selling a current policy form at a higher premium after a specific date. Average premium looks like this:

- Individual buyer average premium is $2,322, as the average purchaser is late 50s [1]

- Worksite buyer average premium is closer to $1100, as the average purchaser at work is in the 40s. [2]

Obviously I wish every employer would offer long-term care insurance so that people would have the opportunity to learn about it as young as possible and the premium would be much more affordable. Fifty-one percent of new sales in 2011 were made in the workplace which is very exciting, and I encourage you to ask your employer to offer long-term care insurance.[3] Recognizing that the majority of people don't have access to an employer-sponsored plan however, this chapter deals with the individual policy buyer. Chapter Five deals with how worksite long-term care insurance works and why it is so important.

How much does long-term care insurance cost?

Now that you understand how the benefits work, we can discuss how much the insurance costs.

By averaging the premiums of major LTCI carriers, let's look at a snapshot of a plan that will pay about 2/3 of the cost of care in most parts of the country for **a couple** - $150 daily benefit ($4500 monthly); a 3 year benefit period, 5% compound inflation, 90 day waiting period period:[4]

Why am I showing you premium for a couple? Because generally it's one check and also because if you and your spouse or partner are in reasonably good health, I don't want you to even think about getting long-term care insurance on just one of you. This is something you do for each other. Early in my career, I especially would hear men say "I want to buy long-term care insurance on my wife, but I don't need it." He is thinking his wife will take care of him, especially if she is younger. I would usually bite my tongue as I wanted to say "Wait a minute. Superman and the president of the United States needed long-term care...and you are special, why?" But what I would say is "Buying long-term care insurance for yourself is how you take care of her. Does she ever sleep? When is the last time she picked you up? Can you see that the only way she can get enough rest to take care of you is if you have the money to hire caregivers to help her?"

"Couple" by the way can mean married, domestic partner, or same-sex partners and carries the deepest discount up to 40% with some carriers. Most plans also have a discount if you are part of a couple and your spouse or partner doesn't apply or applies and can't qualify for coverage. Why? Because couples are typically slower to file a claim as they try to take care of themselves. Single people without a primary caregiver pay the highest premium as they may file a claim sooner rather than later. For a sample single rate, just divide the numbers in the chart below by two and add 20% – 30%, depending on whether or not you can qualify for the preferred health discount.

✹ *CONSUMER ALERT:* Several carriers like Genworth, MedAmerica and Transamerica announced discount reductions for couples in 2012. Some carriers still offer 30% - 40% when both are issued and 15%-20% when one is issued. Some have a two-person or household discount which could be siblings or a parent and adult child.

Age of Couple	Annual Premium Standard	Annual Premium Preferred	Monthly Premium Standard	Monthly Premium Preferred
40	$3,600	$3,500	$320	$300
50	$4,200	$3,900	$370	$350
60	$5,200	$4,800	$460	$430
70	$8,800	$8,000	$780	$700

Even though the insurance carriers are charging quite a bit more for long-term care insurance today, it is still a phenomenal deal compared to paying full price for the care itself. To calculate this for yourself, just multiply the premium of a plan you are considering by 30 years and compare the premium to the benefits you will have in 30 years. For example:

The 50 year old couple above with standard health would pay $126,000 in 30 years ($4200 x 30) vs. a benefit pool of $648,000 each, so $1.3 million for both. How did I arrive at that?

This plan has the 5% compound inflation benefit which you will recall from Chapter Three enables the benefits to double every 15 years. So in 30 years, the $4500 monthly benefit will double twice to $18,000 and the benefit account of $162,000 ($4500 x 36 months) will double twice to $648,000. For additional premium, a couple can have access to each other's benefit pool ("shared care") which really enhances the value of the coverage.

Now, there can be class rate increases along the way as in other insurance products, but not nearly as often with long-term care insurance as with other products. Even so, there's a huge difference between paying $126,000 in premium vs. paying $1.3 million for the cost of six years of care in 30 years, so it's easy to see the concept.

For those of you in higher cost areas of the country, we will look at the same plan except a $250 daily benefit ($7500 monthly benefit). Remember, these rates are for TWO people:[5]

Age of Couple	Annual Premium Standard	Annual Premium Preferred	Monthly Premium Standard	Monthly Premium Preferred
40	$5,800	$5,600	$510	$490
50	$6,600	$6,300	$580	$550
60	$8,200	$7,800	$730	$680
70	$14,000	$13,000	$1,230	$1,140

Now let's do the same calculation for the 50 year old couple in standard health:

$6600 x 30 = $198,000 vs. a benefit pool of initially $270,000 each ($7500 x 36 months) which will double twice in 30 years to $1,080,000 each, or $2.1 million for both.

Of course if either person qualifies for the preferred health discount, these examples will look even better.

✳ CONSUMER ALERT: The preferred health discount is usually 10% but can be as high as 15%. A couple of carriers have either reduced the preferred health discount or eliminated it altogether.

My Advice: Health is fragile. If you are in excellent health today and can qualify for the preferred health discount while it is still available on long-term care insurance, there's no guarantee you will be able to in a couple of years. Therefore, I say shop sooner rather than later for long-term care insurance.

Premiums for long-term care insurance are the same for men and women, but are based on age.

CONSUMER ALERT: Genworth, John Hancock, Mutual of Omaha and Transamerica will begin charging gender-specific rates in 2013. I never thought this would happen with long-term care insurance as it will put women at a distinct disadvantage. Why? Because women live longer and have more claims than men. A couple of other carriers appear to be following this trend.

My Advice: Single women in particular file more claims than men and will be impacted the most by this monumental change in long-term care insurance. Please listen to me on this. SINGLE WOMEN NEED TO SHOP FOR LONG-TERM CARE INSURANCE SOONER RATHER THAN LATER.

Waiver of Premium

Premiums are waived after a specified time of receiving benefits, usually expressed in days of benefit payments. For example, older policies typically waived premiums after 90 days of nursing home benefits. Some policies do not require these days to be consecutive. Newer policies also waive premiums when you receive assisted living, home care or adult day care, and most policies waive premiums on the first day of benefits. The premium only comes back if you get truly better, which typically means you don't need help with at least two daily activities, for 180 consecutive days.

Many plans offer the "dual waiver" or "joint waiver", which means the premium is waived for both spouses when one spouse starts receiving benefits. Generally the couple must buy the same benefits, but it is a very low cost option if you are fine with that. However, is the sick spouse dies, the premium will come back on the well spouse unless the couple bought a benefit called "survivor".

Survivor Benefit—This is a meaningful option as it means a surviving spouse can stop paying premiums after the death of a spouse if the death occurs after the policy has been held a specified period of time with no claims on either spouse, usually 10 years, but it could be less. For example, if the death occurs prior to the 10th year, the surviving spouse would not have a premium waiver. A few policies have a more liberal provision, however, and will waive the premium on the 10th policy anniversary of the surviving spouse. The additional premium is typically about 9%. Many couples decide that is a small amount to pay to get a paid-up policy for the surviving spouse. No surprise, however, is that most carriers won't offer this benefit to a couple with a significant age difference, such as 15+ years.

Trend #2 – Tighter Underwriting

Decline rates for the industry are about 22% but about 10% for applicants under age 50, 15% for 50-59, one in four applicants 60-69, almost 40% for applicants in their 70s and almost two-thirds of applicants 80+.[6]

These percentages are no big surprise when viewed next to characteristics of Medicare beneficiaries:[7]

- Almost half have an income below 200% of poverty level
- 44% have three or more chronic conditions
- 29% have a cognitive issue that limits ability to function independently
- 15% have two or more ADL limitations

A combination annuity/LTC product with less stringent underwriting may be a potential coverage resource for more affluent older Americans.

Policies are available for ages 18+, but most are sold in the 40-79 age range. **No one 18+ is too young to consider long-term care insurance.** A 25-year-old can wind up in a coma after a car accident. Pre-retirement ages are definitely the best time to consider long-term care coverage, because premiums are lower and one's health is usually better at younger ages. Not only that, but the longer you wait, the higher the cost of care will be which means you will need to buy a larger benefit. So you really are facing a triple whammy. You are buying a larger benefit at an older age, plus if you have developed a serious health issue, you could be uninsurable. At that point, no amount of money will buy a policy.

✳ ***CONSUMER ALERT:*** Don't believe ANYONE who tells you to wait until your late 50s or age 60 to buy long-term care insurance.

My advice: Buy it as young as you can. Suze Orman, two-time Emmy Award-winning television host, #1 *New York Times* bestselling author, magazine and online columnist, writer/producer, and one of the top motivational speakers in the world today, used to advise people to wait until age 59. Listen to what she says today:

> *In the past I have recommended you wait until age 59 to purchase an LTC policy. Given recent changes to these policies, I now say that is the latest you should consider making a purchase.[8]*

And in a recent newspaper article, she emphasized:

> *Over the years, I have had some health problems that are fine today.*
> *But, when I went to get my own LTC insurance policy two years ago*
> *I was denied for recent health reasons. If I had just gone one year*
> *earlier, that would not have been the case.*[9]

I've thanked Suze many times for being this transparent with her readers and sharing her story.

Some people say I'm pushing the envelope when I say "If you're over 18, you're not too young to buy long-term care insurance." I don't think so and that's why when my firm does employee education seminars, we always bring up the two families I know with 20-somethings who had automobile accidents while away at college and wound up back home in the care of their parents the rest of their lives. Sometimes parents, like my eye surgeon, buy long-term care insurance on their adult children to avoid being in exactly that position.

We also explain that disability insurance only provides a portion of income so a family can pay its day-to-day bills. It doesn't provide another $3000-$6000 a month to hire caregivers, and it usually ends at age 65.

The True Cost of Waiting

There is a strong financial reason not to wait to buy long-term care insurance. The longer you wait, the more benefit you must purchase because long-term care costs are increasing so rapidly. Please don't miss this! The younger you buy, the longer you will pay, but you will pay less.

Going back to the sample plan we've been using ($4500 a month ($150 per day) with a 90 day waiting period, a three year benefit period, 100% home care and 5% compound inflation), let's look at what happens if a married 50 year old who can qualify for the preferred health discount considers buying this plan but decides to wait, assuming he or she will be insurable at age 60:

A married 50 year old with preferred health can still buy a plan that will pay about 80% ($4,500 a month) with a three year benefit period and the best inflation (5% compound for life) for about $1,730 a year (United of Omaha). Waiting until age 60 means he would have to buy $7,500 a month because that's what it will grow to in 10 years. If he no longer qualifies for the preferred health discount at age 60, which is likely, his premium would then be $4,000 a year.

Developing this example further, buying at age 50 means paying about $52,000 in premium in 30 years to get $700,000 in benefits on that plan. Yes, there will be class rate increases but there's a huge difference between those two numbers so you can still see the concept! And investing the difference of $2,270 over 10 years at 3% to 5% only grows to about $30,000, then you have to subtract taxes and investing fees if applicable.

So the advice to wait until age 60 is causing a 60 year old couple in ok health to have to consider $8,000 a year for coverage when they could have gotten it for only $3,500 a year at age 50 when they were in great health.

I continue to qualify these examples by saying there will be class rate increases but these numbers are so far apart that I think you can still see the concept.

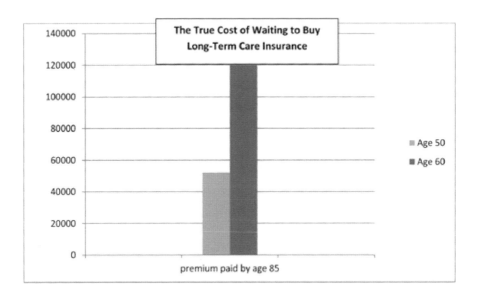

Long-Term Care Insurance Rate Stability

This is a good time to talk about the elephant in the room—long-term care insurance rate increases. LTC insurance is "guaranteed renewable", which means that premiums cannot be increased unless all policyholders in a certain class receive the same increase. The class can't be defined by age or sex. It is typically defined as a specific policy form number and it may be further defined by a certain geographic area.

It's not terrible that a long-term care insurance policy has had rate increases. Some of the newspaper articles have made it sound like it's the end of the world. I say we need to put this into perspective. Many long-term care insurance carriers have been offering it for 20+ years and have had no more than two or three or maybe haven't had a rate increase yet. How many other insurance products can say that? Homeowners, automobile insurance go up periodically especially if we file a claim or two. Do we even need to talk about how often health insurance goes up? My husband and I have seen our health insurance premium go from $337 a month to about $1200 a month in the last 15 years! And you will learn in Chapter Eight that Medicare supplement insurance premium, aka "Medigap", typically increases **every year.**

The problem with public perception has stemmed from insurance agents not making it plain to applicants that the premium can increase on a class basis. I remember thinking when I first started selling long-term care insurance in the late 1980s and heard how some agents weren't explaining this, "This is going to be a real problem someday". Someday is here. I don't doubt this point has been improperly represented in our industry. But some of us made it crystal clear to every applicant.

How to Decide Whether or Not to Accept a Rate Increase

As carriers have implemented rate increases in recent years, they typically send an offer to keep the premium the same by reducing benefits. I recently helped Doug and Brenda Crockett of Gallatin, Tennessee with this decision when their carrier presented them with a 90% rate increase. I didn't sell them their original policy so I had no skin in the game. I simply evaluated their situation and gave them information with which to make an informed decision. Here is their story.

Doug is 65 and Brenda is almost two years younger. They have had their policies since November 2002. Their current benefits are:

- $246 Daily Benefit which has grown from $150 when purchased

- Benefit Period: six years

- Elimination Period: 60 days

- Inflation Option: 5% compound for life

	Current Premium	New Premium
Doug	$1,200	$2,280
Brenda	$1,144	$2,174
Total	$2,345	$4,454

The carrier offered to keep the premium the same if the inflation factor could be decreased from 5% compound to 2.7% compound.

Step 1: Longevity/Alzheimer's Family History Question

I asked if either of them has a family history of Alzheimer's and/or if they have longevity in their family - like several people living to be age 90+? They answered "no" to Alzheimer's. Doug doesn't have longevity in his family, but Brenda's family typically lives into the late 80s. They don't have the type of plan that allows them to access each other's benefits, so I knew it would be good if at least she could keep the six year benefit period.

Step 2: Alternate Plans

I asked Doug to call the insurance company and ask for the premium if they decreased their benefits to one of these three plans:

Requested Benefit Reduction	Premium for Doug	Premium for Brenda	Total	Savings from $4,454
Reduce the daily benefit to $200 and keep the 6 year benefit period	$1,866	$1,780	$3,647	$807
Reduce the daily benefit to $200 with a 5 year benefit period	$1,780	$1,693	$3,473	$981
Reduce the daily benefit to $200 with a 4 year benefit period	$1,606	$1,563	$3,169	$1,285

Step 3: The Analysis

I decided to compare the $200 with the four year benefit period as it represented the most savings in premium, but I could have made the same case with either of the above three scenarios.

- your new premium of $4,454 for you and Brenda X 20 years = $89,100

- your benefits in 20 years will be $679 daily benefit X 2,190 days (6 yrs) = $1,487,010 x 2 = $2,974,020

- premium for $200/4 year benefit period is $3,169 [$1606 + $1,563]

- benefits with the $200/4 year benefit period plan in 20 years = $530 daily benefit x 1,460 days = $773,800 x 2 = $1,547,600

- savings if you take the $200/4 year benefit period = $1,285

- ($4,454 - $3,169)
- savings over 20 years =$25,700 [$1,285 x 20 years]
- benefits lost over 20 years = $1,426,420 [$2,974,020 - $1,547,600]

Step 4: The Summary

"Doug, you are giving up almost $1.5 million in benefits to save $25,700. To lend perspective, I've attached an illustration with another major carrier for the same benefits you and Brenda bought so you can see that plan for a 58 and 57 year old today **with the preferred health discount** is $5,826.17. The standard rate would be $6,854.34. Both are much higher than the $4,454 that your carrier is asking you to accept, and your benefits are much greater now after growing at 5% compounded annually."

Step 5: Future Outlook

"One more thing to take into account, Doug, is that using a projection of $1000 a day in 30 years, the $200 plan would cover about 80% of that as it will grow at 5% compound to $864 in 30 years vs. your current benefit of $246 growing to $1,063. So if you are comfortable with the 80% payout on a daily basis, then you just have to get comfortable with giving up the extra two years of benefits."

Result: They accepted the full rate increase and kept their benefits the same.

I also made sure they understood that this is not a one-time decision. They can decrease their benefits at any point in the future if they decide the premium is unaffordable.

Rate Stabilization Regulatory Activity

The National Association of Insurance Commissioners amended the Long-Term Care Insurance Model Regulation in 2000 to include stiff penalties for insurance companies practicing inappropriate pricing activity.

Highlights of this section of the NAIC Long-Term Care Insurance Model Regulation of 2000 are:

- The 60/40 loss ratio requirement for long-term care insurance, which means that at least 60 cents of every premium dollar must go for benefits, will be eliminated. The NAIC believes that formula is an incentive for rate increases - the higher the premium, the more money available for administrative costs, creating a greater incentive for insurance companies to increase rates.

- Rates must be actuarially certified that they are not expected to increase.

- When a rate increase is approved by the state, 85 cents of each rate increase dollar must go to benefits and only 15 cents can go to administrative costs. This encourages more accurate pricing from the beginning.

- The applicant must sign that he or she understands rates can increase.

- The insurance company has to disclose at time of sale the rate increase history on similar policies for the last ten years.

- If a rate increase is approved by the state then turns out to be unjustified, the insurance company has to refund the money to the policyholders.

- If an insurance company exhibits a pattern of inappropriate rates, the insurance commissioner can prevent the company from doing business in that state for five years.
- Contingent nonforfeiture is required to be included in every policy at no additional premium.

This regulation prevents an insurance company from introducing a new product at a low price with every intention of raising the premium in a few years. There are bad apples in every barrel, and the NAIC is committed to putting regulations in place that prevent the bad apples from spoiling the apple butter. Forty-one states have passed rate stabilization legislation.[10]

My shot of the Capitol when lobbying in Washington DC about The Real Choice Campaign.

States That Have Adopted NAIC Premium Rate Stability Provisions

Alabama	Kentucky	Oklahoma
Arizona	Louisiana	Oregon
Arkansas	Maine	Pennsylvania
California	Maryland	Rhode Island
Colorado	Minnesota	South Carolina
Connecticut	Missouri	South Dakota

Delaware	Montana	Tennessee
Dist. Columbia	Nevada	Texas
Florida	New Hampshire	Utah
Georgia	New Jersey	Vermont
Idaho	New Mexico	Virginia
Illinois	North Carolina	West Virginia
Iowa	North Dakota	Wisconsin
Kansas	Ohio	

However, there have been other reasons for rate increases that are beyond the control of any insurance company.

1. The economy – when rates are determined expecting a 7% return on money invested as reserves and the carrier only earns 2%, you can see how that would have a detrimental impact on that rate determination.

2. More desirable types of care can mean earlier claim activity than the carrier priced for in the rate determination. A great example of this is care in an assisted living facility. Some of them look like country clubs! Plus, they cook and clean for you…what's not to love?

3. Lower than anticipated lapse rates - insurance companies set premium rates based on an assumption that a certain percentage of policies will lapse (be cancelled) before a claim is filed. If a company assumes that 7 to 9% of policies sold will lapse and only 3% do, you can see that many more claims will be payable than the company originally thought.

    History has shown that most policyholders recognize the value of long-term care insurance and are not allowing policies to lapse. Because premiums are determined by age and health status, consumers understand it's more expensive to buy a new policy at an older age, and that any change in health conditions could result in an additional premium charge or decline. This is why many consumers who bought a policy in the past and wish they had purchased a higher benefit find it less expensive to buy a second policy to supplement the first, rather than replacing the first one.

4. Longevity – the Centers for Disease Control and Prevention says that life expectancy at age 65 is 18.4 years. However, you saw in Chapter One that the Census Bureau predicts eight million centenarians by 2050![11] In a nutshell, policyholders are living much longer than insurance companies expected, which means more are living long enough to claim benefits.

    Longevity added to very low lapse rates and a drastic drop in interest rates have resulted in a perfect storm for long-term care insurance carriers. Even after taking these parameters into consideration, however, the regulators are concerned about the rate increases that have occurred after most states had adopted the NAIC rate stabilization provision. The NAIC is now working on more stringent rate stabilization provisions.[12] This could take a couple of years, then states have to decide to adopt it.

✳ **CONSUMER ALERT:** Adding a more stringent rate stabilization provision is extremely likely to make an insurance company introduce a new product with higher premium. Between the time it will take for the NAIC to introduce this provision plus the time for insurance carriers to get a higher-priced product approved in your state can take about three years.

My advice: Shop for long-term care insurance by the end of 2014 or sooner to be safe.

Potential State Legislation to Address Rate Stabilization

Two states have taken matters into their own hands to stabilize long-term care insurance premiums. Both will cause higher premiums if other states decide to adopt them.

Florida

Since 2006, insurance companies are no longer allowed to:

- raise rates on existing policies higher than new policyholders are being asked to pay for the same benefits; and
- cannot deny a claim based on fraud, unless the fraud was discovered in the first two years after the policy was purchased.[13]

The result has been that policies cost more in Florida to absorb these requirements, especially the second one. If someone applies for long-term care insurance, knowing he or she has early signs of dementia, it can be years before the dementia is obvious enough to be detected in the underwriting process. You can see how activity of this nature can torpedo the best attempts of insurance companies to accurately forecast claims payments and establish stable premiums.

California

California Assembly Bill 999 prevents insurers from passing poor investment returns on to policyholders and eliminate the practice of insurers "cherry-picking" a small group of policies to justify large rate increases, in addition to other strong consumer protections. This bill was signed by the Governor on September 28, 2012 with an effective date of January 1, 2013.[14]

A frightening part of this legislation that didn't pass would have prohibited a carrier's ability to raise rates more than every five years for policies issued before July 1, 2002 and every 10 years for policies issued after that date. While that sounds good from a consumer standpoint, it could have caused insurance companies to stop selling long-term care insurance in California as actuaries (the people who determine the rates) would be very uncomfortable giving up that much control to adjust rates in order to maintain the necessary resources to pay claims.

South Carolina

Following in the footsteps of California 999, South Carolina proposes to amend its Long-Term Care Insurance Regulation 69-44:[15]

- Policies issued after July 1, 2013 must be (1) non-cancellable; or (2) paid in full within ten years of issuance; or (3) the total amount of rate increases over the life of the policy cannot increase by more than 50%. Premiums may not be increased after 10 years from date of issuance of the policy.

- Policies issued prior to July 1, 2013: premiums may not be increased if (1) the cumulative increase of the annual premium exceeds 100% of the initial annual premium; or (2) if the policy has been in force for twenty years or more (except upon a finding of the Director that not permitting the requested rate increase will place the insurance company in hazardous financial condition).

"Non-cancellable" is the insurance term that means the rates can never increase which I don't see ever happening in long-term care insurance. This type of proposed legislation is very dangerous to the long-term care insurance industry. No one has a crystal ball and can see ten years into this future as this proposed legislation suggests is possible.

However, there is an opportunity left with a couple of carriers to limit the number of years you pay premium.

Limited Pay Plans

We will be watching the South Carolina situation anxiously but in the past, states have not been friendly towards approving a non-cancellable policy because higher than anticipated demand for long-term care benefits could make it difficult for an insurance company to hold the rate. Some companies offer a limited pay plan that allows the premium to be paid up by age 65, or in ten years. The policyholder is subject to a class rate increase during the premium paying years, but can never be asked for more money after the policy is paid up, regardless of future rate increases on that policy form. Ten years is typically the shortest limited pay plan available.

✴ *CONSUMER ALERT:*   Several well-known long-term care insurance carriers like Genworth, John Hancock, Mutual of Omaha and Transamerica discontinued their limited pay plans in 2012. For those who can afford it, a limited pay plan is a smart thing to do as it protects you from rate increases once it is paid up.

My advice: If you want a paid-off long-term care insurance policy, now is the time to get one while there are still insurance carriers offering it. Two companies that still offer them are MedAmerica and LifeSecure, both subsidiaries of Blue Cross and Blue Shield plans.

Rate Guarantees

Both Transamerica and United of Omaha products are issued with a five year rate guarantee in states that allow it, plus you have the option to pay additional premium to buy a six, seven, eight, nine or ten year rate guarantee.

It's worth reminding you that the above section about rate increases and rate guarantees applies only to traditional (standalone) long-term care insurance plans. The combination plans we discussed in Chapter Two provide long-term care insurance premiums that are guaranteed for life.

If you want to see the rate increase history of a particular insurance company, the California Department of Insurance publishes a national rate increase history of long-term care insurance carriers at http://www.insurance.ca.gov/0100-consumers/0060-information-guides/0050-health/ltc-rate-history-guide/index.cfm whether or not that company offers long-term care insurance in California. There's also a rate comparison page on that site.

How Underwriting Affects Rate Stability

The type of underwriting, whether liberal or conservative, plays a major role in an insurance company's rate stability. "Underwriting" refers to the type of health conditions that an insurance company will accept when a person applies for coverage. Below-market premiums, liberal underwriting (i.e., accepting people with major health problems), and a small asset base can make rate increase a higher probability. I won't say there haven't been any companies that have done these things. As in any industry, a few bad apples can spoil the pie, and that's when the regulators are bound to get involved. Be assured, the regulators have been on this issue like a duck on a June bug for over a decade. (If you don't know what that means, you don't want to be the June bug!)

Underwriting

One of the saddest things I have to do is tell someone that he or she can't qualify for long-term care insurance so there's no use in submitting an application. Equally as sad is to pre-qualify the person with an insurance company only to find out there are more health issues than we thought after the person applies and isn't accepted. In third place is the adult child who calls to get her parent "with a few memory issues, not much" covered on long-term care insurance. No insurance company will issue a long-term care insurance policy to someone who already has dementia. Does "the house is already on fire" ring a bell? All policies today cover mental conditions which are of an organic nature, such as Alzheimer's and other dementias, but only when it develops after coverage is issued.

✳ **CONSUMER ALERT:** **Do not EVER casually mention to your doctor that you are having trouble keeping up with things.** When applicants say something to their doctor along the lines of "Well, I've been forgetting where I put the keys and it's worrying me," they could have just nailed the lid on the coffin for their long-term care insurance application. The doctor may think nothing of it and view them as cognitively fit, but the medical record now has a note that screams "memory loss...Alzheimer's just around the corner", and they will most likely be declined.

My advice: Be very careful about what you share with your doctor about any type of memory loss. It's also a good idea to monitor the notes in your medical records to be certain information is correct, just like you do with your credit report. You have a legal right to see any of your medical records today. All you have to do is ask.

You have to be in reasonably good health to qualify for individual long-term care insurance, and a general rule of thumb is you must be stable with no medication changes in the last six months. Progressive conditions such as Alzheimer's, Parkinson's disease, AIDS, etc. are uninsurable, although at least one company (MedAmerica) will consider applicants who are HIV positive. Applicants must be ambulatory to qualify for coverage, and must not need assistance with activities of daily living (bathing, dressing, transferring, toileting, continence, eating).

Heart surgery, cancer or one mild stroke may be acceptable risks after recovery periods of usually between two and five years, depending on the insurance company. Conditions such as hypertension (high blood pressure) or high cholesterol are acceptable if controlled. People who take an antidepressant or anti-anxiety medication usually can get a policy if their health otherwise is good. A mental condition like bipolar is difficult, but not impossible, to insure if health is otherwise excellent.

Carriers report that the top reasons for decline are:[16]

- Musculoskeletal/arthritis-related conditions
- Diabetes with heart/circulatory problems
- Cerebrovascular (stroke)

Diabetes

Diabetes has become one of the most difficult conditions to work with because it ties directly into the second and third most common reasons for nonacceptance. The risk for stroke is two to four times higher for diabetics, and other strong complications are heart disease, kidney disease, neuropathy (numbness in hands and feet), amputation and blindness.[17] Most of these conditions are likely to make someone meet the criteria to get a long-term care insurance claim paid. It's not an automatic decline, but underwriters are cautious. Diabetes (contracted later in life, not during childhood) can be insurable if it is controlled by diet or oral medication. A few companies will accept 50-70 units of insulin per day as long as height and weight are reasonable and the diabetes is under control. Glycohemoglobin is a blood test that checks the amount of sugar (glucose) bound to hemoglobin. The glycohemoglobin A1C test is used to diagnose and monitor diabetes.

In screening and diagnosis, some results that may be seen include:[18]

- A nondiabetic person will have an A1C result between 4% and 6%
- Diabetes: A1C level is 6.5%
- Increased risk of developing diabetes in the future: A1C of 5.7% to 6.4%

An underwriter wants to see the A1C number less than 8.0 for an extended period of time such as a year with little or no fluctuation, and some companies insist on less than 7.0. But that's not enough. There can't be any associated conditions like neuropathy (numbness in hands and feet), retinopathy, high blood pressure not under control, and height and weight have to be in proportion. That leads to a chicken or egg discussion; i.e. which comes first?

Does diabetes lead to obesity or does obesity lead to diabetes?

An indepth study published by the Society of Actuaries reported that 12 percent of the people who eventually satisfy the criteria for collecting long-term care insurance benefits were attributable to diabetes; however 20 percent of diabetes was attributable to obesity/overweight. It further said that obesity at age 50 was associated with large increases in diabetes and disability.[19]

The really startling statistic is that according to the American Diabetes Association, one in four Americans over age 65 have diabetes, which is another strong justification for applying for long-term care insurance much younger.[20]

Now you can see why long-term care insurance underwriters are more cautious than ever about accepting applicants with diabetes and when combined with excess weight, the approval rate really goes down.

The Obesity Epidemic

Something to take very seriously in the long-term care insurance underwriting process is the height and weight ratio. Two-thirds of adults and a third of children are obese or overweight and racking up about $190 billion a year in related health costs, or 20.6 percent of U.S. health care expenditures.[21]

People who are obese have a higher risk of contracting conditions like high blood pressure, heart disease, sleep apnea, stroke and ultimately severe joint deterioration that can lead to immobility. Can you see how obesity also leads to the above main reasons for long-term care insurance application declines? Insurance carriers have height and weight tables that are generous as most people look at reasonable height and weight ratios but they are strictly observed. A carrier like Mutual of Omaha/ United of Omaha may have a substandard rate of an additional 25% for more weight-challenged people but most carriers don't. Even so, obesity combined with other serious health issues can still result in a decline.

Co-Morbid Conditions

This is the term for multiple health issues. One condition by itself might not be a big deal but when combined with two or more conditions, it can knock someone out of getting long-term care insurance.

If you are not sure if you will qualify, most insurance companies allow the insurance professional who is helping you to submit your information to pre-qualify you to see if you should submit an application. This process won't guarantee you will be accepted, but it lets you know if you can try. When you want to find out if you are insurable, here is the information the insurance company will want to know:

- age and gender
- height and weight
- medications
    - name
    - dosage and frequency

- o   reason you are taking it
- o   how long you've taken it
- surgery in the past 12 months and if so why?
- physical therapy in the last 12 months and when was the last visit?

Some companies have substandard rates but not many. Now that more claims experience is available, the insurance companies are being cautious so they can afford to cover as many people as possible without having to ask for rate increases.

The standard basis for underwriting is medical records, instead of a physical exam, although some insurance companies are utilizing paramedical or "face-to-face" exams. A paramedical exam means a home health nurse visits to check blood pressure, height, weight, and to do an assessment of the applicant's overall physical and mental health.

✷ *CONSUMER ALERT:*   A delicate way to say this is that the paramedical exam historically has not required fluid to leave your body. This is about to change as soon this exam will likely require a blood and urine sample. Why do you suppose this might be happening?

In 2008, President George W. Bush signed the Genetic Information Nondiscrimination Act (GINA) into law. Under GINA, employers and health insurers can no longer discriminate against individuals based upon their genetic information. ***This law does not cover life insurance, disability insurance and long-term care insurance.***[22] Genetic testing in the long-term care insurance underwriting process isn't being done today but could happen in the foreseeable future. A blood and urine sample can open up any number of health conditions to an underwriter, but currently, cardiovascular conditions are a primary target as they rank closely behind Alzheimer's as a reason people file LTC insurance claims.

With the expense today of ordering medical records and conducting face-to-face exams, a preliminary telephone interview is common to determine exactly what information is needed. Some insurance companies are using a national drug database as a cost-effective underwriting tool. This database gives a complete history of a person's prescriptions which the underwriter can match against conditions for which the applicant is likely to be taking the medication. "Hits" on a condition that would lead to a long-term care claim can then be validated by getting medical records and/or ordering a face-to-face exam.

A face-to-face exam means that someone personally interviews the applicant to be sure he or she is in good mental health. Most companies require face-to-face exams for applicants in their 70s and older, but can require them for younger applicants based on the telephone interview.

Important: The underwriting telephone call is an integral part of the underwriting process and without it, your application cannot move forward. There are really two reasons for the call:

1. You may be asked some of the same questions you were asked during the application process; sometimes the insurance company is checking to be sure your agent is doing a thorough job in completing the application.

2. The larger reason for the call is to be sure you are mentally sharp, so please don't joke about losing your car keys or any other memory

lapses! (Think of this call as like going through Security in the airport. You wouldn't dream of joking about ANYTHING as you go through the check point.)

Knock-Out Questions

The application is also an integral part of the underwriting process for long-term care insurance. The health questions are typically divided into three categories:

- "knock-out" questions which means if you answer "yes" to any of them, you will not be allowed to apply; e.g. do you currently need help with daily living activities or use equipment such as a wheelchair, walker, electric scooter, quad cane or oxygen, or have you received physical therapy or home care visits or care in an assisted living facility or nursing home over the past year?

- questions that address serious conditions like cancer, diabetes, circulatory

- a catch-all question that asks if you have been to a physician for any condition not mentioned to that point on the application.

✸ **CONSUMER ALERT:** In 2013, you will see family history questions required on some long-term care insurance applications, starting with Genworth.

My advice: If you have a family history of Alzheimer's especially with your parents, you need to apply for long-term care insurance sooner rather than later. At some point, your family history could keep you from qualifying for long-term care insurance!

In going through the application process for long-term care insurance, there's no sense trying to hold anything back. With all of the above methods of underwriting, it's going to come out, especially with the national drug database. However, sometimes people don't mention certain things because they think aren't important. Here is a list that my staff and I have heard people forget to mention that can dramatically impact their chances of getting long-term care insurance:

- C-PAP machines which are used to treat sleep apnea, especially when they are used with oxygen.

- using physical therapy as a form of exercise/maintenance when the person could be using a gym/trainer, etc. It may seem like a good idea as health insurance may pay for some visits, but it often postpones applying for LTC insurance up to 12 months after the last session.

- history of falling . . .explaining that your middle name isn't "Grace" doesn't help.

- hepatitis episodes from the distant past or "in remission" since it was so long ago

- "infrequent" narcotic pain medication – most carriers won't accept any narcotic use.

- multiple joint replacements—it's not so much having more than one, it's the additional issues as one gentleman had who contacted me for help. His medical records showed that he has a leaky heart valve, diabetes, high blood pressure, back issues, neck numbness and arthritis…and he tips the scales in the wrong direction. Sigh.

People with diabetes and stroke have become especially difficult to insure as carriers have seen the impact these conditions have on claims experience.

Some carriers won't accept either condition under any circumstance, especially as part of the simplified underwriting in the group/multi-life space which we will study in the next chapter.

I hope you have found this section helpful. The most important thing about underwriting is that the younger the applicant, the better chance he or she has to qualify for a policy. **No amount of money will purchase long-term care insurance once someone is uninsurable due to a significant physical or mental health problem.** Premiums are lower at younger ages and are locked in at the age of application, unless there is a rate increase for an entire classification of policyholders. On the other hand, don't assume you won't qualify without checking with an insurance professional who is knowledgeable about long-term care insurance. There is nothing to lose and everything to gain to see if you can qualify for a policy offering even limited coverage.

Tip: Please don't make the mistake of saying you won't accept coverage if your spouse or partner can't get it. That's when you may need it more than ever! If one of you can't qualify for coverage, your resources will likely be spent taking care of that one, and the healthier one may wind up with very little to live on. But wait, there's another idea for an uninsurable spouse and it's a well-kept secret in the long-term care insurance industry.

The Contingent Insured Benefit, aka The Spouse Security Benefit

For an additional 60% in premium, an additional 60% in benefits will be paid while the policyowner is receiving benefits **without reducing the benefit account.** This provides additional money to pay for care for the spouse who was uninsurable at the time the policyholder bought. This benefit is available on the Mutual of Omaha/United of Omaha products for ages 18-69. Here's how that works:

> *Mary has had epileptic seizures with a history of falling for 40 years. Harold, her husband, is still in excellent health at age 58. A plan that will pay $4500 a month with a three year benefit and 5% compound inflation is $2,603 with the preferred health discount. Adding the spouse security benefit brings the premium to $4,166 which will provide additional funding for Mary's care in the event Harold has a claim.*

Being able to qualify for long-term care insurance is a precious gift. If you can get it, do so and don't let anyone talk you out of it. Your children may not understand at first but later when they need help to care for you, they will love you for it.

Claims

The criteria for getting a claim paid is the same for all types of policies as it is Federally controlled in order for the premiums to be tax-free and enjoy other tax incentives, according to IRS guidelines implemented January 1, 1997 as part of the Health Insurance Portability and Accountability Act of 1996 (HIPAA). Just like you can need care physically or mentally, you can trigger the benefits in one of those two ways:

Physically – a licensed health care practitioner (physician, Registered Nurse or licensed social worker) must tell the insurance company that you are expected to need help with at least two activities of daily living for at least 90 days.

Please note that the 90 day expectation of need is not a waiting period. You could have bought a 30 day waiting period, and if you are expected to need help at least 90 days, the benefits will begin on the 31st day. To be clear, **long-term care insurance isn't intended to pay for a broken arm or even a broken hip with today's technology as conditions like these will not generally require someone to need help at least 90 days.**

The 90-day certification assures that long-term care insurance will be preserved to pay for truly long-term conditions. Short-term conditions like fractures and mild strokes usually require skilled care such as physical, speech or occupational therapy. Health insurance and Medicare pay only for skilled care and will cover most of these short-term conditions, called "sub-acute" or "post-acute" care.

Mentally – the licensed health care practitioner must certify to the insurance company that you are impaired to the point of being a threat to yourself or someone else. For example, if you have high blood pressure and can't remember to take your medicine, you could cause yourself to have a stroke. If you will walk out in the middle of the interstate, you could cause 20 other people to have a stroke ☺

If either the physical or mental deficiency just described is present, the person is considered "chronically ill", which is the criterion specified by HIPAA that allows an insurance company to pay a claim.

The six ADLs set forth by HIPAA are:

- Bathing
- Dressing

- Toileting
- Transferring
- Eating
- Continence

With either method of certification, the licensed health care practitioner must work out a 12 month plan of care for you and you must stick to that. For example, if your plan of care said you can be cared for safely at home but on a Sunday afternoon you start climbing out the windows, your spouse can't pack your bags and move you into an assisted living facility without getting the plan of care changed and approved by your health care practitioner and the insurance company.

The following story illustrates how a cognitively-impaired person can be a threat to someone else.

My cousin Ann married a successful surgeon who loved her dearly and wanted to give her everything. He did, including a beautiful country estate on 25 acres and a 25 ft. waterfall at the entrance of the property which tumbled with joyous abandon into a placid pond, surrounded by beautiful flowers. He was very intelligent, a wise investor and businessman with a shrewd eye for real estate. Ann knew both his parents had endured extended bouts with Alzheimer's so they were receptive when I suggested long-term care insurance. His symptoms appeared in the 8th year of their marriage. Sporadic at first, Ann knew it was time to file a claim when he forgot how to turn off the riding lawn mower. She had learned not to leave him alone and fortunately saw it happen. She had to run as fast as she could and jump up beside him to stop the motor just before he drove them *over the rocks into the pond. At that point, he had paid in $18,090 in premium in the six years after purchasing the policy, all of which he got back in only 3.5 months. Words can't express the relief Ann is experiencing when those checks come in and she can pay people with whom he is familiar to help with his care.*

Mental Conditions and Cognitive Impairments

Policies today all cover cognitive impairment, such as Alzheimer's disease. However, some policies will not cover mental conditions of a non-organic nature such as schizophrenia, manic-depressive disorders, etc. Some cover all types of mental conditions. Why is this important? Sometimes at older ages, the lines can blur between dementia and depression, for example. A company that covers all types of mental disorders may be more likely to pay a claim, rather than holding a claim up while attempting to determine if the problem if organic or non-organic.

Tax-Qualified or Non-Tax Qualified

Non-tax-qualified policies are still being offered by a few insurance companies because they don't require the 90 day certification, which means they will pay for short-term care.

The taxation issue often is presented as the center of the controversy on whether to purchase a tax-qualified (TQ) or non-tax-qualified (NTQ) policy, i.e., will the IRS ever rule that benefits from a non-tax-qualified policy are taxable income? This uncertainty has apparently outweighed the desire to pay for short-term care as over 99 percent of long-term care insurance policies being purchased today are tax-qualified policies.[23]

Insurance companies are required to provide Form 1099-LTC to anyone who receives benefits from any type of long-term care insurance policy, tax-qualified or non-tax-qualified. The insured is required to report benefits paid from any type of long-term care insurance policy to the IRS on Form 8853, Medical Savings Accounts and Long-Term Care Insurance Contracts. The only tax-free benefits a policyholder is allowed to report on that form are those paid from a TQ policy. The IRS matches up these 1099s with individual tax filings and sends letters requesting an explanation from people who failed to report benefits received from long-term care insurance policies. This is also the form that monitors the annual tax-free threshold for LTCI benefits.

Beware of advice that the cost of care is a deductible medical expense and will offset the taxable income. IRS Form 1040: Schedule A - Itemized Deductions plainly states in the block marked "Medical and Dental Expenses": *Caution: Do not include expenses reimbursed or paid by others.* This means that any amount reimbursed by a non-tax-qualified policy cannot be deducted as a medical expense.

In other words, tax-qualified policies restore long-term care insurance to its original purpose, which is to pay for long-term conditions. For this reason, though no ruling has thus far been made, there's an excellent chance that improved tax deductions for long-term care insurance premiums will continue to apply only to tax-qualified policies. A recent example is the tax incentives in the Pension Protection Act that we discussed in Chapter Two apply only to tax-qualified policies.

How do you know a policy is tax-qualified? Simple. There will be a notice on the first page that it is intended to be and the 90 day certification language will be in the benefit trigger section.

Getting a Claim Paid

Most carriers have tried to streamline the claims filing procedure. Many provide an 800 number so the insured can notify the company that the need for long-term care has arisen. Most carriers want to know as early as possible about a potential claim so they can start managing the process effectively. Upon notification, the care coordinator at the insurance company will assist with the necessary paperwork and help obtain the 90-day certification from the appropriate medical practitioner to establish benefit eligibility and the 12 month plan of care to initiate benefits. The services of the insurance company's care coordinator are free. The care coordinator can also arrange to have the insured's need evaluated on a local level to ensure the appropriate level of care is being provided in the best setting for the policyholder's condition, i.e., home care, adult day care, assisted living or nursing home care. As mentioned earlier, a policy may provide a benefit to hire a private care coordinator who is not employed by the insurance company. (Most Prudential policyholders have this benefit as it was included at no extra cost.)

A Common Claims Complaint

Three common reasons why benefits are not paid when long-term care insurance policyholders submit a claim are:

- They are at home but don't meet the criteria to get a claim paid; i.e. being expected to need help with at least two daily living activities for at least 90 days or having a severe cognitive impairment that makes them a threat to themselves or others.

- They have moved into an assisted living facility but don't meet the above criteria. They think merely moving into the assisted living facility is enough to start receiving benefits.

- They haven't satisfied their waiting period. Some policies, especially older ones, require a charge for an eligible expense to be incurred each day of the waiting period. Even if it is for two hours of paid home care provided by a licensed home care professional, a charge has to be incurred.

The last one leads into a very common issue policyholders are facing when it comes time to collect benefits. There are home care services springing up around the nation that provide only sitters and companions to meet the escalating demand spawned by the aging baby boomer population. Often, the care recipient doesn't require a licensed caregiver, especially dementia patients. They just need to be watched closely so they don't hurt themselves or anyone else. Many long-term care insurance plans will not pay these workers as they typically are not licensed professionals. Traditional long-term care insurance plans require home care to be provided by licensed caregivers, at least on the level of a home health aide, commonly called a Certified Nurse Assistant (CNA). The home health professional doesn't always have to be provided through a home health agency, especially if a home health agency isn't nearby, such as within a 40 mile radius. He or she could be a CNA, Licensed Practical Nurse or Registered Nurse working as a freelancer, but some type of licensure is required, as well as a government ID, tax ID or Social Security number.

The insurance company receives the complaint phone call when the family files a claim, expecting to use a trusted caregiver who has helped other family members or friends and whom they consider totally trustworthy. It can be difficult for a family to hear that a claim won't be paid unless the trusted caregiver is replaced with a licensed professional. Some families even pay for trusted caregivers to become a CNA. Most attempt to locate a person who meets the criteria of the insurance company. On the other hand, using non-licensed caregivers may have a propensity for greater abuse so you can see why some companies continue to require licensure.

Plans with a full or partial cash benefit provide a strong advantage to address this common complaint. Once the policyholder has been certified as chronically ill, the insured receives a check each month, without having to verify charges or services. The insured or responsible party signs a statement once a month that the policyholder still meets the benefit trigger criteria, and that's all there is to it.

If the insured receives benefits above the Federal threshold of $320 per day in 2013 ($9,700 per month), it will be necessary to prove that the money is being spent for qualified long-term care services, but anything less than that does not require an accounting. (Again, "qualified" in this context means the care meets the tax-qualified benefit triggers of either the need for help with two or more Activities of Daily Living (ADL) for at least 90 days or severe cognitive impairment.)

Policyholders with a cash benefit can pay for the agencies that employ the non-licensed caregivers such as sitters and companions without worrying about the tax ramifications. The agency for which they work is the employer, does the background checks and keeps a worker coming to the home so the client doesn't have to worry about having to find alternate caregivers during sick or vacation time. However, if you are hiring caregivers and controlling their time, the IRS is likely to view you as an employer. Then you will be responsible for contributing to the employee's FICA, Medicare and unemployment taxes.

As we discussed in the home care section of this chapter, if you want to use your own informal caregivers and don't want to deal with an agency like this, you can use a resource such as Hire Family (www.hirefamily.com or 877-775-5516) to help you manage the taxation end.

Caution: If you are considering a cash plan, make sure you have someone trustworthy to manage the money.

When claims are paid, the benefit checks are usually made payable to the insured, but some insurance companies will allow the insured to assign payment to the provider. If benefits are assigned, it's a good idea to have someone trusted by the insured to audit the bills and claim payments every month to ensure proper billing for the services received.

Whichever type of policy the claimant owns, it is really important for the insured to sign the necessary documents so that the claims representatives with the insurance company can talk to family members or even the agent if the family wishes the agent to be included in the communication process.

Coordination with Medicare and Other Insurance—Tax-qualified policies are not allowed to make a payment if Medicare pays or if Medicare would pay in the absence of a deductible or coinsurance. Some companies interpret this provision in its strictest sense, i.e., if Medicare makes a payment on days 21-100 for nursing home care, the long-term care insurance policy will not make a payment, even though you are responsible for a daily co-payment for those days. Most people, however, have coverage to supplement Medicare for the first 100 days—either a

Medicare supplement, retiree plan or a Medicare Advantage plan. (This is further evidence that Congress intends long-term care insurance to pay for long-term conditions beyond three months, not short-term recovery conditions.)

A few policies won't duplicate benefits paid by any other health insurance, which could include another long-term care insurance policy but rarely does. Some companies police it another way: They won't sell you a daily or monthly benefit that, together with the policy you already have, would exceed the maximum daily or monthly benefit they offer.

Claims Regulatory Activity

What happens if you submit a claim to your long-term care insurance carrier and it is denied? The National Association of Insurance Commissioners (NAIC) has established a meaningful appeals process that will result in the claim being reviewed by an Independent Review Organization (IRO) not connected to the insurance company. The NAIC language applies to both individual and group and requires the claimant to contact the insurer within 120 days after adjudication. As with other NAIC amendments, states have to incorporate these provisions into their insurance rules.

If you believe a claim has been denied unjustly and you can't resolve it with the insurance company, you always have the right to file a complaint with the policyholder service area of your state's department of insurance. You can do that on the NAIC website. The complaint history for each long-term care insurance carrier is on that site as well. Just click on the box on the home page of the National Association of Insurance Commissioners (www.naic.org) that says:

CONSUMER INFORMATION SOURCE (CIS): *Insurance company, complaint & financial data*

The direct link is https://eapps.naic.org/cis/

While you're there, you can order a free copy of the NAIC's "A Shopper's Guide to Long-Term Care Insurance" at this link: https://eapps.naic.org/forms/ipsd/Consumer_info.jsp

Or, you can get one from your insurance professional. It contains a complete list of contacts for your state's department of insurance, agency on aging and State Health Insurance Assistance Programs (SHIP). SHIP is a government funded organization to provide insurance counseling, but my experience is they are more proficient in the world of Medicare and Medicare supplemental coverage than in long-term care insurance. It's not their fault. Resources for training in state government are so scarce that it's difficult to keep them trained. Feel free to share this book with any of them. They are wonderful people and my hat goes off to them every day for their diligent efforts to help families.

Characteristics of Long-Term Care Insurance Claims

So how much has long-term care insurance paid out, you say? The answer is somewhere around $55 billion has been incurred out of collected premium of $137 billion. This is cumulative since the beginning of the

LTCI industry.[24] The top ten long term care insurance carriers paid almost $11 million a day in benefits in 2010 and about 250,000 policyholders are currently claiming benefits from all carriers. The largest open claim is $1.7 million which has been going on over 15 years![25] Only about 20% of home care claimants transfer to an assisted living facility or a nursing home.[26]

In fact, **long-term care insurance may be the only thing that keeps people out of a nursing home or certainly makes it the care option of last resort.**

July 18, 1991 was a big day for Ella, age 59 and Fred, age 66. It was the day their long-term care insurance coverage was effective. Ella's premium of $832.40 ended when she had a severe stroke just before her 65th birthday in 1996 and spent her 65th birthday in a skilled nursing facility. She never recovered from this devastating stroke and required 24 hour care. Her family was able to do this because her policy paid almost half the cost. She received $304,597.00 between 2002 and her death on May 27, 2010. She was home the entire time.[27]

The Value Proposition of Long-Term Care Insurance

I'm going to end this chapter by inviting you to ask your financial professional for a long-term care insurance illustration that will pay either $100, $150 or $200 a day for either three or five years, with the 5% compound inflation factor.* Then use the chart on the next page to

---

*$100 a day may seem really low but it will pay for care in an average assisted living facility or for about five hours a day of home care. These benefits could be enough to keep a person out of a nursing home when combined with good inflation coverage.

evaluate that plan. Just multiply the premium x 30 years and use the chart to see where the benefits will be at that time.

That's all well and good, you say, IF you ever need care and use your policy. Here's some new information just in from DaVinci Consulting Group in an analysis for the American Association for Long-Term Care Insurance:

> *The lifetime chance of using policy benefits for someone who buys a policy at age 60 with a 90 day waiting period is one in three.*[28]

Some of you are saying "But I'll be in the 2/3 who don't need care." Maybe you will be and I certainly hope you are. But here's the thing. If you take the policy and never ever need it, yes, you could say you made a mistake equal to the premium you paid out. But if you don't take the policy and you do need care, couldn't you say you made a much larger mistake equal to the cost of care you have to pay out at future costs, not current costs?

I'll take the little mistake any day.

The overall message of higher premium combined with tighter underwriting is that applicants need to apply as young as possible, so what are you waiting for? If you are in reasonably good health, please contact your insurance professional today for help with planning for long-term care.

How to Evaluate the Value of Your Long-Term Care Insurance Plan with a 5% Compound Inflation Factor

Year	Daily Benefit	Daily Benefit x 3 years	Daily Benefit x 5 years	Daily Benefit	Daily Benefit x 3 years	Daily Benefit x 5 years	Daily Benefit	Daily Benefit x 3 years	Daily Benefit x 5 years
1	$100.00	$109,500.00	$182,500.00	$150.00	$164,250.00	$273,750.00	$200.00	$219,000.00	$365,000.00
2	$105.00	$114,975.00	$191,625.00	$157.50	$172,462.50	$287,437.50	$210.00	$229,950.00	$383,250.00
3	$110.25	$120,723.75	$201,206.25	$165.38	$181,085.63	$301,809.38	$220.50	$241,447.50	$402,412.50
4	$115.76	$126,759.94	$211,266.56	$173.64	$190,139.91	$316,899.84	$231.53	$253,519.88	$422,533.13
5	$121.55	$133,097.93	$221,829.89	$182.33	$199,646.90	$332,744.84	$243.10	$266,195.87	$443,659.78
6	$127.63	$139,752.83	$232,921.39	$191.44	$209,629.25	$349,382.08	$255.26	$279,505.66	$465,842.77
7	$134.01	$146,740.47	$244,567.45	$201.01	$220,110.71	$366,851.18	$268.02	$293,480.95	$489,134.91
8	$140.71	$154,077.50	$256,795.83	$211.07	$231,116.24	$385,193.74	$281.42	$308,154.99	$513,591.65
9	$147.75	$161,781.37	$269,635.62	$221.62	$242,672.06	$404,453.43	$295.49	$323,562.74	$539,271.24
10	$155.13	$169,870.44	$283,117.40	$232.70	$254,805.66	$424,676.10	$310.27	$339,740.88	$566,234.80
11	$162.89	$178,363.96	$297,273.27	$244.33	$267,545.94	$445,909.90	$325.78	$356,727.92	$594,546.54
12	$171.03	$187,282.16	$312,136.93	$256.55	$280,923.24	$468,205.40	$342.07	$374,564.32	$624,273.87
13	$179.59	$196,646.27	$327,743.78	$269.38	$294,969.40	$491,615.67	$359.17	$393,292.54	$655,487.56
14	$188.56	$206,478.58	$344,130.97	$282.85	$309,717.87	$516,196.45	$377.13	$412,957.16	$688,261.94
15	$197.99	$216,802.51	$361,337.52	$296.99	$325,203.77	$542,006.28	$395.99	$433,605.02	$722,675.03
16	$207.89	$227,642.64	$379,404.39	$311.84	$341,463.95	$569,106.59	$415.79	$455,285.27	$758,808.79
17	$218.29	$239,024.77	$398,374.61	$327.43	$358,537.15	$597,561.92	$436.57	$478,049.53	$796,749.22
18	$229.20	$250,976.01	$418,293.34	$343.80	$376,464.01	$627,440.01	$458.40	$501,952.01	$836,586.69
19	$240.66	$263,524.81	$439,208.01	$360.99	$395,287.21	$658,812.02	$481.32	$527,049.61	$878,416.02
20	$252.70	$276,701.05	$461,168.41	$379.04	$415,051.57	$691,752.62	$505.39	$553,402.09	$922,336.82
21	$265.33	$290,536.10	$484,226.83	$397.99	$435,804.15	$726,340.25	$530.66	$581,072.20	$968,453.66
22	$278.60	$305,062.90	$508,438.17	$417.89	$457,594.36	$762,657.26	$557.19	$610,125.81	$1,016,876.35
23	$292.53	$320,316.05	$533,860.08	$438.79	$480,474.07	$800,790.12	$585.05	$640,632.10	$1,067,720.16
24	$307.15	$336,331.85	$560,553.09	$460.73	$504,497.78	$840,829.63	$614.30	$672,663.70	$1,121,106.17
25	$322.51	$353,148.44	$588,580.74	$483.76	$529,722.67	$882,871.11	$645.02	$706,296.89	$1,177,161.48
26	$338.64	$370,805.87	$618,009.78	$507.95	$556,208.80	$927,014.67	$677.27	$741,611.73	$1,236,019.55
27	$355.57	$389,346.16	$648,910.27	$533.35	$584,019.24	$973,365.40	$711.13	$778,692.32	$1,297,820.53
28	$373.35	$408,813.47	$681,355.78	$560.02	$613,220.20	$1,022,033.67	$746.69	$817,626.93	$1,362,711.56
29	$392.01	$429,254.14	$715,423.57	$588.02	$643,881.21	$1,073,135.35	$784.03	$858,508.28	$1,430,847.14
30	$411.61	$450,716.85	$751,194.75	$617.42	$676,075.27	$1,126,792.12	$823.23	$901,433.70	$1,502,389.49

*your premium is subject to a class rate increase, which means it can only go up on an entire class, not just on you personally

I had the great opportunity to share my Real Choice idea with Gov. Mike Huckabee at the President's Summit at Oral Roberts University on November 17, 2012. You can see it at http://www.ltcconsultants.com/articles/2012/real-choice

Chapter Five:

EMPLOYERS: WHY YOU HAVE TO LEAD, NOT FOLLOW

—⟨⟨⟨⟩⟩⟩—

A grayer workforce is a trend that is continuing to pick up speed.
—Steven Pozzi. "Never Can Say Goodbye",
BEST'S REVIEW, June 2012, p. 60

Section One: Long-Term Care Insurance is Productivity Insurance for the Employer

Your telephone rings and it's one of your employees. Her voice is trembling and you immediately know something is very wrong.

Umm…we just found out my mother has Alzheimer's for sure. The doctor says she can't be left alone because she might wander off or start a fire. I know I've used up all my vacation on her doctor visits this year, but someone needs to stay with her while I come to work. I called Medicare and her Medicare Supplement and found out they won't pay for someone to stay with her. I'm not really sure what we're going to do.

The next day another employee calls with this question.

We keep getting these letters in the mail about long-term care insurance. I know it's something we need because my sister had to take care of my father for three years and now she and I don't get along. My husband says he absolutely doesn't want anyone coming to our house to talk to us about it. I was wondering if the company offers anything?

Yet another employee has this question.

I think the company offers long-term care insurance. My wife was just diagnosed with Parkinson's disease and I don't want to miss anymore work. We didn't take it when it was first offered, but can we still get it?

How comfortable are you in answering these questions? If just between you and me you are experiencing a little of the "deer in headlights" syndrome, this chapter will help you.

- What should an employer look for in a group LTCi policy?

- What do you need to know about employee education for LTC insurance, especially if your company is offering it for the first time?

- Are there any options to do something special for executives without doing it for all employees?

But first, let's explore why employer-sponsored long-term care insurance, aka "worksite LTCI" has resulted in almost half the long-term care insurance sales for the last several years.[1] It's not difficult to understand when you look at the caregiving tsunami that is about to overtake our nation and dramatically impact the level of productivity in the workplace.

Caregiving Today and Tomorrow

A major study published by the National Alliance for Caregiving in collaboration with AARP paints this startling picture of caregiving in America:

- A third of American households – about 36 million – provide care today.[2]

- Sixty-six percent take care of one person; 24% two; 10% three or more![3]

Number of Care Recipients

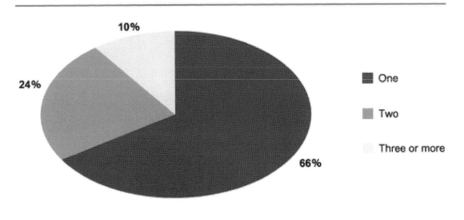

Source: *Caregivers in the U.S. 2009*, National Alliance for Caregiving/AARP, 11/09

- The average duration of caregiving is 4.6 years, and three in ten have taken care of their loved one five years or more. [4]

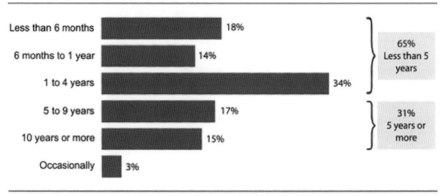

Source: *Caregivers in the U.S. 2009*, National Alliance for Caregiving/AARP, 11/09

- To compound this situation, more than one third (37%) also have children or grandchildren under age 18 in the household. [5] It's no wonder that one-third of caregivers report they are highly stressed! [6]

A June 2011 report said:

The percentage of adult children providing personal care and/or financial assistance to a parent has more than tripled over the past 15 years. Currently, a quarter of adult children, mainly Baby Boomers, provide these types of care to a parent. [7]

You can see in the chart on the following page how dramatically the percent of men and women providing basic parental care has grown between 1994 and 2008: [8]

Percent of Men and Women Providing Basic Parental Care, 1994 versus 2008 *

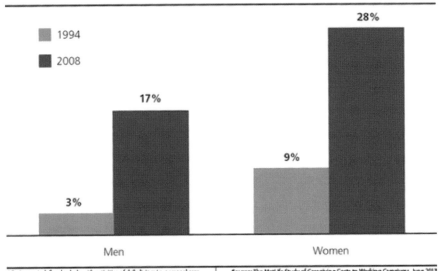

* Basic care is defined as help with activities of daily living; i.e. personal care.　　|　　Source: The MetLife Study of Caregiving Costs to Working Caregivers, June 2011

A National Public Radio interview with AARP Senior Vice President Cheryl Matheis said that leaving a job to care for someone results in an average loss of $325,000 in lifetime income from lost wages, Social Security and pensions.[9]

Can you see why many employers have come to recognize that long-term care insurance can be "Productivity Insurance?" Let's do a quick review of what we stated in Chapter One and hopefully it will mean more to the employers reading this chapter.

- The fastest growing cohort of the US work base is made up of employees aged 55+. This age group is projected to grow over five times as fast as the overall labor force and make up nearly one-quarter of the labor force in 2020.[10] Why is this significant? Because this age group represents the prime caregiving years. Most will wind up becoming caregivers for spouses or aging family members, but some will become care recipients with early long-term care events brought about by strokes, Lou Gehrig's disease, early Parkinson's or Alzheimer's, and the like.

Women's participation in the labor force has increased dramatically; in fact, it has increased more than 50% in the past 15 years.[11] Today, women make up almost half of the workforce in the United States (47%).[12] Why is this significant? Because women make up two-thirds of the nation's caregivers.[13]

The number of people with Alzheimer's is expected to grow 50% in the next 20 years.[14]

Caregiving duties have the following impact on the employee and his or her employer:[15]

- repeated workday interruptions to handle medical visits and phone calls;

- increased absenteeism and leave of work to help the ailing loved one;

- decreased motivation and morale;

- increased and ongoing stress which can lead to caregiver health problems (increasing health insurance claims as well as reducing on-the-job productivity); and

- requests for part-time work or a decision to resign altogether (adding to replacement costs).

At least seven out of ten working caregivers leave the workforce entirely or make a substantial change such as reducing hours or transferring into a less demanding job.[16,17] Since women tend to provide more personal care such as help with bathing and dressing than men, they are more likely to leave jobs than reduce hours.[18,19]

Some forward-thinking employers are starting to wonder what will happen to their productivity level if a large number of female employees start making adjustments to work schedules or even drop out of the work force to accommodate caregiving responsibilities. The average caregiver for adults over age 18 is 49 years old, so you can see how a mass exodus of women in their peak working years over the next 20-30 years could have a detrimental impact on our nation's economy.[20]

It really boils down to how much time caregiving really takes. The chart below will show you that one out of four caregivers provide care more than 20 hours a week and about one in seven provide more than 40 hours.[21]

Hours of Care Provided

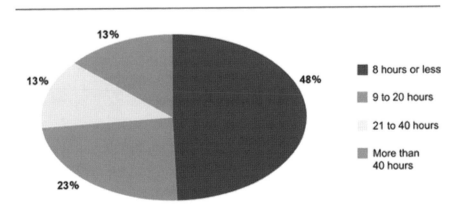

Source: *Caregivers in the U.S. 2009*, National Alliance for Caregiving/AARP, 11/09

It's no surprise that the caregiving time increases in relation to the number of Activities of Daily Living (ADLs) the care recipient needs help with. When you zero in on primary caregivers who live with the person they are taking care of, as many as a third are classified as "High Burden" which means they spend an average of 47 hours a week providing help with three or more ADLs. Another 19% are categorized as "Medium Burden" which means they provide help with two or more ADLs.[22]

The Impact of Caregiving on Work

As many as 73 percent of caregivers were employed in the 12 months preceding the NAC/AARP survey, but the number dropped to 57% by the time the survey was finished: 46% full-time and 11% part-time.[23] The chart below affirms that seven in ten caregivers reported making changes such as cutting back on their working hours, changing jobs, stopping work entirely, taking a leave of absence, or other such changes as a result of their caregiving role.[24] However, 83% of the caregivers in the "high burden" category had to make these types of changes.[25]

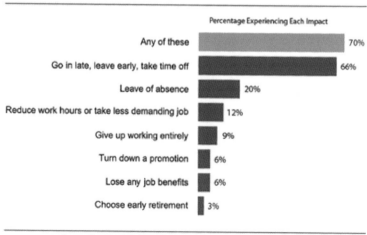

Work Accommodations Due to Caregiving

Percentage Experiencing Each Impact

Any of these	70%
Go in late, leave early, take time off	66%
Leave of absence	20%
Reduce work hours or take less demanding job	12%
Give up working entirely	9%
Turn down a promotion	6%
Lose any job benefits	6%
Choose early retirement	3%

Source: *Caregivers in the U.S. 2009,* National Alliance for Caregiving/AARP, 11/09

Making a Difference with Long-Term Care Insurance

Since 51% of the caregivers in this major study provided help with two or more ADLs which is one of the requirements to get a LTCi claim paid, can you see how LTC insurance could impact the lives of a large number of caregivers in our country if it can be put into place before the caregiving event occurs?[26] It wouldn't have helped the entire 51% of caregivers in this example because one in seven were caring for a disabled child under age 18, but it's safe to say it would have helped many of them.[27] The critical point I want to make with you now is that **employers must offer long-term care insurance to employees ages 18+ so that almost all employees and spouses can qualify with good health at younger ages.** And with proper employee education, many extended family members will also purchase while they are still insurable.

It is surprising how many people in their 50's can't qualify for long-term care insurance. The average employee purchaser is 48; [28] however when an employer is kind enough to offer long-term care insurance to employees and their families, young employees who understand the need buy it.

Robert was 27 years old and his young wife was only 24. He called for a personal consultation for help in choosing the benefits when his employer offered long-term care insurance. When the insurance producer who took the call asked him why he was interested, he gave this compelling reply: "My father just had a stroke and moved in with us. I have a four-year-old son. I don't want him to EVER go through this.[29]

Overall, employees buying LTCI today on themselves, their spouses and eligible family members who can pass underwriting can help maintain the productivity of the workforce in several ways.

- First, the employer benefits by knowing that if a significant illness or injury should strike the spouse or eligible family member of an employee, the insurance will provide money for caregivers who will allow the employee to remain on the job and have peace of mind that the loved one is being taken care of. Employees with peace of mind make better workers and most importantly, caregivers whose family members have long-term care insurance are TWICE AS LIKELY to stay in the workforce as those whose family members do not.[30]

- Second, LTCI carriers allow extended family members such as parents, siblings and adult children to apply for coverage even when the employee doesn't. They are allowed to apply with full underwriting, and those who can qualify ultimately mean decreased distractions for the employee due to the need to care for an ailing family member.

- Third, the June 2011 MetLife study said that "adult children 50+ who work and provide care to a parent are more likely to have fair or poor health than those who do not provide care to their parents." [31] A February 2010 MetLife study said that caregiving employees cost employers 8% more in increased health care costs, potentially costing U.S. employers an extra estimated $13.4 billion per year.[32]

- Finally, future generations of employees will be relieved of work distractions and be able to stay on the job because their parents took advantage of the opportunity to insure themselves through their employer.

> *The goal is for employers to acknowledge the caregiving Tsunami that is coming and make long-term care insurance a standard benefit offering in the workplace as a way to stand against it.*

Section Two: LTCI Tax Incentives for Employer-Sponsored Plans

A common objection I hear from employers when asked to offer long-term care insurance is there's no money for a new employee benefit offering. I hasten to assure the employer that there is no requirement to contribute to the premium, but there are tax incentives that favor the employer that does so. There may be an underwriting incentive as well but this section will provide a quick summary of the LTCI tax incentives for employers offering long-term care insurance to their employees that we covered in detail as you learned in Chapter Two.

- 100 percent of premiums for employees, spouses and dependents are a tax-deductible business expense to employers of all types just like health insurance.

- Deductibility varies for the owners, however, by type of corporation: self-employed business owners can deduct an age-based amount of premium on themselves, their spouses and dependents as part of their self-employed health insurance deduction and owners of C-Corporations can deduct 100%, including limited pay premium of 10 years or longer.

- Employers can select by class (tenure, salary, job title) for an employer contribution or for the offering itself.

- Premium contributions are not taxable income to employees.

- Benefits up to $320 a day in 2013 ($9,700 per month) are tax free to employees whether or not the employer contributes to the premium. This amount typically increases each January. Greater amounts are tax-free as long as the benefit doesn't exceed the cost of qualified care. This is a tremendous advantage LTC insurance has over disability income insurance, plus disability insurance ends at age 65. Long-term care insurance is 100% portable at the same benefits and premium.

- Employers can make long-term care insurance more affordable for employees by offering Health Savings Accounts since an age-based amount of long-term care insurance premium can be paid with pre-tax dollars through an HSA.

I don't think an employer should base the decision to contribute to long-term care insurance premium solely on tax incentives. Contributing to the premium not only demonstrates the importance the employer attaches to the benefit, but please consider that it also frees up dollars that employees can use to purchase coverage for spouses and other eligible family members. Many employers are deciding it is more cost effective to contribute to the premium for a worksite LTCI plan rather than incurring costs due to caregiver absences and distractions. Now do you see why I continue to hammer on the point that long-term care insurance is Productivity Insurance for employers? And that's a perfect segue to the next section.

Section Three: How Long-Term Care Insurance Helps Employers Retain Employees

Retention was the top benefits objective cited by employers until it became second to controlling benefits costs in the 2010 and 2011 MetLife employee benefits surveys.[33] Long-term care insurance can be an especially effective way to retain and reward key executives since the tax deductibility extends to a "10-pay plan" – a plan that is paid up in ten years. Unlike a cash bonus that creates a taxable event for the executive, a 10-pay LTCI plan is a significant tax-free financial gift. Benefits are tax-free AND it protects the employee from rate increases after the plan is paid up.

> *Corporations who are interested in attracting, retaining and rewarding key executives now have a way to do so by increasing and protecting retirement income benefits as LTC insurance restores losses through IRS limits on qualified plans. Long-term care insurance can be the employee benefit differentiator for a progressive employer as C-Corporations can now deduct 100% of the premium for limited pay plans as an employee benefit for employees, including owners. This is an excellent way to retain key executives as neither the employer contribution nor the benefits are taxable income to the employee or the corporation owner(s). [34]*

✳ ***CONSUMER ALERT:*** You saw this in Chapter Three but it is so important that I repeat it here. *Limited pay plans have been discontinued by many companies. An employer who wants to retain key executives with this incredibly valuable benefit should act immediately to get a limited pay plan for them!*

In addition, I believe that the employer who **really** wants to protect productivity will pay the premium on the executive's spouse as well to keep the employee on the job if a spouse needs long-term care.

Non-Financial Concerns about Caregiving Outrank Financial

The emotional side of this gift is too important to overlook. A March 2010 Age Wave/Harris Interactive survey said that when asked their greatest fear about having a long-term illness, people are twice as concerned about being a burden on their family as protecting their assets. [35]

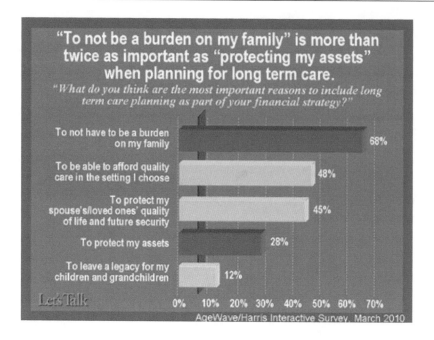

Surprisingly, this same survey said the greatest concern of becoming a caregiver is the emotional strain – even more than the financial costs.

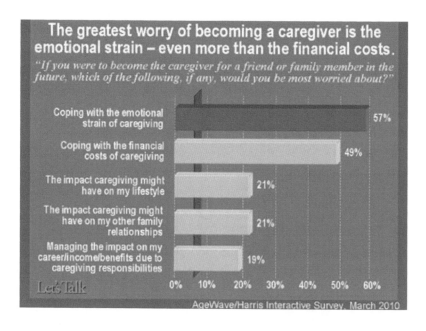

The employer that can lift this worry for an executive and his or her spouse or partner will incur greater loyalty and enjoy higher retention rates.

Section Four: Characteristics of the Worksite LTCI Market

The Bureau of Labor Statistics reports about 155 million people working in the nation as of September 2012.[36] How many have access to long-term care insurance?

Number of Employees Who Have Access to Long-Term Care Insurance by Size of Firm[37]	
<100 employees	8%
100+ employees	26%
100-499 employees	18%
500+ employees	35%

There are 5.9 million firms in the United States and 5.8 million of them have less than 100 employees.[38]

Number of employees	Number of firms with employees
0-4	3,575,240
5-9	968,075
10-19	617,089
< 20	5,160,404
20-99	475,125
100-499	81,773
< 500	5,717,302
500+	17,236
Total:	5,734,538

With this information, you may be able to understand better why less than three million long-term care insurance policies have been sold through employer-sponsored programs, whether true group or multi-life (see definitions below).[39] I am hoping you will also start to understand the huge role employers can play in being part of the solution to the tidal wave of caregiving that is about to consume our nation and workplaces.

True Group Vs. Multi-Life

Size matters. When we say that almost half of the long-term care insurance policies were bought at work, we are talking about a combination of true group and multi-life. Multi-life generally applies to the market below 100 employees and can extend up to 1,000. What is the difference?

Multi-life LTCI is simply offering an individual long-term care insurance product to employees and their eligible family members with a premium discount and usually simplified underwriting (SI) which means limited health questions.

✳ ***CONSUMER ALERT:*** It is extremely important to tell employees that the simplified underwriting is a ONE-TIME opportunity that will not be repeated with that carrier. The only insurance companies offering multi-life today are LifeSecure, MedAmerica and Transamerica. John Hancock may return to this market in late 2013. All require a minimum number of employees who can say "no" to the limited health questions.

True group: Like a group health insurance plan, the employer is the master policyholder of a true group LTC insurance plan and the employees receive certificates of coverage instead of policies. True group plans generally have fewer benefit choices but are guaranteed issue or only ask a few health questions.

✳ **CONSUMER ALERT:** In today's market, there is only one insurance carrier offering true group and that carrier (Genworth) only offers guaranteed issue to companies with 1000 employees or more.

The following chart will explain each major difference.

	Multi-Life (Individual policies)	True Group
Eligibility in Addition to Employee	More flexible: spouse/ partner; parents; grandparents; siblings; adult children 18+; all respective in-laws	Employer can choose to not offer to domestic partners. May or may not be offered to siblings or adult children. Active employees from 20 hours per week.
Underwriting - Voluntary	Typically 6-9 questions and participation requirement of at least 10 employees who can say "no" to the limited questions OR the greater of 15 apps or 10% of employees over age 45 and over $35K salary	Guaranteed issue for 1000+ with good demographics* (see description at the bottom of this chart); i.e. desirable age, salary & education. No participation requirement. Modified Guaranteed Issue (2 questions plus height & weight for groups of 300-999).
Underwriting – Spouse/ Partner	Simplified available for working spouses/ partners with no premium contribution by the employer	Simplified available for all spouses/ partners plus height & weight
Rates	No preferred or substandard, but varies based on marital status. Could be two tier (single and married) whether spouse/partner applies or not or could be single, married 1 or married 2. Discounts range from 5%-15% for multi-life and up to 40% for couples.	Usually blended which means one rate regardless of marital status; no preferred or substandard; the Federal LTCI Program did this to treat everyone equally and true group carriers follow that model.
Rate Increases	Class rate increase unless there is a rate guarantee in place…options range up to 10 years and some have 3-5 years built in for no extra premium	Rate increase would apply to the entire group block; not to the claims experience for one employer.

Benefit Choices	Most flexible as it will be all the daily/monthly benefits and benefit periods up to a cap less than is available with full underwriting; e.g. $6000-$9000 monthly benefit; 5-6 years benefit period or $500,000 benefit account	Usually one or two benefit periods and 3-5 daily or monthly benefits
Informal Caregivers	Could be all cash or a cash alternative	If approved by the insurance carrier
Employee Education	The insurance professional does it	The carrier does it (see addendum at the end of this section)
Enrollment Method	Could be all online for all applicants or split case with a call center with app emailed to the applicant for an electronic signature. Some carriers are all paper for all applicants.	Online with electronic signature for employee and spouse/partner; family members enroll online and print the application for signature then mail it in.
Portability	Yes - same benefits and premium	Yes – same benefits and premium
List bill	Yes – typically minimum of 10	Yes – typically minimum of 50
Request for Proposal (RFP)	Broker does it as individual carriers don't provide this service	Carrier does it

They Don't Take All Comers

It's easy to think that insurance companies have it so tough today that any employer wanting to offer long-term care insurance would be welcomed with open arms.

Not so.

There's still a huge stigma in this country that long-term care insurance is nursing home insurance for old folks, so it takes a focused and consistent effort to educate employees to buy it as young as possible on themselves, their spouses and to encourage eligible family members to buy it. As benevolent as some companies may be, the bottom line question for insurance companies and employee benefit advisors is "will this group produce enough revenue to make it worthwhile to offer this benefit?" There may be a minimum participation to hit as well. Experience has made it possible for the long-term care insurance industry to compile a list of criteria for a successful enrollment. I will present it here like a checklist so you can easily ascertain where your employee population falls as a desirable prospect for a worksite long-term care insurance offering.

- At least 40 percent of the employees over age 40
- At least 40 percent of the employees make over $40,000-$50,000 ($70,000 for higher cost parts of the country like New England and parts of California)
- Do a large percentage of employees have post-high school education?
- Nature of the industry (nothing extremely hazardous)
- Are the employers planners; i.e. do most participate in the retirement plan and other voluntary benefits?

The most important factor on the above list is the education level of the employees. Insurance carriers use the nature of the industry along with the position title of the employees to help determine education levels. About 70% of LTC insurance buyers are college-educated.[40] If income and age demographic is borderline, the carrier may still agree to issue a proposal if education is high and if the employees are planners; i.e. they are contributing to a qualified retirement plan such as a 401(k) and participate well in other voluntary products. To make this determination, carriers must have date of birth, gender, salary and preferably job title on the census. Regarding gender, it does not help if the majority of the employees are female as decision-making ability comes into question.

If there is doubt about the level of interest in an LTCI worksite offering, the employee benefit advisor may ask you to survey your employees to gauge their interest level. But why wait for that? My advice is to use my employee survey on the next page to quickly find out for yourself. After all, your time is valuable and you want to spend it on offering employee benefits that are truly appreciated. My experience is that a lot more employees are interested than you as an employer even realize. If you are going to do this, please use my employee survey. It will do no good to send around the question "Are you interested in long-term care insurance?" Most employees will say "no" due to the widespread perception that it is nursing home insurance for old people. My survey tells them what it is and emphasizes the impact of long-term care on their lifestyle, their family and on their retirement savings so they can make an informed decision. When I train insurance agents how to sell long-term care insurance, I often encourage them to take the emphasis off what long-term care insurance IS and put it on what long-term care insurance DOES.

Employee Survey *(to be sent by employer)*

Dear *[Fellow Employee/Associate]:*

Because you are a valuable member of the *(Name of Company)* team, we are letting you know about an important new voluntary employee benefit that we are considering. It is **long-term care insurance**, and we need your input before making a decision to offer it.

Perhaps you know someone whose life has been completely disrupted by the demands of caring for a spouse, parent, or in-law who requires daily long-term care. Perhaps your own life has already been affected by such a situation, or you may need long-term care yourself one day.

The need may be created by a tragic accident, a debilitating illness **at any age**, or advanced age. Whatever the reason, providing long-term care can be devastating financially and emotionally. **To maintain a career and to provide daily long-term care for a family member is very difficult. This type of care is very expensive–up to** *[insert average annual cost for your area]* **annually in this area–and it can have a serious, negative impact on your lifestyle and your ability to hold a job.** It can also affect the quality of your life in your retirement.

Long-term care insurance can supply the financial resources necessary to get the help you need if you should need long-term care or find yourself responsible for the long-term care needs of a spouse, parent or in-law. It can pay for home care, assisted living, adult day care and even nursing home care.

There are many advantages to enrolling in a group long-term care insurance plan now, such as **discounted group rates,** a one-time opportunity for **limited** *[or no]* **health questions** and the convenience of **payroll deduction.** It would also be available to certain family members with full medical underwriting. You will be hearing more about this new employee benefit, and if there is enough interest to offer it, we can hold informational meetings in the coming weeks. **I urge you to share this information with your family and make a decision together.**

Please let us know if you would like to learn more about this new benefit:

_____ YES, I am interested in learning more
_____ YES, I may have a family member(s) who may be interested in learning more.
_____ No, I am not interested at this time

Please return this form to *(Employer Contact)* no later than *[insert date]*.

General Discussion of Multi-Life vs. True Group

The significant attraction of a true group plan is guaranteed issue underwriting with no participation requirement and online enrollment, especially when employees are located in multiple states and the producer doesn't have to seek individual state licenses and carrier appointments. The website stays open year round and family members from any state can apply through the website.

Whether you are offering a multi-life or true group plan to your employees, **it is very important to stress that limited underwriting is a one-time opportunity of 30, 60 or 90 days** when the plan is first offered. New hires have this opportunity for a certain time period after their hire date. Some employers like to offer it once a year in order to ensure that new employees are thoroughly educated. If you feel that way, you can ask if the insurance carrier allows that.

Plans with simplified underwriting typically don't ask about common health issues like high blood pressure or cholesterol and most don't ask height and weight. Employees report greater levels of appreciation for LTCI plans with simplified underwriting or guaranteed acceptance. This is truly a gift from the employer as many employees could never qualify for long-term care insurance in the individual market due to excessive weight or progressive health conditions.

I can't emphasize enough that it is essential to emphasize this one-time opportunity heavily throughout the open enrollment period so that employees don't think they can get it next year or the year after as is the case with many employee benefits. To do this, I suggest that you emphasize it in an announcement letter sent to the homes of your employees and then do several follow-up emails prior to holding employee meetings or webinars about the plan. Why would you send the announcement letter to the homes? To make sure the spouse sees it, especially if you have a significant percentage of male employees. Let's face it. Men simply do not take information home. Just stating a fact ☺ Of course, you will also want to be clear that eligible family members have to go through full underwriting, but that's all the more reason why they need to apply as young as possible in order to qualify medically. A few plans do allow spouses to enroll with limited underwriting. I think it's just as important for spouses to get long-term care insurance as employees. As an employer, you should think it is even more important because if the spouse needs extended care, your employee may have to leave the workforce to become a primary caregiver or experience financial and emotional difficulty trying to find and pay caregivers.

Employer Contribution: Employers can pay the entire premium of course but may wish to contribute a flat amount, a defined benefit or a percentage of premium. Often an employer may not believe a flat amount if equitable to all so may elect to pay a base plan instead, such as $1500 a month, a $50,000 benefit account and 3% compound inflation. Some employers want to pay a percentage of premium; i.e. 50% and the carrier isn't able to do that. The simple fix is the carrier bills the employer for 100% of the premium and the employer payroll deducts the employee's share.

Employee Education: You can have the most reputable carrier, the most competitive product, the most supportive employer, and without an excellent employee education plan, your enrollment will suffer greatly. As noted above, multi-life plans put the insurance professional in the driver's seat to conduct a highly effective employee education campaign. True group carriers typically start the education shortly before the first meeting by mailing an announcement letter to the home and following it with a rate kit that shows the low rate based on Future Purchase Option (FPO) inflation. A couple of reminder postcards are usually sent out in addition to a couple of "deadline approaching" emails round out the carriers' employee education program. In my opinion, these efforts aren't nearly enough to make sure your employees truly understand the gift of long-term care insurance and take maximum advantage of the one-time opportunity for limited health questions.

To amplify this process, please strongly encourage your employees to attend employee education meetings or webinars, even though the carrier you are working with may be offering online enrollment. The meeting or webinar will help them get a first-hand explanation of long-term care issues and the product offered. For maximum attendance and ultimate enrollment, consider pre-educating the employees with several short articles about the need for long-term care insurance and how the policy features work in the six to eight week period prior to the employee education seminars. Post all of the communication pieces on the company website to make it easy for employees and their families to access this valuable information.

The Congressional Research Service said that the average participation in worksite long-term care insurance is 4%.[41] Employers who enhance the carrier's program by adding their own messaging, allowing employee education meetings or webinars on the clock are able to educate the employees more effectively and will see these percentages increase dramatically. The icing on the cake to this process is to allow personal consultations if the financial professional offers to do them. The consultations can be onsite or via telephone and/or internet.

Family members should be made to feel welcome at any of these educational activities as make no mistake about it...**long-term care impacts the entire family.**

The most successful employee education campaigns will emphasize long-term care as **Lifestyle Insurance,** not just as another employee benefit. Without long-term care insurance, someone usually has to give up a life to be a primary caregiver. If that someone is one of your employees, it's fairly likely that you will lose that employee much sooner than you would like.

Rate Increases: Be sure to communicate whenever appropriate that rates can increase on a class basis, and not on the claims experience of just that group. The employees and their family members will see the rate increase history of the carrier on the personal worksheet in the application, but the employer should make sure this point is made in the pre-education materials, in the employee meetings and in one-on-one consultations.

Plan Design: The true group carriers limit the number of choices intentionally to make enrollment less confusing as they have to plan for no personal contact with the group, especially a large one.

Section Five: Worksite LTCI Plan Designs

If you are offering a true group plan, you will be asked to choose which benefits to offer your employees by staying within the carrier's template of a limited number of choices:

- Daily/monthly benefits – be sure to take into account the cost of care in your area, but an affordable minimum choice should be enough the cover the cost of an assisted living facility in your area and five hours of home care (at least $3000 a month in most parts of the country)

- Benefit periods/benefit accounts – be sure to have the minimum choice for the lower income employees and that is typically a two-year benefit period or the cash equivalent

- Inflation options – be sure to offer a compound inflation option. I'll explain why this is especially important in Chapter Seven when we discuss The Long-Term Care Partnership. For now, just know that people who want the asset protection provided to Long-Term Care Partnership policyholders must buy compound inflation if they are under age 61 as most employees are.

Inflation Coverage – Encourage the employees to **BUY INFLATION COVERAGE.** As you saw in Chapter One, the cost of care has more than tripled in the last 20 years to $222 today ($6,750 per month) for 10 hours of daily home care or semi-private care in a nursing facility.[42] The national average cost of care in 1987 was $56 a day.[43] At that growth rate, the cost of care will be over $27,000 a month in 30 years, or about $880 per day. Obviously the 5% compound for life is still a desirable inflation option but it has become more costly.

To make long-term care insurance more affordable, most carriers especially true group carriers offer a future purchase option (FPO) as one of the choices. It may be called a Guaranteed Purchase Option (GPO). This means the employees will have low premiums now and a chance to buy additional coverage in the future. **Be clear with any education you do that the FPO/GPO is not Partnership-compliant for applicants under age 61 and may not be for applicants under age 76.** The insurance company will be able to tell you the inflation requirements for your state. Therefore, you should also offer the automatic increase option that grows with compounded interest (not simple interest) each year.

New Inflation Options

There are new versions of the compound benefit to keep the premium more affordable such as 5% compound to age 61 or 65, then it switches to 5% simple. Another example of a more affordable option is the 2 times compound option that allows the benefit to double in 15 years then stop growing. This can be a viable offering if you encourage the employees to start with a higher monthly benefit. For example, a $3000 monthly benefit with an unlimited 5% compound inflation benefit will take 30 years to reach $12,000. A $6,000 monthly benefit with 2X compound would get there in 15 years and could cost less than the $3000 with unlimited inflation. Ask if any of these inflation options are Partnership-compliant in your state for applicants who are under age 61.

The 3% compound option has become a favorite due to affordability and is Partnership-compliant for all ages in almost all states. However as we discussed in Chapter Three, 3% takes 24 years to double whereas 5% compound doubles in 15 years. This means that in 30 years, the benefit with the 3% compound factor is about half of the benefit with the 5% compound factor. A creative way to use 3% yet keep it more affordable might be to start the monthly benefit higher as with the 5% compound 2X above. For example, using $7500 with 3% compound instead of

$4500 with 5% compound is a viable option when you consider that it will take about 25 years for the two monthly benefits to equalize.

Many states have approved guaranteed annual increases based on the Consumer Price Index (Urban for all items) for under age 61. Before offering that method, consider the current growth rate of the CPI in recent years:

Consumer Price Index (CPI) –All Urban Consumers (All Items) [44]	
1998	1.6%
1999	2.7%
2000	3.4%
2001	1.6%
2002	2.4%
2003	1.9%
2004	3.3%
2005	3.4%
2006	2.5%
2007	4.1%
2008	0.1%
2009	2.7%
2010	1.5%

However, some employees are not at a point in their lives to be able to afford a compound option even though you have communicated to them clearly that an FPO/GPO is not Partnership-compliant. You can point out in the group meetings that a high daily/monthly benefit with FPO enables them to lock in that much coverage at their current age. If the plan allows the insured to switch to compound without underwriting, you definitely want to highlight that in your education efforts and just encourage the employees who need to start with FPO/GPO to make that switch as soon as they can.

Waiver of Premium: The premium stops at claim time on the insured and some companies offer an option for it to stop on both spouses/partners for a small additional premium. With a compound inflation feature, the benefits continue to grow during a claim and the insured is no longer required to pay premium.

Daily or Monthly Benefit – Ask your employee benefit advisor or whoever is handling the employee education, to be clear about how this benefit works at claim time. Here are points to explain:

- Will it reimburse eligible charges up to the daily/monthly benefit? This is called a **reimbursement** plan as we discussed in Chapter Three.

- Will it pay the entire daily/monthly benefit regardless of the charge? This is called an **indemnity** plan.

- Does the insured have to incur charges and prove services from qualified caregivers before benefits begin?

- Is part or all of the daily or monthly benefit available in **cash**? If so, you can explain the potential for the IRS to view the insured as an employer and the employer's contribution of the caregiver's Social Security, Medicare and unemployment taxes. Or, the insured can simply use an organization that provides these services or provides caregivers and not worry about it.

The monthly benefit is more flexible for home care so you can include that if it's an option rather than making the employees think about it. The insured might need more hours of home care on certain days due to family caregiver availability and it is easier to max out a daily cap than a monthly cap.

To make coverage choices easier to understand, consider asking your employee benefit advisor to make up a sheet with four sample plans. Don't show more than four daily/monthly benefits in the sample plans. Here is a suggestion for the minimum choice on the first sample plan in order to provide a meaningful foundation for the employee or family member with limited resources.

- The daily or monthly benefit equal to the cost of assisted living or five hours of home care in your area;
- a one or two year benefit period; and
- a compound inflation option.

Home Health Care/Adult Day Care – Benefits that cover long-term care outside of the nursing home, such as home health care, adult day care, foster home care, etc. are the most popular, especially when you explain in your employee education efforts that nursing home care makes up only 15% of the long-term care picture.[45] With the baby boomers' aversion to nursing home care, it is expected research will provide more ways to provide care in the community.

If you have a choice between offering a home care benefit that pays less than the nursing home benefit (i.e., 50%) and one that pays equal to the nursing home benefit, choose the one that is equal (the best choice), or at least 75%-80%, since home care costs can equal and even exceed nursing home costs. If you are offering a cash plan, a lower home care option can be a viable way to reduce the premium as the benefit can be used to pay for informal caregivers, who normally cost less than licensed professionals.

Elimination Period/Waiting Period – In the worksite world, a one-time 90 day elimination period/waiting period is the norm. It's one less decision the employees have to deal with. Most people are more worried about how to pay for care that lasts three years, not three months. With newer plans, this is truly a waiting period that starts on the date of benefit certification and requires no charges to meet. If charges are required, it might be one service to start the waiting period or perhaps one service a week, and the charge could be for a minimal amount of care such as four hours of home care. These requirements are much better than forcing the insured to incur a charge every day of the waiting period.

Benefit Period/Benefit Account – Some plans express the lifetime maximum in time; e.g. one, two, three, four, five or six years. Some express it in money such as $50,000, 100,000, $200,000, $300,000 or $500,000. If you are offering a reimbursement plan, explain how the benefit period/benefit account can last longer if charges do not consume 100% of the benefit each month. Encourage this to be the last decision as it is more important that the employee select a daily/monthly benefit and an inflation factor that will enable him or her to make up the difference at claim time. However, when insureds can no longer make up the difference, they can apply for Medicaid benefits in Partnership states and protect assets equal to the benefits paid out at that time. (Oklahoma and Montana residents must exhaust their LTC insurance benefits first.)

Shared Care – A popular option that helps employees feel more comfortable about buying shorter benefit periods than unlimited by allowing couples to have access to each other's benefit period/benefit account and to inherit unused benefits from the deceased spouse/partner.

Common Worksite Benefit Options

As I mentioned earlier, it is easier for your employees if you offer four "pre-packaged" plans in the employee education meetings and in the pre-education material prior to the meetings, then employees can customize the benefits based on their specific needs during a one-on-one consultation that follows the employee education seminar.

How do I know this? My firm was responsible for conducting the employee education for the initial offering of long-term care insurance by the Federal government. We had to do 2,020 employee education meetings in 42 states and 210 cities in 4.5 months so we got plenty of practice at presenting the information! I personally made sure the presentations were perfect for the Hawaii meetings ☺ Fortunately the man in charge of this program with the Office of Personnel Management had us offer four pre-packaged plans as he called them and it made the information and choices so much easier for the Federal employees and their family members to understand. In addition to a meaningful minimum plan as mentioned above, here are ideas for three additional plans:

- Plan 2 might be one that pays 2/3 of the cost for 8 hours of home care or care in a nursing facility with a three year benefit period;

- Plan 3 might pay 80% of the cost with a three year benefit period do; and

- Plan 4 might pay 80% of the cost with a four year benefit period.

If you need help determining the cost of care in your area, most of the long-term care insurance carriers maintain a map of average LTC costs on their website. A good resource for this is also provided by the Mature Market Institute at MetLife, even though MetLife doesn't offer long-term care insurance anymore. You can find that at https://www.metlife.com/assets/cao/mmi/publications/studies/2012/studies/mmi-2012-market-survey-long-term-care-costs.pdf.

After making the basic benefit decisions of monthly benefit, benefit period or account and inflation option, employees and their eligible family members usually have access to a few more options. Here are common options available in today's worksite offerings:

Restoration of Benefits – this benefit says that if the insured becomes truly better for at least 180 consecutive days, all benefits paid for that claim will be restored. While this benefit may not be as meaningful for older applicants, it can be very meaningful for younger worksite applicants, especially those who can only afford short benefit periods. It is reasonably priced.

Shared Waiver – Another reasonably priced addition, this option stops the premium on both spouses/partners when one is receiving benefits; however the premium will resume on the healthy spouse/partner if the sick one recovers or dies, unless the survivor option has been purchased.

Survivor – in most plans, this option gives a surviving spouse/partner a paid up policy/certificate if the coverage has been held at least 10 years and usually adds about 9 percent to the premium.

Limited Pay Options – These options typically accelerate the premium in order to pay it up during the employee's working years. (Remember my earlier consumer alert that these are going away.)

Additional years of rate guarantee – some plans build in an initial rate guarantee such as three or five years then allow the applicant to buy additional years. Again, the appropriate core benefit level is the first consideration.

Shortened Benefit Period – For additional premium, this feature requires the carrier to pay a claim at any point in the future equal to the greater of the premium paid or 30 X the daily benefit if the insured terminates coverage after at least three years even though the coverage is no longer in force. I'm not a fan of this benefit because for no additional premium, today's plans include contingent non-forfeiture which gives this feature to insured's if the rates go beyond a certain percentage based on issue age. The table is included in the Outline of Coverage and again in the policy or certificate that each applicant receives when coverage is issued.

Return of Premium Benefit - Some plans include a return of premium at death benefit and you have no choice but to offer it. Others offer this benefit as an option. If extra premium is charged for this privilege, analyze carefully if the extra premium is a wise expenditure for the employees. The odds are great that they will use the coverage, never get any money back, and they will have paid the extra premium for nothing. They might be better off using the extra premium to buy a better inflation option or an increased dollar amount of coverage, or putting it into their retirement fund.

Evaluating Older Group LTCI Plans

The typical group LTCI offering in the 1990s was three daily benefits, two benefit periods, 50% home care, and the FPO inflation option. Some didn't offer a compound inflation option. A couple offered the ability to pay informal caregivers, but most didn't.

Should employees replace? Typically no. The same amount of coverage today would cost a lot more, not only because they are older but because long-term care insurance costs more today due to revised pricing methods. Rather than replace the older plan, the employee can just add to it with the new employer-sponsored plan. He or she may be able to buy a smaller plan to supplement the original plan. Check the coordination of benefits language in the new plan as it may pay in addition to the old plan, or it may pay secondary in order to pay the eligible charge at 100%.

(Caution: Plans issued prior to January 1, 1997 were grandfathered to be tax-qualified plans and increasing benefits on such a plan will cause it to lose its tax-qualified status.)

Transferring Reserves

If you are transferring from one true group product to another, the older one may transfer the reserves to the newer one. If that doesn't happen, the new carrier must treat the employees as completely new customers and base the premium on their current age. If a reserve transfer occurs, the new carrier can apply a premium credit and charge less for any additional coverage the employees may want to buy. You can discuss this with your employee benefit advisor to see if it is a possibility for your group.

Section Six: Trends That Are Making the LTCI Worksite Market Grow

Thanks to growing consumer awareness efforts about the need to plan for long-term care, we're finally starting to see a time in which a wider age group of employees is aware of it. What are those efforts and when did they start?

1) 2002: The Federal Long-Term Care Insurance Program. When the largest employer group in the world started offering long-term care insurance as an employee benefit, a strong message was sent to the private sector about its importance.

2) 2006: The Deficit Reduction Act signed by the president on February 8, 2006 made it possible for all states to participate in the Long-Term Care Partnership which satisfies the #1 reason non-buyers might buy long-term care insurance as we discussed in Chapter One.

3) 2006: The *Own Your Future* program. The Deficit Reduction Act allocated $3 million per year through 2010 for states to conduct a consumer awareness program on the importance of planning for long-term care with help from the federal government and 24 states did that. You can learn much of this information at www.longtermcare.gov.

4) 2006: Long-term care insurance carrier national advertising really started happening as several major LTCI carriers paid for national television advertising.

5) 2010: The most extensive health care reform bill ever to pass in the United States was signed by the President on March 23, 2010 as The Patient Protection and Affordable Care Act. PPACA included the Community Living Assistance Services and Supports (CLASS) Act. It did not survive, but it called a lot of attention to the need for employers to offer long-term care insurance as a voluntary benefit whether or not there is an employer contribution. There was also some funding to continue consumer education efforts that were originally funded by the Deficit Reduction Act to educate consumers about the Long-Term Care Partnership.

6) 2011: Well-known media personalities like Suze Orman started changing their message to say 59 is the latest one should buy long-term care insurance, instead of advising their followers to wait until that age to buy. [46] Dave Ramsey, well-known author of **Financial Peace** and nationally-syndicated host of *The Money Game,* maintains one doesn't need to buy long-term care insurance until age 60 because of the limited number of young people in nursing homes. Actually, about 10% of nursing home patients are under age 65, but that's not the point.[47] Most people are never in nursing homes, so we shouldn't be gauging the need for long-term care by how many people need nursing home care. Most people are cared for by their families and someone has to give up a life to be the primary caregiver, often to the detriment of that person's children and spouse. There are two main points to be made about why people should buy long-term care insurance as young as possible:

1. By age 60, many people can't qualify medically for long-term care insurance and many more can't afford today's higher premiums for that age bracket. Buying young locks in one's insurability and the insurance costs less since the premium is mostly based on age.

2. **Anyone at any age can need long-term care.** I myself was bowled over when I saw this research:[48]

A healthy 35 year old office worker has a:

*   24% (female) 21% (male) chance of becoming disabled for 3 months or longer; and a

*   38% chance that the disability will last 5 years or longer (both genders).

You learned in Chapter One that care expected to last longer than three months is the definition of long-term care. You also learned that health insurance and Medicare typically don't pay for this extended care. You also learned that disability insurance only provides a portion of an employee's salary to help with living expenses. It doesn't provide an additional $3000 - $6000 a month to pay for caregivers and it ends at age 65. In case you are seeing workers compensation as a payment option, the same article asserts that "three times as many disabling injuries occur off the job as on the job, and are therefore not covered by workers' compensation".[49]

7) Thanks to an aging population, **personal experience with long-term care is higher than it has ever been,** and that is having a significant impact on buying behavior. The major industry study below clarified that the #1 reason employees and their families buy long-term care insurance is to keep from being a burden on their family, just as the Age Wave/Harris Interactive survey pointed out in Section Two of this chapter.[50]

The Call to Action

The 2010 Buyer/Non-Buyer study published by America's Health Insurance Plans reported that 57% of individuals say they have never been contacted about LTCI.[51] This is an extremely dangerous statistic as my best guess is that only about 5% of the 80 million baby boomers have purchased long-term care insurance, when you consider that less than ten million LTCI policies are in force today![52] This in combination with the 2014 Medicaid expansion to younger Americans with incomes up to 133% of the poverty level will suck priceless dollars from our state budgets that could have gone to the starving education funds that are desperately needed to make us a more competitive world economy.

As an employer, you have the best opportunity of any segment of the population to make a difference in this staggering disservice to Americans by offering long-term care insurance to all of your employees, age 18+, and their eligible family members. At least give employees the information with which to make an informed decision. Fifty-two percent of U.S. employers now offer financial education to their employees, according to a 2012 survey by the Society for Human Resource Management (SHRM).[53]

Does this information include planning for long-term care? My guess is not often enough. And if the employer doesn't make it happen, for most people, it doesn't happen. A Nationwide/Harris Interactive poll reported that only one in five consumers discussed health care costs in retirement not covered by Medicare with a financial advisor.[54]

Especially since most employers simply can't offer retiree health insurance anymore, the information on how to pay for health care costs in retirement becomes an even more valuable service that employers can provide to their employees.

The Really Big Picture

It's my opinion that only employers can make a difference fast enough to help states contain the explosive Medicaid growth and the resulting cuts in state services when money has to be used for Medicaid instead of education, transportation, services for the poor elderly and children, and for all the other services we need states to provide.

This is the day I gave Gov. Haslam my idea about The Real Choice Campaign to allow employers to lead the way in educating families to plan for long-term care.

Chapter Six:

ALTERNATIVES TO LTC INSURANCE

———— ✥ ————

Other ways people consider financing long-term care are through accelerated death riders to life insurance policies, life settlements, reverse mortgages and critical illness policies. These options may also be useful to supplement an existing long-term care insurance policy. Perhaps the cost of care has risen faster than you thought it would and you believe you need more coverage. Or you have an older policy with a 50% home care benefit and you want more home care benefits. You get the idea. An overview of each of these options is presented in this chapter as additional information for the long-term care planning process.

Accelerated Death Benefits

An alternative to purchasing a long-term care insurance policy is to purchase a life insurance policy that will provide cash advances against all or a portion of the death benefit to pay for long-term care expenses while the insured is still living. Because the death benefit can be paid out early, this form of long-term care payment as a part of a life insurance policy is commonly referred to as an accelerated death benefit, but it can also be referred to as a "living needs" benefit. Early versions paid only if the policyholder suffered from a terminal illness. Most policies today make the benefit available for chronically ill people as well. Some pay only for permanent confinement in a nursing home, but others pay for home and community-based care, like assisted living.

The accelerated death benefit is an alternative to traditional LTC insurance policies for some people because this provision can be added to a life insurance policy for little or no cost. It also can help someone who cannot qualify for a traditional LTC insurance policy at an older age, if the benefit was included in the policyholder's life insurance at time of purchase, as is the case with many younger purchasers of life insurance today. And, a few life insurance policies will even allow you to add an accelerated death feature after you become sick.

Typically, monthly benefits for long-term care will equal 2% of the face value. For example, if the face value of the policy is $150,000, the benefit would be $3,000 a month.

Newer policies tend to be reimbursement policies. This means they will only pay for actual charges up to the available benefit equal to 2% of the face value. Older policies were commonly indemnity plans, which paid out the 2% amount, regardless of the charge. The Health Insurance Portability and Accountability Act of 1996 (HIPAA) is primarily responsible for this change. Since benefit payments in excess of $320 per day in 2013 (or the monthly equivalent) that exceed the actual cost of care will be taxed as income, the majority of long-term care insurance policies pay only the actual charges for services received. This helps policyholders avoid a precarious tax situation.

What are the pitfalls? At 2% of the face value, the monthly benefit payments are likely to be lower than traditional LTC insurance products, because many people do not have life insurance policies with large face amounts. So if the life insurance policy has a face value of $100,000, the monthly benefit would be $2,000. If the policy advanced the entire $100,000 in this example, the benefit duration would be about four years. That sounds good until you realize that this benefit would pay less than a third of the cost of daily eight-hour shifts of home health care or care in a nursing facility.

Other pitfalls are that some policies pay a lower benefit for home health care, typically 50 percent. An especially serious problem is that inflation may not be addressed. Also, if the primary need is for life insurance, utilizing the death benefit for long-term care expenses defeats the purpose of the insurance by leaving the survivors with little or no death benefit after the insured is deceased. Newer policies have a residual death benefit, which means that a percentage of the original death benefit is paid at death even if the entire death benefit had been accelerated for long-term care. A residual death benefit of 10 percent is common.

The Health Insurance Portability and Accountability Act of 1996 provided much needed clarification that accelerated death benefits will be treated as if they were the proceeds payable on account of death; i.e. income-tax free, if the benefits meet the criteria of HIPAA. Non-qualified versions are being sold, so check carefully to see if the sales brochures, sample policies, etc., have notification that the policy is tax-qualified. Policies that are intended to be tax-qualified are required to be clearly marked.

Since the cost to add an accelerated death benefit option to a life insurance policy is minimal with most policies, this can be a very good purchasing decision, especially for parents of small children when every penny counts.

It can also make it possible to buy a smaller long-term care insurance benefit later on in life if it is simply unaffordable to buy both policies at the same time. See the Mass Mutual example on p. 57.

Life Settlements

Today older Americans who have life insurance (group, individual, term, whole life, and universal life) can sell their policies to a life settlement company for their present value. This can present a significant estate planning tool as well as providing the money to pay for long-term care.

These are people who no longer need a death benefit because the original reason they bought life insurance doesn't exist anymore (for example, college tuition, change in estate size, sale of a business or divorce) or perhaps they can't afford the premium after retirement, a classic problem with term life insurance.

Policies of almost any size can be sold, from $250,000-$100 million, but the most common range is $250,000 to $10 million. The most common age range is 75 and older. Policies purchased include those held in irrevocable life insurance trusts, buy-sell agreements, and "key-person" policies. The proceeds from the policy sale are unrestricted, so the money can be used to pay long-term care expenses for someone who is uninsurable and to fund the purchase of long-term care insurance for a spouse who is insurable. High net worth individuals also may want to use the funds for such options as:

- making cash gifts to family members
- purchasing a minority interest in a closely held business to reduce estate taxes

- facilitate the transfer of a business to the next generation

- funding the purchase of permanent life insurance that will insure a spouse to cover estate taxes

- making charitable gifts and funding planned giving techniques

- purchasing a business

- paying down debt

- investing the proceeds

As you can see, disposition of the funds is up to the imagination and simply represents a way to use life insurance while living. A common use of a life settlement transaction is to use the proceeds to purchase a new insurance product. Life insurance has gone down as life expectancies have crept up, so it's not unusual to be able to buy the same or a higher death benefit for a lower premium even though the policyholder is older.

Although the normal age range is 75 and older, a few life settlement companies will even purchase a life insurance policy from someone as young as 60 years old, if the life expectancy is in the 12 year range, which may be the case with certain health conditions.

Here is an example of using proceeds from a life settlement for long-term care:

An 80-year old gentleman, with some health concerns, had a $400,000 universal life insurance policy that had very little cash value. Making the premium payments was becoming a financial burden, and he and his wife were concerned about long-term care for each of them.

Unfortunately, he did not qualify for long-term care insurance because of his health problems. A life settlement gave him $175,000. The sale of this policy not only relieved this couple of the monthly premium payments but the life settlement funds enabled the client to purchase a long-term care insurance policy for his wife, a second-to-die policy on the two of them with a $200,000 death benefit, and also provided funds for his own long-term care needs.[1]

Another example involves one of my clients who became my client because she and her husband were able to recoup some lost assets through a life settlement:

A victim of an embezzler who specialized in celebrity investments, an 89-year-old gentleman was left with two 12 year old universal life insurance policies with a total death benefit of $800,000 that he was about to lose as he and his wife simply didn't have the money to continue the premiums. Thankfully, they were able to sell them for $308,000 just before they were to lapse. A nice touch to this story is the money came in on the client's 90th birthday. An even nicer touch is that since he had actually paid in more in premium than he received in the life settlement, their tax advisor believes they will not owe income tax on the proceeds. The 64 year old spouse was able to buy a long-term care insurance policy supplemental to the one the embezzler had sold her with an inadequate inflation benefit to protect her as she begins to age.

Concerning taxation issues, the IRS released Revenue Ruling 2009-13 on life settlements (Seller-Owner) which says life settlement payments can incur tax liability to the original policyholder as ordinary income limited to the amount of income that would be recognized if the policy were surrendered. However, if that amount exceeds the "inside build-up" under the policy, the excess may be taxed as capital gain. Revenue Ruling 2009-14 was also released which applies to the purchaser of a life settlement. For a discussion of these rulings and Revenue Ruling 2009-25 11/30/09 Addendum, see www.lisa.org.

Of course, you should discuss any individual tax situation with a professional tax advisor.

Note that a lump sum received from any source could and probably would affect the ability to qualify for Medicaid as it would be counted as an asset. We will discuss Medicaid eligibility in the next chapter.

Another major concern that had to be put to rest was Stranger Owned Life Insurance. This practice occurred when investors would lend older people the money to buy life insurance with the promise that the policy owner would sell the policy in a few years. Sounds like a plot for a good murder mystery, doesn't it? The National Association of Insurance Commissioners passed a ruling in December 2006 that prohibits a person or entity loaning the money to an older American to buy a life insurance policy just for the purpose of selling it in a couple of years. You can see a thorough examination of life settlement regulations in "Life Insurance Settlements: Regulatory Inconsistencies May Pose a Number of Challenges" provided by the Government Accountability Office in July 2010 http://www.gao.gov/new.items/d10775.pdf. Many states have since passed legislation that prohibits a life settlement within a certain number of years of the effective date of the policy without a good reason such as chronic or terminal illness, death or divorce of a spouse, retirement, and so forth.

If this process interests you, please see The Life Settlement Process at the end of this chapter.

Critical Illness

Critical illness policies were introduced in the United States in the mid-1990s and pay a lump-sum upon diagnosis of one of a dozen or so conditions including Alzheimer's, multiple sclerosis, heart attack, stroke when effects of the neurological injury last for at least 30 days, life threatening cancer (malignant and growing uncontrollably outside its original location), major organ transplant, paralysis, kidney failure requiring dialysis, blindness, deafness, and perhaps severe burns. Some policies have a return of premium benefit, which means the premium will be returned to a beneficiary less any benefits paid out if the policyholder dies without receiving all of the benefits.

A partial benefit, perhaps 25 percent, is paid for conditions such as malignant cancer in one location; heart angioplasty and heart bypass surgery.

You may be charged a higher premium if one or more of your immediate family members (parents and siblings) have had any of these conditions.

Common issue ages are 20-64 but you can keep the policy as long as you live. However, benefits usually reduce to 50 percent at age 65 or five years after the effective date if you were older than 60 when you purchased the policy.

The lump-sum benefit can pay anywhere from $25,000 to $1 million, depending on how much you purchase when you buy the policy. One company recommends three to five times the annual salary for employed people plus any outstanding mortgage balance.

Critical illness policies can be standalone, or some are sold as an optional benefit with a life insurance policy or annuity. If sold in the workplace, there may be only a few medical questions in order to qualify.

The lump-sum benefit of a critical illness policy can be used to cover the miscellaneous expenses connected to a major illness such as:

- insurance deductibles and co-pays
- travel expenses such as meals, lodging and airfare to seek additional medical treatment
- experimental treatment and/or drugs
- treatment outside of a managed care network
- child care or elder care
- salary replacement for time away from work
- household help like cooking, cleaning and laundry
- home modifications
- mortgage payments and other debts

The point is the lump-sum benefit of a critical illness policy is a cash benefit that can be used for anything.

Critical Illness Insurance vs. Long-Term Care Insurance

Can critical illness coverage be an alternative payment option for long-term care? Possibly, especially if you are not able to qualify for long-term care insurance and you are able to get a critical illness policy through your employer with simplified underwriting, which means just a few medical questions.

What are the pitfalls?

1. Access to benefits is tougher in some situations; e.g. Alzheimer's patients could have to need help with at least three activities of daily living (ADLs) in addition to requiring permanent daily supervision as diagnosed by a board-certified neurologist. Long-term care insurance policies use a safety evaluation for self and others to award benefits to a policyholder with Alzheimer's, not an ADL evaluation.

2. The critical illness benefit is a lump-sum cash benefit which can bring a strong temptation to spend it for things other than long-term care services.

3. A lump-sum cash benefit may be difficult to budget so that it lasts throughout a long-term condition. According to the Alzheimer's Association, the lifespan of an Alzheimer's patient can be four to 20 years.[2]

4. Benefits may reduce at age 65, and a long-term care insurance policy is sometimes most needed at older ages.

On the positive side, critical illness insurance can be relatively inexpensive at younger ages, especially if it is a rider on a life insurance policy, and the benefit would be invaluable if long-term care is needed at a young age. At any age, critical illness makes a good supplement to long-term care insurance as the money can be used for any need.

Reverse Mortgages

First, what is a reverse mortgage? Because many older Americans have most of their savings invested in their home, the federal government established a home equity conversion loan program in 1988 to help Americans age 62 and older on fixed incomes convert part of the equity in their home into tax-free income without having to sell the home, give up the title, or take on a new monthly mortgage payment. Administered by the U.S. Department of Housing and Urban Development (HUD), **these loans are called reverse mortgages** as no repayment of the loan is ever required until the borrower dies, sells the home, or permanently leaves the residence for 12 months or more. In other words, people are able to tap the value of the home without giving it up as long as they live in it.

One must be a homeowner, which can include a single family residence, condominium, townhouse, duplex, triplex, or four-plex, as long as the development meets FHA guidelines. There are no income qualifications and limited credit qualifications, because unlike an equity loan from a bank, a reverse mortgage requires no monthly payments. The homeowner is responsible only for keeping up payments for homeowner's insurance and property taxes, and to maintain the condition of the home. The home can be sold at any time; e.g. if the owner decides to move.

How Funds are Disbursed and Tax Implications

The funds available to the homeowner are tax free and don't count as income for Social Security eligibility purposes. The balance due grows as funds are disbursed to the homeowner. The available cash can be taken in a lump sum, monthly payments, or as a line of credit which can be accessed as needed. Or, the money can be available as a combination of regular monthly payments and a line of credit. The line of credit is popular because no interest is charged on the money until it is used, and it allows the homeowner to decide when he or she needs the money and how much.

The interest rates on reverse mortgages are adjustable. Monthly adjustments to the interest rate will not affect monthly payments, unless the owner has chosen to take his or her money as a line of credit. Otherwise, fluctuating interest rates will only affect how much money is owed when the owner dies, moves out of the home, or sells the home. Since interest adds to the balance that will be owed when the property is sold, a fixed rate can be tempting in the current economy with lower interest rates, but the downside is it requires the borrower to take the full amount of equity upfront.[3] Also, the new Saver program explained a little later in this section may likely carry a higher fixed rate than the standard loan due to the significantly lower upfront fees.[4] It's common sense to realize that the higher interest rate can cause the money saved on fees to backfire if the borrower holds the reverse mortgage a long time.

Barb Stucki, CEO of NestCare FPA and formerly the reverse mortgage authority for the National Council on Aging, cautions seniors against taking a lump sum from a reverse mortgage and parking it in the bank to augment savings. The fees for taking out a reverse mortgage are much higher than the interest the borrower could earn at a bank.[5]

The Payback Process

When sold, any balance due on the reverse mortgage is paid and the remaining equity goes to the owner or in the case of death, to his or her estate. The amount of equity remaining depends on how long the borrower was able to stay in the home and the value of the home at the time of sale.

An especially attractive feature with the way the program was set up was that at no time would repayment exceed the value of the home, which became even more attractive as housing values declined. Because this was true regardless of whom the home was sold to – strangers or family members like the children - this feature made reverse mortgages **non-recourse loans**, which means the loan is secured only by the property. If the house sells for less than the balance due, the lender will accept that as long as it is a bona fide sale. Behind the scenes, the lender turns the loan over to the government at that point and HUD has to repay the difference to the lender.

This desirable feature for the homeowner isn't without a price. An insurance premium of an upfront fee of 2% of the loan and 1.25% annually is required. Criticism of excess fees surrounding reverse mortgages culminated in **The Housing and Economic Recovery Act of 2008**, effective October 1, 2008 which capped the origination fee at two percent of the first $200,000 borrowed and one percent on the balance, with a maximum of $6,000 (subject to increases in the CPI as determined by the Bureau of Labor Statistics in $500 increments).

After a booming private reverse mortgage market, the down economy led to almost all of the reverse mortgages today being the Home Equity Conversion Mortgage (HECM), the only one insured by the Federal Housing Administration (FHA). The older one is and the more valuable the home is increases the amount that can be borrowed. The maximum lending limit in 2013 is $625,500.[6]

The Impact of the HECM Saver on the Reverse Mortgage Market

In response to the criticism about the fees, FHA introduced the HECM Saver in **HUD Mortgagee Letter 2010-34** dated September 21, 2010, a new loan that charges .01% (.0001) instead of the 2% (2.0) upfront mortgage premium. The annual premium will continue to be 1.25% of the unpaid loan balance for both programs. For example, the fee with a Saver is very small such as $25 on a $250,000 loan, instead of $5,000 on a HECM Standard loan. HUD does this by approving loans at 10%-18% less than with the HECM, and the Saver is available for all types of disbursement and for fixed or adjustable interest rates. The HECM Standard is a better deal for people who are able to stay in their homes a long time, as there is more time to amortize the fees.

> You can research any of the HUD Mortgagee Letters mentioned in this section at this link:
>
> http://www.hud.gov/offices/adm/hudclips/letters/mortgagee/

A big change in the demographics of reverse mortgagors: The average age of the borrower was 79 in the early years of this program but now it's early 70s. Thanks to the easy credit that preceded a sagging economy, many new entrants are 62 year old baby boomers who are strapped with debt. A reverse mortgage looks like an oasis in the desert for these early baby boomers. Generally there is no cash out-of-pocket. The proceeds can be used to pay off an outstanding first mortgage or any other debt on the home. The associated fees such as the origination fee, an appraisal fee and other standard closing costs may be financed as part of the reverse mortgage. The caution is to ensure there is enough money to pay property tax and homeowners' insurance on an ongoing basis.[7]

Several dangerous pitfalls have emerged:

1. The money is taken as a lump sum and spent quickly to eliminate debt, then the money isn't there to keep the home up. In the past, lenders would roll the property tax and insurance into the loan but guidelines in Mortgagee Letter 2011-01 dated January 3, 2011 said HUD can't use taxpayer dollars for this purpose. The homeowner has 24 months to catch up these expenses or face foreclosure. Bank of America and Wells Fargo, the two largest banks that issued reverse mortgages withdrew from this market in February and June 2011 respectively as they had no way of establishing a borrower's ability to keep up with homeowners' insurance and property taxes.[8] MetLife exited the reverse mortgage in April 2012, leaving smaller mortgage brokers and lenders to fill the void of these major players.[9]

2. One spouse is under age 62. Financial straits make it hard to delay the application, so the reverse mortgage has to be put in the name of the age-qualifying spouse. The couple doesn't have the money to refinance when the younger one turns 62 so it stays in the name of the older spouse. When that spouse dies, the loan has to be paid off for the widow(er) to remain in the home.[10]

3. Another spouse issue is that a spouse whose name isn't on the deed is not required to go through HUD counseling and may not know the loan will become due when the homeowner spouse dies. This can easily happen with remarriage.[11]

A Maelstrom of Protest

AARP filed a lawsuit against HUD on March 8, 2011 on behalf of three surviving spouses, but the spouse issues were only part of the basis for the suit.[12] HUD had come to regret the decision to allow all buyers the ability to pay back no more than the value of the home, especially after the Katrina debacle which set off a chain reaction of declining home values. Congress was concerned that too many homes were hitting the crossover point at which the loan balance exceeds the value of the home and that the need for HUD to pay off the difference between the loan balance and the value of the home was happening more frequently. This raised the concern that the losses to the Federal Housing Administration Insurance Fund which insures the loans were becoming too great and would eventually roll back on the taxpayer. This policy created a moral hazard, HUD said, as it provided a perverse incentive for people to not keep their home up since the lower the home value, the lower the balance that had to be paid back on the reverse mortgage.[13]

It came to light that HUD "clarified" the definition of a non-recourse loan in **Mortgagee Letter 2008-38** dated December 5, 2008 and started requiring spouses and family members who wanted to keep the house after the borrower died to pay the full balance, even if it exceeded the value of the home. Other buyers not related to the borrower could buy it for **the lesser of** the unpaid mortgage balance or 95% of the appraised value. That combined with the problem of surviving spouses not being named as a borrower and facing foreclosure unless they either paid off the full loan balance or sold the home to a third party and moved out created a maelstrom of protest. AARP also charged that lenders encouraged younger spouses not to be named as a borrower as older homeowners applying alone are granted higher monthly payments since they aren't expected to collect as long as younger borrowers.[14] The lenders mostly sided with AARP and HUD rescinded Mortgagee Letter 2008-38 in **Mortgagee Letter 2011-16** dated April 5, 2011.[15]

With that issue put to rest, the popularity of the new HECM Saver has taken the reverse mortgage out of the "loan of last resort" position for lending institutions as well as older homeowners. Small community banks that were seeing them as competition to home equity loans are now wanting to offer them with reduced or no origination fees. While upfront fees may be lowered by about 40%, a *Wall St. Journal* article points to an example of a New York resident who would receive about $262,000 with a Saver on a $500,000 home versus $331,500 with the standard HECM version.[16]

> You can compare HECM Standard and HECM Saver options at www. reversemortgage.org.

Much of the cash from the various plans has been used for home modifications, home repairs, to weatherize homes, to make homes accessible for the handicapped, for supplemental retirement income, and some of the money is being used to fund long-term care services. Very little has been used to purchase long-term care insurance, according to Peter Bell, President and CEO of the Reverse Mortgage Lenders Association.[17] This is really unfortunate, as long-term care insurance complements a reverse mortgage by making the reverse mortgage money last longer, as the insurance negates the need to depend on the reverse mortgage money to pay 100% of care costs.

Buying Insurance Products with the Proceeds of a Reverse Mortgage

A common misconception is that The Housing and Economic Recovery Act of 2008 prohibits the purchase of financial products with the money from a reverse mortgage. This isn't true. It said that the same individual can't receive compensation for selling the reverse mortgage and financial products. It also said that lenders can't require borrowers to purchase insurance, annuities, or other products as a condition for getting a reverse mortgage.[18]

Reverse Mortgages and Long-Term Care Insurance

Rather than pay for long-term care services directly, much more mileage can be obtained from the money by purchasing long-term care insurance if the owner is insurable. He or she can purchase a long-term care insurance policy outright by paying a monthly, semi-annual or annual premium. Some borrowers take the reverse mortgage as a line of credit, and then use the interest growth each year to pay their long-term care insurance premiums. Or, a lump-sum obtained from a reverse mortgage can be used to purchase an annuity, which can then be set up to pay the LTC insurance premiums for the rest of the insured's life. Or, the lump sum can be used to purchase a combination life insurance or annuity long-term care insurance policy as described in Chapter Two that pays LTC expenses with a premium guaranteed never to increase.

Consumer Protection Features in a Long-Term Care Insurance Policy

It's important to remember that the loan becomes due within 12 months after a borrower leaves the home to go to an assisted living or nursing facility (or leaves for any reason).[19] So if moving to a facility and losing the reverse mortgage money to pay the premium will jeopardize the plan, it's important for a couple to purchase the option in many policies today that allows the premium to stop on both spouses/partners when only one of them starts receiving benefits. This is called the "shared waiver". However, the premium will come back on the spouse not on claim if the LTC spouse passes away. The survivor benefit can also be purchased which says if one spouse/partner dies after the insurance has been held 10 years, the surviving spouse has a paid-up policy.

To make it easier for children to keep the home when the reverse mortgage comes due, some people (or their children) purchase a life insurance policy on the homeowner when the reverse mortgage is obtained so the children can use the death benefit to pay off the mortgage and keep the house.

For a list of lenders that offer reverse mortgages in your state, call the National Reverse Mortgage Lenders Association at 866-264-4466 or visit the website at www.reversemortgage.org and click on "Find a Lender". This website also contains a calculator that you can use to estimate how much a borrower may be able to obtain through a reverse mortgage and to compare the standard HECM with the new HECM Saver program.

To make sure families understand the program, FHA requires a free individual information meeting with a HUD-approved housing agency separate from the lender so he or she can learn about the program objectively and decide if it's right for them. To obtain the name of a local counseling agency or qualified telephone counselor from a reverse mortgage lender or by calling AARP (888-687-2277), or HUD's Housing Counseling Clearinghouse (800-569-4287). According to the National Reverse Mortgage Lenders Association, the counseling session costs homeowners about $125-$150, as lenders are not allowed to pay for counseling.[20]

✳ **CONSUMER ALERT:** Please be sure the reverse mortgage is done in the name of both spouses if you are married. Otherwise, when the spouse whose name it is in dies, the reverse mortgage comes due for the surviving spouse **immediately.** If this can't be done because one spouse is under age 62, get it done as soon as that spouse turns 62. I can't think of a better thing to do on that 62nd birthday than to be sure that spouse doesn't lose that home someday because she wasn't on the reverse mortgage!

Continuing Care Retirement Communities (CCRCs)

CCRC's were originally designed to "be all things to all retired people" in their infancy by setting up a community that provided care throughout the various stages of retired life in exchange for a substantial down-payment. However, as life spans continue to expand and interest rates on investments have continued to drop, many have found that proposition impossible to fulfill.

Today's CCRCs still typically require the hefty down-payment, but it's good advice to have an attorney look over the contract before signing. I had a client once tell me she had moved into a CCRC and asked my advice about keeping her long-term care insurance policy. I steeled myself to tell her she could give it up. (The reason I steeled myself was because her premium represented the largest case I had ever sold as she was age 79 when she bought it, and the renewals were 10% forever!) But before I did, I asked to see the CCRC contract. Imagine my amazement when I read that not only would no care be provided in her unit, the basic contract her $400,000 had purchased provided only 365 days of care in the CCRC's nursing home section. She had purchased a long-term care insurance policy from me with a $180 daily benefit and a lifetime benefit period. I quickly advised her (with copies to her two sons – a surgeon in California and a writer in Manhattan) to keep her policy. It was a good lesson to me about how much CCRC's have reduced what was once perceived to be a lifetime commitment to care for those who purchased units.

Advantages of LTC Insurance vs. Continuing Care Retirement Communities

The down payment: Rather than part with a few hundred thousand to buy into a CCRC, a long-term care insurance policy allows one to retain one's assets.

Health: A common perception is that one can buy into a CCRC with poor health. This is not normally the case because the CCRC is "on the hook" for the agreed-upon amount of care and like an insurance company, the CCRC's pricing is partially predicated on not all residents needing care. One of my clients wanted to move into a CCRC with a seven year waiting list. I advised her to keep her long-term care insurance policy certainly through the seven years because if she had a stroke or some other significant health event, there would have been an excellent chance the CCRC would not have accepted her.

Home care benefits: A typical CCRC contract will provide some timeframe of care in its nursing home section, but it's not unusual for there to be no coverage in the unit, so long-term care insurance home care benefits could be very helpful to prolong the time the resident can stay in the unit. And if it becomes necessary to leave the unit, is there an assisted living section or does the resident have to go straight to the nursing home section?

In addition to finding out specifically what long-term care coverage to expect from the CCRC, clients really need to think about the lifestyle change that results from moving into a CCRC. Can they really adjust to living quarters of 900 square feet, for example, when they've been living in a home with 3,000 square feet?

To reiterate, please be sure to have an attorney review the information you obtain from a CCRC that you are seriously considering moving into. A

U.S. Senate Special Committee on Aging report spells out the information you are entitled to from any CCRC:[21]

Financial

1. audited financial reports;

2. information on accreditation, if applicable;

3. key financial indicators on the ability of the CCRC to meet obligations to residents (i.e., debt levels and debt service, liquidity, capital for improvements, etc);

4. financial forecasts for future years, including financial statement projections and actuarial studies;

5. occupancy trends;

6. average length of time for payment of entrance fee refunds;

7. a narrative disclosure from the CCRC regarding its financial condition, including an explanation of complex financial terms and concepts and an in-person meeting session with residents to discuss and allow for questions and answers;

8. fee schedules to consumers, including entrance fees, monthly fees, and fees for other CCRC amenities;

9. fee adjustment policies to consumers, including the manner in which increases occur and increase trends;

10. reserve funding levels and sources;

11. expected source of funds for development, repair, or replacement of facilities;

12. refund policies and revenue sources; and

13. the status of a resident claim on CCRC assets in case of bankruptcy or insolvency.

Non-Financial

CCRCs should provide information about the provider and management to the consumer including:

1. governing structure and ownership;

2. names of board members/trustees;

3. history of the CCRC;

4. for- or non-profit status;

5. relationships with any outside companies for management or other reasons;

6. affiliations with any religious or charitable groups to consumers;

7. recent state examinations including health and safety inspections to consumers;

8. a description of the physical CCRC property, including amenities and services to consumers;

9. a copy of the CCRC contract including termination provisions to the consumer;

10. financial assistance policies in the event that a resident has financial difficulties;

11. requirements for admission or discharge from different levels of care (i.e., independent living, assisted living, and nursing facility), including policies on involuntary transfers to a higher level of care;

12. rules and regulations of the CCRC to consumers;

13. policies regarding life changes such as marriage or death of a spouse to the consumer; and

14. annual or operating reports to consumers.

VA Benefits

As a long-distance caregiver for my Aunt Jeannette who was a photographer in the Air Force in World War II, I was surprised to learn that as a veteran receiving the Medicaid nursing home benefit, she was entitled to keep $90 a month instead of the $40 per month that the Tennessee Medicaid program allows. As her Power of Attorney, I had to apply for it on her behalf with the local Veterans Administration office and it took about a year to obtain, but eventually she was awarded that amount. Here is the description of this benefit:

The Department of Veterans Affairs (DVA) limits monthly Veterans benefits (VA) to $90 for any Medicaid eligible:

- veteran who is a long term care resident, and who does not have a spouse or child; **or**
- veteran's surviving spouse who is a long term care resident, and who does not have a child.

As for actually paying for home care and nursing home care, CMS reports that the VA pays less than 2%.[22]

Many retired veterans believe veteran benefits, administered through the Veterans Administration (VA), will cover any long-term care need a veteran may face in the future. However, many veterans have never actually reviewed the "Federal Benefits for Veterans, Dependents and Survivors" handbook which outlines exactly how veteran "Extended Care" (long-term care) benefits work and what it takes to qualify. You can see and download this information at www.va.gov/opa/publications/benefits_book.asp

Priority Groups

The VA begins by assigning each veteran to a priority group. Priority groups are used to balance the demand for VA health care enrollments, with the actual resources that are available. Priority attention is given to the groups who have the highest **service-connected** disability ratings and ends with those who have no **service-connected** disability but simply lack the financial means to meet their basic health care needs. Based on the actual resources the VA has available at any given time, qualifying for benefits may be even tougher.

Priority Groups are based on the severity of a physical or psychological disability followed by a financial assessment, for the purpose of determining who receives access to care services first.

Who is Eligible for VA Nursing Home Care?

In a nutshell, nursing home care is available for veterans who need nursing home care for a service-connected disability, and those rated 60 percent service-connected and unemployable; or Veterans or who have a 70 percent or greater service-connected disability. VA-provided nursing home care for all other Veterans is based on available resources.

Non-Institutional Long-Term Care

In addition to nursing home care, VA offers a variety of other long-term care services either directly or by contract with community-based agencies. Such services include adult day health care, respite care, geriatric evaluation and management, hospice and palliative care, skilled nursing and other skilled professional services at home, home health aide services, and home based primary care. Veterans receiving these services may be subject to a copay.

VA social workers will assist veterans in interpreting their eligibility and co-pay requirements when necessary. Veterans are required to pay co-pays from $0 to $97 per day for extended care services based on the available resources between the veteran and his or her spouse.

Financial Assessment

In order to determine if a veteran must pay a co-pay for extended care, it is necessary to identify all household income and assets. You will see in the next chapter that this assessment is stricter than applicants for the Medicaid long-term care benefits have to satisfy. Spousal income is protected for the healthy spouse of a Medicaid applicant, whereas the income for a veteran and his or her spouse is considered as joint income.

In addition to the home and any other property, countable assets include:

- cash
- bank accounts, checking and savings accounts, certificates of deposit, money market accounts
- all retirement accounts

- stock, bonds, annuities, notes
- art, rare coins, stamp collections, collectibles, gold, silver

Veterans Aid & Attendance and Housebound Benefits

The most popular potential source of assistance to pay for long-term care services for veterans today seems to be the Aid and Attendance (A&A) and Housebound benefits. These benefits which are sometimes called the Aid & Attendance Pension, are explained in Chapter 3 of the Federal Benefits handbook. They may be available to veterans who served during a time of war, have limited or no income, and are age 65 or older or permanently and totally disabled. A veteran can receive either the A&A benefit or the Housebound benefit, but cannot receive both at the same time. The A&A benefit is higher than the Housebound benefit because it requires a greater loss of functionality.

A veteran may be eligible for the A&A benefit when:

1. the veteran requires the aid of another person in order to perform personal functions required in everyday living, such as bathing, feeding, dressing, attending to the wants of nature, adjusting prosthetic devices, or protecting himself/herself from the hazards of his/her daily environment; or

2. the veteran is bedridden, in that his/her disability or disabilities requires that he/she remain in bed apart from any prescribed course of convalescence or treatment; or

3. the veteran is a patient in a nursing home due to mental or physical incapacity; or

4. the veteran is blind, or so nearly blind as to have corrected visual acuity of 5/200 or less, in both eyes, or concentric contraction of the visual field to 5 degrees or less.

A veteran may be eligible for the Housebound benefit when:

1. the veteran has a single permanent disability evaluated as 100-percent disabling **AND**, due to such disability, he/she is permanently and substantially confined to his/her immediate premises, **OR**,

2. the veteran has a single permanent disability evaluated as 100-percent disabling **AND**, another disability, or disabilities, evaluated as 60 percent or more disabling.

If a veteran is eligible for the A&A or Housebound benefit, the amount of the benefit is determined by a formula. The formula starts with the maximum benefit amount and reduces the maximum benefit amount by the veteran's "countable income", which basically is any income received by the veteran and the veteran's dependents. Deductions can include unreimbursed medical expenses that are not reimbursed by Medicare or private medical insurance, such as the cost of long-term care. In addition, assets above a certain level not counting the primary residence can disqualify a veteran for the A&A or Housebound benefit. Whether or not assets are deemed excessive depend upon the facts of each individual case but generally would be in the $80,000 range.

The current maximum benefit was determined on December 1, 2012, and like social security payments, will generally increase a little each year. The current maximum A&A benefit is $20,447 per year ($1,703 per month) for veterans without dependents and $24,239 per year ($2,020 per month) for veterans with one dependent. The current maximum Housebound benefit is $14,978 per year ($1,248 per month) for veterans without dependents and $18,773 per year ($1,564 per month) for veterans with one dependent.

The $90 per month that I mentioned at the beginning of this section that a veteran who is receiving nursing home care paid by Medicaid is in addition to the personal needs allowance to which Medicaid patients are entitled and any other pension benefit. It is for the veteran's personal needs and can't be used to offset the cost of care.

For veterans who are uninsurable for private long-term care insurance, the A&A benefit can be a great thing to help the veteran afford care in an assisted living facility, for example. However, since the maximum A&A benefit is only about $2,000 per month, it should not be considered an alternative to private long-term care insurance for those veterans who are eligible for private coverage. That amount barely pays half of the cost of an assisted living facility today and only about a third of daily eight hour shifts of home care or care in a nursing facility.[23]

Family Caregiver Benefits

Under the Caregivers and Veterans Omnibus Health Services Act of 2010, the Department of Veterans Affairs (VA) launched a series of new and enhanced services supporting family caregivers of seriously ill and injured Veterans. The Act is especially targeted to provide a wide range of new benefits to support certain caregivers of eligible post-September 11, 2001 veterans.

Some of the new benefits include:

- a monthly stipend (direct payments to a family caregiver based on wages of a home health aide in the area where the Veteran resides);

- access to health care insurance (if the Caregiver is not already entitled to care or services under a health care plan);

- travel expenses, including lodging and per diem while accompanying Veterans undergoing care;

- respite care (not less than 30 days per year, including 24/7 in-home care); and

- mental health services and counseling (including individual or group psychotherapy).

Each VA medical center has designated caregiver support coordinators who will assist eligible Veterans and caregivers in understanding and applying for the new benefits. To download an application, visit http://www.caregiver.va.gov/apply or call 1-877-222 VETS (8387). The VA has also published a fact sheet that is available here: http://www.caregiver.va.gov/pdfs/CaregiverFactSheet_Apply.pdf.

The VA has a Caregiver Support Web page at www.caregiver.va.gov.

THE LIFE SETTLEMENT PROCESS

THE PLAYERS

Issuer – the insurance company that issued the policy

Life settlor – the seller (individual or trust, corporation, Partnership, LLC)

Life settlement provider – licensed in states to buy policies

Escrow agent – holding tank for the money

Funder (Purchaser) – third party that ultimately owns the policy (not shared with Life Settlor)

TYPE OF POLICIES THAT CAN BE SOLD

- On individuals primarily age 70+ (younger considered if significant health problems)
- Generally $250,000+ face value
- Term,* whole, variable, universal, variable universal (individual or group)
- Owned by individual, trust, corporation
- Must be older than 24 months unless one of these situations exist:**
    o Owner or insured was diagnosed as terminally or chronically ill after the issuance of the policy
    o Owner's spouse has died
    o Owner divorces his or her spouse
    o Owner retires from full-time employment

---

*if it is convertible to permanent life insurance in order to stabilize the premium for the Purchaser
**Four years in Minnesota and five years in Iowa, Nebraska, Nevada, North Dakota, Ohio, Oregon, Vermont, West Virginia, Wisconsin.

- o Owner has a physician-certified disability that prevents owner from maintaining full-time employment
- o Owner experiences an unexpected significant decrease in income and is unable to pay the premium
- o Owner disposes of ownership interests in a closely held corporation

FORMS REQUIRED FOR A LIFE SETTLEMENT

1. Initial life settlement application (Beneficiary, loans, ever assigned, major health issues, doctors, life expectancy less than 24 months… 36 in IN or MA, ADL deficiency or cognitive impairment)
2. Durable Power of Attorney for life settlement provider to deal with insurance company
3. HIPAA Authorization to Release Medical Records
4. Authorization for Life Insurance Company to Release:
   a. Inforce illustration
   b. Annual statement
   c. Verification of Coverage dated within 30 days of closing and showing the policy in good standing (not in grace period)
   d. Copy of complete policy, including master policy and employee certificate if group policy); "complete" means it includes a copy of the application
   e. Change of ownership and beneficiary forms, collateral assignment
   f. Possibly a copy of medical records the insurance company used to underwrite the policy

5. Beneficiary's Consent to Transfer, Waiver of Interest and Release of Claims

6. Spousal Release of Beneficiary

7. Physician's Letter of Competency (must be an original)

8. Life Settlor's Acknowledgement (all info about the policy is true and notably, that it wasn't purchased with the intent to sell it)

9. Copy of Life Settlor's Social Security card and driver license or government ID

10. Settlement statement (how money is to be paid…wire transfer, cashier's check)

11. Escrow Agreement (entity that handles the money and documents… e.g. Wells Fargo…agree to release funds to Life Settlor within 3 business days of receiving the change of ownership & beneficiary forms from the insurance company that insurance company has 30 days to provide)

12. Disclosures to Life Settlor that there may other options like accelerated death benefit, cash value and that life settlement money can be attached by creditors; may affect Medicaid eligibility

13. Primary Designee to be contacted for periodic health reports on the Life Settlor

14. W-9 for Life Settlor

THE PROCESS

The Life Settlement Provider bundles all these forms along with the life settlement contract and submits to the Life Settlor for signatures then to the purchaser. The Verification of Coverage has to be current to show the policy is in good standing and not in a grace period. The change of ownership and beneficiary forms are sent to the insurance company. The Life Settlement Provider deposits the money into the escrow account. The escrow agent pays the Life Settlor per the terms of the Settlement Statement (wire transfer or cashier's check) within 3 days after notification from the Life Settlement Provider that the change forms are accepted by the insurance company. The insurance company has 30 days to process the change forms but usually does it much faster. If the insurance company fails to accept these within 45 days, the deal is off (rarely ever happens).

RIGHT TO RESCIND (CONSUMER PROTECTION)

The Life Settlor has the right to rescind the contract within 30 days from the date of the contract or within 15 days after receiving the funds. If the Life Settlor dies within this rescission period, the contract is automatically rescinded and the entire death benefit goes to the beneficiary as soon as the recipient of the funds pays the money back to the Life Settlement Provider.

TAX IMPLICATIONS

Viatical settlements – tax-free to someone who is chronically ill or terminally ill with a life expectancy of 24 months or less per HIPAA, January 1, 1997.

Life settlements – general view is taxed as ordinary income for the difference between premiums paid and cash value then taxed as capital gain for amount received above cash value. (Consult a professional tax advisor for a final determination.)

WHAT'S IN IT FOR THE LIFE SETTLOR

- **PURCHASE LONG-TERM CARE INSURANCE** for self and/or spouse
- Provide immediate source of income
- Provide funds for retirement
- Eliminate costly premium payments
- Receive more cash than the cash surrender value
- Tax efficient solution
- Fund a charitable gift
- Pay gift taxes
- Take a dream vacation

"Anyone would be lucky to have Phyllis Shelton in their corner. Her expertise and ability to navigate the very complex details of a life settlement is truly amazing. Phyllis, who never gives up, found creative and successful solutions for me. And I will always be grateful to her for the difference she made in my life."

Keren Saks, client, New York

Congressman Lee Terry (NE) was kind enough to listen to my idea about The Real Choice Campaign. You can see it at http://www.ltcconsultants.com/articles/2012/real-choice

Chapter Seven:

PEOPLE WHO DO NOT QUALIFY FOR LTC INSURANCE

———∞∞∞———

It's always with great sadness when I have to tell someone he or she doesn't qualify medically for long-term care insurance. It's especially difficult when the person could have qualified, say 10 years earlier, but now there is an issue like multiple sclerosis or degenerative disk disease that has developed. Now the person is simply uninsurable for long-term care insurance, either traditional or the combination annuity/long-term care insurance policy that we discussed in Chapter Two that can be a little easier to get.

The first thing I recommend is for an uninsurable person who is still working to ask the employer if a worksite long-term care insurance plan can be offered with limited or no underwriting. You learned in Chapter Five that a true "guaranteed issue" plan typically requires a company with 1000 employees so if you work for a company that size, it's worth a trip or phone call to the HR Director. Who knows? The management of your company might be considering a long-term care insurance offering and a call from an interested employee might make it happen. If you get a "no" to a long-term care insurance offering or if you work for a smaller company, ask if a critical illness product offering with limited health questions might be in the works.

If any type of employer offering isn't an option, there could still be a silver lining here. If the uninsurable person was insurable at one time, there's a chance there might be other coverage in place that can help.

Life insurance or annuities: Check your policy or ask your insurance professional or the insurance company if you will be able to accelerate the death benefit or annuity account value if you ever need help with at least two activities of daily living or have a severe cognitive impairment. If the answer is "yes", ask how much it will pay. The answer will likely be a certain percentage of the death benefit or annuity account value per month. If you have any type of life insurance that builds cash value, you can ask if there is an option to have the growth buy additional death benefit instead of all going to increase the cash value. If so, that will create a larger amount available for long-term care in the future if you can accelerate the death benefit for long-term care. This option is commonly known as "paid-up additions" since it means that you are buying more death benefit over time. Of course you want to be careful about this and not use the death benefit of your life insurance policy or the annuity account value to fund your long-term care if you have a beneficiary who needs this money when you die.

Life settlement: If there is no provision in your life insurance policy that allows you to use the death benefit for long-term care and/or you don't have a beneficiary depending on the death benefit, you may be able to sell it for much more than you would receive if you just tried to use the cash value. Please review "The Life Settlement Process" at the end of the last chapter to see if this might be an option for you. If so, you can check with my good friends at Asset Servicing Group (theasg.net) to find out for sure. Asset Servicing Group is the only independent third party servicer in the life settlement industry and I have known Tom Moran, the

President and CEO for many years. Asset Servicing Group manages over 6,000 policies with a total face value of over $4 billion that have been through the settlement process.

Also, we didn't discuss Viatical Settlements in Chapter Six but anyone at any age with a life expectancy of 24 months or less is allowed to sell a life insurance policy and use the benefits tax-free however the money is needed per the Health Insurance Portability and Accountability Act of 1996, which is the same legislation that governs today's tax incentives for long-term care insurance.

Reverse mortgage: Although I would rather see people do this when they are still insurable if they otherwise can't afford long-term care insurance, a reverse mortgage can also be a valuable source of funding for extended care itself. If you are married, just be sure to get it in your spouse's name as well as yours so that it won't have to be paid back immediately if one of you dies or needs to go to a long-term care facility.

A long-term care immediate annuity: This can be an option for an older person 75-99 who is already receiving long-term care, even if that person is in a nursing home. This concept involves buying a single premium immediate annuity which is converted into a monthly income guaranteed for the life of the policyholder. You can fund it with a CD, mutual fund, savings, money market, IRA or other qualified funds. You can even select an annual rate for the payment to increase anywhere from one to ten percent to provide for inflation.

Why would anyone want to do this and what makes this type of annuity different than a regular immediate annuity? Here's the main reason: a regular immediate annuity is not medically underwritten and the same life expectancy tables are applied to everyone, regardless of medical condition. With this product, the applicant is medically underwritten, and the poorer the person's health is, the higher the monthly benefit will be. In other words, the sicker the better! Bet you never thought you would hear that phrase applied to an insurance product, did you? Here's an example:

An 82-year-old male desiring a monthly income of $3,000 would normally have to pay about $295,000 in a single premium. However, if he had dementia, this special long-term care immediate annuity would require only $155,000 to obtain the same $3,000 monthly benefit. Another example would be an 87-year-old female with Alzheimer's disease. A $5,500 monthly benefit could be obtained for a deposit of $238,000 instead of $436,000 in a regular immediate annuity.* You can even structure the annuity so the beneficiary will receive all or a portion of the money if the insured dies earlier than the insurance company projected, particularly if he or she dies within the first six months of purchase.

This product is called ImmediateCare and it is underwritten by State Life, which is owned by OneAmerica. You can find out more about it at www. oneamerica.com.

Other annuities that are not underwritten: Check with your financial professional about an annuity that will provide a greater payout if long-term care is needed. They may not leverage your money as much as the one mentioned above, but can still be worth considering.

---

*examples based on interest rates in effect 12/9/12

Short-term care products: As long-term care insurance premium has climbed, products that pay 6 months, 9 months or a year have begun to proliferate. They can be a little easier to get from an underwriting standpoint since the insurance company isn't on the hook for as much coverage as a long-term care insurance plan. Inflation benefits are available on these plans as well. Two good ones to check out are Recovery Care II underwritten by Standard Life and Accident (www.slaico.com) and Transitions, underwritten by MedAmerica Insurance Company (www.medamericaltc.com).

You can also seek the advice of a good elder-law attorney and your State Agency on Aging. Contact www.ElderLawAnswers.com or www.naela. org for a national registry of elder-law attorneys.

It's also my job to tell you how Medicaid functions as the largest public payer of long-term care.

Medicaid Benefits for Long-Term Care

Medicaid is the country's public assistance program for health care. It is funded by taxpayer dollars so it is means-tested. This means Medicaid will pay secondary to a designated share of the patient's income, after the family has spent most of its savings. As we discussed in Chapter One, public dollars are scarce and states are struggling. Medicaid already pays for almost two-thirds of all long-term care in the United States.[1] The more Medicaid has to pay for long-term care, the more services the state will have to cut and the higher taxes the residents of that state will have to pay.

In addition to essential services like K-12 and higher education, crime enforcement, transportation, road-building, state employees' salaries, etc., states will have to reduce long-term care services as well. This means there can be waiting lists for home care which can make it necessary for Medicaid patients to receive care in nursing homes. Choices are even more limited there, such as no private room and the person needing care goes wherever a bed is available, sometimes hours away from the family. Medicaid typically doesn't pay for the really nice assisted living facilities that are so popular. Most of us would agree there are always more choices as a private pay patient, so most people would rather use Medicaid as a last resort, not as a first resort.

Income and Asset Eligibility (2013)

Medicaid long-term care benefits are intended for people with low income and very low assets. This means that an applicant has to meet both income and asset criteria to qualify for Medicaid benefits, in addition to medical criteria. This means that the Medicaid applicant has to either need help with the number of Activities of Daily Living (ADLs) required by the state and that can vary. One state might require help with two and another state might require help with four. If the applicant doesn't need help with the required number of ADLs, he or she must have the required level of cognitive deficiency. In other words, being poor isn't enough to qualify for the Medicaid LTC benefit.

Since over half of Medicaid's long-term care payments for older people and adults with physical disabilities are for nursing home patients, this module will explain the financial eligibility qualification process for nursing home benefits. [2] It's not unusual for eligibility for home care patients to be stricter. [3]

Asset Eligibility

The person applying for Medicaid has to spend assets down to $2000 in most states. These states have different amounts:

Connecticut	$1,600	New York	$4,150
Indiana	$1,500	North Dakota	$3000
Minnesota	$3,000	Ohio	$1,500
Missouri	$1000	Pennsylvania	$2400
Nebraska	$4000	Rhode Island	$4000
New Hampshire	$2,500		

In the following states, the healthy spouse can keep $115,920, no questions asked:

Alaska, California, Colorado, Connecticut, Florida, Georgia, Hawaii, Illinois, Louisiana, Maine, Mississippi, North Dakota, Vermont, Wyoming and the District of Columbia.

In the following states, the healthy spouse can keep half the assets with a minimum of $23,184 up to $115,920.

Arizona, Arkansas, Idaho, Indiana, Kansas, Maryland, Massachusetts, Michigan, Missouri, Montana, Nebraska, Nevada, New Hampshire, New Jersey, North Carolina, Ohio, Oregon, Pennsylvania, Rhode Island, South Dakota, Tennessee, Texas, Utah, Virginia, West Virginia.

In all states, excess assets have to be spent before Medicaid will approve long-term care benefits. Assuming the long-term care spouse is allowed to keep $2,000, here are three examples:

Example #1: $30,000 in assets – half is $15,000 but the healthy spouse keeps the minimum of $23,184 and the couple has to spend down $4,816 which leaves the LTC spouse with $2,000.

Example #2: $120,000 in assets – the healthy spouse keeps half ($60,000) and the couple must spend down $58,000.

Example #3: $500,000 in assets – half is $250,000, but the healthy spouse can keep no more than $115,920 and the couple must spend down $382,080.

A few other states have minimums in between:

Alabama	$25,000	New York	$74,820
Delaware	$25,000	Oklahoma	$25,000
Idaho	$20,000	South Carolina	$66,480
Iowa	$24,000	South Dakota	$20,000
Kentucky	$22,000	Washington	$41,493
Minnesota	$31,094	Wisconsin	$50,000
New Mexico	$31,290		

Example (South Carolina): $100,000 in assets – healthy spouse keeps $66,480 and the couple must spend $31,520.

Assets do not include the house and a car but do include anything money can be taken out of whether there's a loss or a penalty to take it out. **Assets in either spouse's name count, regardless of the presence or absence of a prenuptial agreement.** The Deficit Reduction Act of 2005 (DRA) which was enacted February 8, 2006 set a home equity limit of $500,000, but it doesn't apply if there is a spouse or a blind or disabled child under 21 still living in the house. States had the right to increase the limit up to $750,000, but most did not do so. (These amounts began increasing in 2011 based on the Consumer Price Index for all items. Effective January 1, 2013, they changed to $536,000 and $802,000.)[4] The single applicant will have to pull excess equity out of the home and spend it for acceptable reasons, such as the cost of care, in order to qualify for Medicaid's long-term care benefit.

Countable assets include any resource that is available to either spouse. In other words, anything that money can be taken out of, even if it results in a surrender charge; e.g. an annuity that is only a couple of years old, or has to be sold at a loss; e.g. stock or property other than the primary residence. Here's a partial list of assets that count:

- cash (checking and savings accounts)
- certificates of deposit (CDs)
- money market accounts
- mutual funds
- stocks
- bonds
- deferred annuities
- property outside the home*
- cash value in life insurance for policies with a face value of $1,500 or more *(varies by state but generally a very low amount)*
- revocable trust (a living trust, for example)
- burial trusts beyond a minimum amount, unless they are irrevocable**
- retirement accounts like 401(k), Keoghs, SEPS, IRA plans, etc.

---

*Some states won't count property outside the home as an asset if rented, but those states usually count the rental income toward the income eligibility requirements. Also, income-producing property outside the home, such as a business location or a working ranch or farm, usually is not counted.
**Varies by state.

> With all of the states, the difference between the spousal asset alloca-
> tion and the asset amount the institutionalized spouse is allowed to keep
> must be spent down before the institutionalized spouse qualifies for the
> Medicaid nursing home benefit.

Income Eligibility Criteria

States are almost evenly split on how this works. Twenty-nine states allow
the Medicaid applicant to have income up to the cost of care and allow
certain deductions to get the income below that amount, such as:

- A personal needs allowance, usually $30-$50 a month

- insurance premiums related to health; e.g. Medicare Advantage,
  Medicare Supplement, retiree

- medical expenses not approved by Medicaid; e.g. a new drug

- income needed for a spouse subject to a range established by
  Medicaid, which is a minimum of $1,892* up to a maximum of
  $2,898, if the healthy spouse's income is less than that amount

Whatever is left over after all deductions have been made goes to the
nursing home, and Medicaid makes up the difference up to the Medicaid
approved rate, which varies by facility but is less than the private-pay
rate in most states. Can you see why private-pay patients might be more
attractive to nursing homes?

Twenty-one states cap the income at $2,130 a month but allow the
Medicaid applicant to put all or just the excess income in a qualified
income trust, commonly referred to as a Miller trust. This is an irrevocable

trust designed for the purpose of helping someone whose assets qualify for Medicaid, but income is greater than the cap but not enough to pay privately. The trust pays the nursing home the agreed upon amount after subtracting allowable deductions. Any money left in the trust at death belongs to the state to pay Medicaid back (see "Estate Recovery" later in this chapter).

The following states are income cap states: Alabama, Alaska, Arizona, Arkansas, Colorado, Delaware, Florida, Georgia, Idaho, Iowa, Louisiana, Mississippi, Nevada, New Mexico, Oklahoma, Oregon, South Carolina, South Dakota, Tennessee, Texas, and Wyoming

The following states allow the LTC spouse to transfer the entire maximum of $2,898 to the healthy spouse:

Alaska	California
Georgia	Hawaii
Illinois	Iowa
Louisiana	Mississippi
Nebraska	New York
North Dakota	Oklahoma
South Carolina	Texas
Wyoming	

How is income determined? First, "the name on the check" rule applies. Social Security or pension income is easily attributable. Trust or investment income that is directed jointly to a married couple is divided 50/50.

You're wondering how the spouse at home can receive more than the minimum monthly income allowance. Some states just use the maximum and allow the spouse at home to keep that much income if the couple has that much income between them. The states that allow the maximum income allowance for the spouse at home are:

Alaska	Nebraska
California	New York
Georgia	North Dakota
Hawaii	Oklahoma
Illinois	South Carolina
Iowa	Texas
Louisiana	Wisconsin
Mississippi	Wyoming
District of Columbia	

The remaining states require the spouse at home to justify the need for additional income above the minimum of $1,892* per month. Those states allow the spouse to keep additional income equal to shelter costs that exceed $567* a month up to the maximum of $2,898. Shelter costs include rent, a mortgage payment, homeowner's insurance, property taxes, a condominium maintenance fee, utilities, etc. If these shelter costs are less than $567*, the spouse can't have more than the spousal minimum of $1,892* a month.

Here's how it works:

The difference between the total shelter costs ($900 a month, for example) and the Excess Shelter Allowance $567 is added to the $1,892, which makes the monthly allowance become $2,225 for the spouse in this example:

---

*This amount changes each July.

Spousal Excess Shelter Allowance	
$900	Total monthly "shelter" costs
- $567	Excess Shelter Allowance
$333	Additional spousal income allowable
+ $1,892	Minimum monthly spousal income allowance
$2,225	Total monthly spousal income allowance

Assets and Income Retained by the Healthy Spouse

A surprising note is that while spousal assets are not protected above the maximum spousal asset share as explained in the preceding section, spousal income IS protected. This means that a spouse can have an income much higher than the spousal income maximum of $2,898 for and not be required to contribute to the cost of care for the LTC spouse. It just means that the LTC spouse wouldn't transfer any income to the healthy spouse, and more of the LTC spouse's income would go to the nursing home. A few states like New York, will ask the spouse to contribute at least a portion of his or her income, but the spouse can simply refuse to do so, with no repercussions under today's laws. Pressure is building to change this to protect starving state budgets.

The Deficit Reduction Act of 2005 (DRA) also established a uniform method of calculating the spousal income allocation. Prior to the DRA, some states were allowing couples to retain more resources to generate the above allowable monthly income. This is called the "asset first" or "resource first" rule. This means a couple could retain enough assets to generate the community spouse's income shortfall by the investment income for the retained assets. The DRA requires all states to practice the income first rule, which means the state won't allow a couple to retain resources to generate income for the spouse until the nursing home spouse has shifted all possible income to the spouse at home.[5] Then if the spouse's income is still below the minimum, the state will allow additional income from retained resources. The income first rule keeps the amount of resources retained for this purpose as small as possible. The DRA thus overruled a 2002 Supreme Court decision that states could choose whether to use the income first rule or the resource first rule.[6]

Estate Recovery

Since 1993, states are required to recover assets from the estate of anyone age 55+ who receives any type of Medicaid long-term care benefits including home and community care, at the death of the second spouse. Some states have extended this recovery effort to include assets that are passed to others outside of probate; for example, assets passed to a spouse or adult child through joint tenancy, tenancy in common, survivorship, life estate, living trust, or other arrangement. Check with an experienced elder law attorney in your state to find out if your state goes outside of probate. The elder law attorney can also tell you if your state places a lien on the primary residence or won't allow probate until Medicaid benefits are paid back. A good resource is Elder Law Answers (www.elderlawanswers.com) to look for an elder law attorney in your area who specializes in Medicaid eligibility and estate recovery.

Some people decide to give the house to the children more than 60 months before they might need to apply for Medicaid to avoid estate recovery. Giving the house to children and continuing to live in it without them can mean the children wind up paying a steep capital gains tax when the house is sold if they don't adhere to the capital gains exclusion rules of having to live in the house at least two of the last five years before the house is sold.

As the states are dealing with an aging population and the prospect of paying for the baby boomers' long-term care needs, estate recovery efforts are growing in intensity. For example, in my state of Tennessee, families can't probate a will without a letter of release from TennCare (Medicaid) that no money is owed to pay the state back for long-term care, and willed property to heirs does not circumvent this requirement as a result of a Tennessee Supreme Court ruling on May 30, 2012.[7] Also, common sense will tell you that states that utilize private contractors to conduct estate recovery tend to be more aggressive, as the private contractors typically receive a percentage of the recovery.

Reverse Mortgages and Medicaid

Medicaid and a reverse mortgage can co-exist within these parameters:

1. A lump sum disbursement will count as an asset, the worst thing that can happen if one is seeking Medicaid eligibility, so taking the reverse mortgage money as monthly income or as a line of credit would be smarter if you intend to apply for Medicaid to pay for LTC.[8]

2. Monthly payments won't count as income as long as the money is spent in the month in which it is received.[9]

3. A line of credit can be held open and Medicaid won't force the homeowner to tap it.[10]

4. A home that has a reverse mortgage on it will not be available for a Medicaid lien in the first position.[11] If a state attaches a lien in the second position, it means when the house is sold to pay off the reverse mortgage that any excess equity will belong to the state beyond the protected amount of $536,000 or $802,000.[12]

A long-term care insurance Partnership plan provides a significant advantage to the homeowner as the protected assets can be designated to protect the home from estate recovery with or without a reverse mortgage.

Transferring Assets - The Myth

The aging population combined with the escalating cost of long- term care and loopholes in Medicaid eligibility laws have encouraged a growing number of older Americans to transfer assets to capture public funding for long-term care expenses. However, shrinking tax dollars caused by the severe decline in the ratio of workers to Social Security beneficiaries, due to the aging population, have caused dire financial straits for the Medicaid program just as it has for Medicare. Here's where we are:[13]

1960	4.9 workers paying Social Security tax for each person receiving benefits
Today	2.8 workers for each beneficiary
2035	1.9 workers for each beneficiary

Assets transferred for less than fair market value within 60 months prior to the application for Medicaid will cause a penalty period equal to the amount of time the applicant could have paid had he not transferred the money.[14] The length of the penalty period is determined by dividing the amount of the transfer by the monthly cost of care, as determined by the state. This is called a penalty period divisor.

For example, a $300,000 transfer divided by a $5,000 average monthly cost of care equals 60 months (five years) of ineligibility. The penalty period begins on the date of application for Medicaid.[15]

The reason the money was transferred doesn't matter. For example, transferring $13,000 per year ($26,000 if you are married) to your children and grandchildren to stay within the federal gift-tax exclusion will result in a penalty period, during which Medicaid won't pay. Donating money to the Red Cross or a religious organization will result in a penalty period. The thought process is "he or she had the money to pay for care but chose to give it away".

Transfers can be done in more subtle ways:

- Setting up a joint checking account with a son or daughter, then removing the parent's name from the account.

- Putting a home in the name of a son or daughter or other family member or friend.

- Purchasing a "life estate" in an adult child's home by paying off the adult child's mortgage. The DRA has made a life estate countable as an asset unless the purchaser lives in the house at least one year after the date of purchase.[16]

- Transferring assets into an immediate annuity, which changes the assets into income. Medicaid compares the amount of the annuity with your life expectancy. Any projected payout that exceeds life expectancy is treated as a transfer and will trigger a period of ineligibility. Pre-DRA, some people got around that by purchasing a "balloon annuity" that has a small payout each year and then pays the remaining money in a lump sum in the last year of life expectancy. (Since the life expectancy tables have nothing to do with the health of the annuitant, the idea is that he or she will probably be deceased by the time the last payment is made.) Keeping the payout small until then preserves principal to maximize the lump-sum payout to the beneficiary. The DRA outlawed balloon annuities.[17]

- Transferring assets into a single premium immediate annuity (SPIA) and producing a monthly income for the healthy spouse. Since spousal income is protected as I told you in the above section *Assets and Income Retained by the Healthy Spouse,* this worked pre-DRA as the amount of principal transferred into the immediate annuity for the spouse would no longer count as an asset for Medicaid eligibility purposes. However, the DRA says that for annuities issued or changed on or after February 8, 2006 on either spouse, the state must be named as remainder beneficiary or remainder beneficiary in the second position if a spouse or minor or disabled child is in first position.[18] Are you confused yet? The first time I read this I thought I was at a Tennessee family reunion!

  This is not to say that people don't continue this practice. It does mean however that as primary beneficiary, the state will get paid back what Medicaid paid on the sick spouse from the SPIA when the healthy spouse dies. If the healthy spouse passes away in a shorter time frame, the state will get some or all of its money back and any remaining payments will go to the contingent beneficiary.[19] If you have any doubt about that and you find yourself with insomnia some night, check out the Tax Relief and Health Care Act of 2006, H.R. 6111, enacted December 20, 2006, which made it clear that the state as the beneficiary intends to collect up to the full amount that Medicaid paid out on the nursing home spouse.[20]

- Setting up a trust that will benefit a charity after your death, so you can receive the income while you are alive.

- Setting up a trust that will benefit a charity with regular income before your death, then the principal will go to a family member when you die.

- Donating to a "pooled-income fund"—similar to a mutual fund operated by a charity for smaller investors to reap the tax benefits of charitable giving without having to invest large amounts.

All of these methods can count as a transfer of assets and trigger a penalty period, which means a period of ineligibility for Medicaid benefits. To reiterate, the motive of the transfer has no bearing on this process.

Note: Setting up a special trust for a disabled dependent is an acceptable transfer and will not cause a penalty period if it is designated that the principal will revert to the state at the death of the disabled dependent. This is called a special needs trust. The advice of an elder law attorney should be consulted with this or any other type of trust.

The biggest problem with transferring assets is that when one can no longer access assets, he or she loses the one thing that matters the most-- **independence and control.**

Please refer to my website at http://www.ltcconsultants.com/general/ wyslyk to see your state's Medicaid information.

Medicaid Home Care

As we discussed earlier, over half of Medicaid dollars spent on long-term care go to nursing facilities.[21] This varies by state. For example, in FY 2010, spending on home care was 76 percent of all Medicaid long-term care spending in Oregon and 24 percent of all Medicaid long-term care spending in Mississippi.[22] The Patient Protection and Affordability Care Act of 2010 (PPACA) continued the expansion of Medicare home care benefits that was started in the Deficit Reduction Act of 2006 by enhancing federal matching funds if states:

- transition Medicaid patients from nursing homes to home care (Money Follows the Person-reauthorized through 2016)

- implement the Community First Choice Option that provides statewide coverage for home care attendants for people with incomes up to 300% of SSI $2,130 who require nursing home level care (effective October 1, 2011);

- will try to balance Medicaid dollars more equally between home care and nursing home care (State Balancing Incentive Program – effective October 1, 2011); and

- expand home care services and extend full Medicaid benefits to home care patients.[23, 24]

As altruistic as these provisions sound, they crumble in the face of reality which says that nursing home care for Medicaid patients is an entitlement and can't be cut by states, whereas home care is a discretionary benefit.[25] An AARP report that analyzed the impact of the PPACA forecasted that budgetary pressures may cause some states to cut certain home care services to achieve immediate savings.[26]

Indeed, there were 511,174 people on waiting lists for home and community based waiver services in 2011, a 19 percent increase over 2010. The average time people spent on waiting list was over 2 years, with wide variations among populations to be served and type of service.[27]

Long-Term Care Insurance - A Better Way to Stay Home

For people who truly want to be cared for at home as long as possible, long-term care insurance is the better choice. Less than 15% of long-term care is even provided in a nursing home nationally.[28] According to a study that tracked new claims opened in 2010 from four leading insurance carriers, 73 percent of LTCI claims were for paid care at home or in an assisted living facility. The remaining claims were for care in a nursing home.[29]

> *If clients ever need to turn to Medicaid for help, a Long-Term Care Partnership policy provides the additional bonus of asset protection equal to the benefits paid out at the time of the Medicaid application.*

The Long-Term Care Partnership

The Partnership for Long-Term Care is a public/private alliance between state governments and insurance companies that was originally funded with $14 million in grants from the nation's then largest health care philanthropy, the Robert Wood Johnson Foundation. Prior to 2006, the program was operational in Connecticut, New York, Indiana, California and approved in Iowa, but Iowa never fully implemented its Partnership program when the other four states did. Variations of the Partnership were approved in Illinois, Massachusetts and Washington, but the main Partnership activity continued to reside in the original four states until President Bush signed the Deficit Reduction Act of 2005 (DRA) on February 8, 2006.

This landmark legislation made it possible for other states to participate in The Partnership for Long-Term Care. Forty states have chosen to participate as of December, 2012:

Alabama, Arizona, Arkansas, California, Colorado, Connecticut, Florida, Georgia, Idaho, Indiana, Iowa, Kansas, Kentucky, Louisiana, Maine, Maryland, Minnesota, Missouri, Montana, Nebraska, Nevada, New Hampshire, New Jersey, New York, North Carolina, North Dakota, Ohio, Oklahoma, Oregon, Pennsylvania, Rhode Island, South Carolina, South Dakota, Tennessee, Texas, Virginia, Washington, West Virginia, Wisconsin and Wyoming.

The idea of the partnership is to provide a way for the Medicaid program to work together with private long-term care insurance to help those people who are caught in the middle: they can't afford to pay the cost of the care or even the cost of a long-term care insurance policy with unlimited benefits, yet their assets are too high to qualify for Medicaid to pay their long-term care expenses. Many middle-income workers and retirees find themselves in this position.

Participating insurance companies in the Partnership recognize the needs of these middle-income Americans by providing LTC insurance policies that have built-in consumer protection benefit standards, and participating states cooperate by allowing these policyholders to access Medicaid without spending down their assets almost to poverty level if the insurance benefits aren't enough.

Without the Partnership, people have three choices to pay for long-term care:

1. Pay for care out of assets and income, which can lead to financial ruin if long-term care costs wipe out savings.

2. Transfer assets to qualify for Medicaid either to children or other family members or to a trust—either way means losing control of the money and losing financial independence.

3. Buy a standard long-term care insurance policy which works—unless the policy runs out of benefits or the benefit isn't enough to cover the cost of care. This can happen because you bought what you could afford, and it turns out not to be enough when you need it. (For example, you couldn't afford the premium for inflation coverage, you could only afford a one- or two-year benefit period, or you bought a daily or monthly benefit significantly lower than the cost of care in your area and you couldn't make up the difference at claim time.)

A fourth option is available with the Partnership for Long-Term Care. Now consumers can purchase a state-approved LTCI policy that provides asset protection if the benefits aren't enough. Here's how it works in Connecticut, Indiana and California with a dollar-for-dollar asset protection model:

*   A special Partnership policy must be purchased from an insurance professional. For every dollar in benefits paid by the policy, a dollar in assets will be sheltered. For example, if a policy pays $100,000 in benefits, and if the Medicaid asset eligibility in your state requires

the insured to spend down to $2,000, in this example the insured would be able to qualify for Medicaid when his or her assets reach $102,000, not $2,000. In other words, he or she would get to keep, or "shelter" $100,000 of assets and still qualify for Medicaid to begin paying long-term care expenses if policy benefits are not enough.

New York has two types of Partnership plans.

1. Dollar-for-Dollar - the same concept as above except the applicant chooses one of two plans: 1.5 years of nursing home benefits and three years of home care benefits paid at 50 percent of the nursing home daily benefit OR two years of nursing home benefits and two years of home care benefits paid at 100 percent of the nursing home daily benefit.

2. Total Asset Protection - These Partnership plans provide that once benefits are exhausted, the policyholder can qualify for Medicaid regardless of the amount of assets. There are two plans to choose from for this type as well: three years of nursing home benefits and six years of home care benefits paid at 50 percent of the nursing home daily benefit OR four years of nursing home benefits and four years of home care benefits paid at 100 percent of the nursing home benefit. While New York offers two unlimited asset protection plans, this desirable feature only happens after the benefits of the policy have been used up. A danger is that if a daily benefit is chosen which is inadequate for the policyholder's needs, he or she could exhaust most or all assets paying the difference between the policy's benefit and the cost of care before the benefits are used up.

For example, in 2013 New York requires new Partnership policy purchasers to purchase a minimum of $265 for the daily nursing home benefit. Long Island averages $390 for a semi-private room. If only the minimum is purchased, the policyholder could easily wind up paying $125 per day or more out of pocket, which amounts to almost $140,000 over the three-year benefit period for nursing home care. Based on the map below provided by The New York State Long-Term Care Partnership, it's easy to guess that the cost of care, while lower in some regions of New York, can easily run as high as $400 per day.

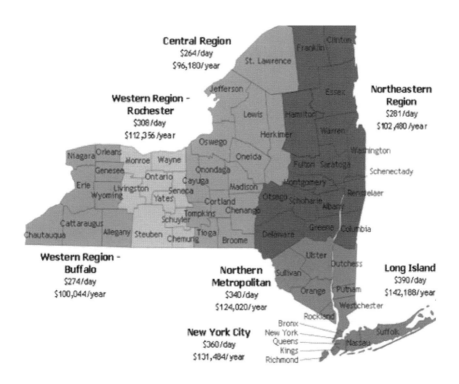

Indiana provides a combination of these two models. The combo plan provides the dollar-for-dollar asset protection, but if the policyholder purchases a benefit maximum that will pay about four years of benefits, the policy will provide total asset protection like the New York option. Since $291,050 represents about four years of benefits at current costs, purchasing a policy that would pay out that much in benefits would qualify for the total asset protection feature in Indiana. (The $291,050 is the 2013 amount and will increase each year to account for inflation.) Here are three possible scenarios to meet the 2013 requirement:

- a daily benefit of $200 with a four year benefit period, as $200 x 365 x 4 = $292,000;

- a daily benefit of $270 with a three year benefit period as $270 x 365 x 3 = $295,650; or

- a daily benefit of $400 with a two year benefit period as $400 x 365 x 2 = $292,000.

The Indiana Partnership maintains a list of agents who have had special Partnership training and publishes the names in a directory for consumers. Call the Indiana Partnership telephone number or access the website listed at the end of this chapter for information on how to be listed in the directory of approved agents.

Massachusetts offers another variation: Medicaid guidelines have to be met as usual so there is no up-front asset protection, but the house is not subject to estate recovery if the policyholder purchases a long-term care insurance policy with a minimum daily benefit of $125 and a minimum two-year benefit period.

In all states, your income goes to pay for the cost of care once you qualify for Medicaid. So the Partnership program protects assets, not income. But income is important for three reasons:

1. If your income is greater than your long-term care costs, you won't qualify for Medicaid and wouldn't benefit from a Partnership policy. People in this situation can consider a standard long-term care insurance policy—perhaps with an unlimited benefit maximum.

2. Income can guide you to a benefit selection. For example, if care averages $200 per day in your area, and you can afford to pay $30 a day from your income, you might purchase a policy for $170 a day for a lower premium than a $200/day policy. (In higher cost areas like New York, Connecticut or California, you would probably be purchasing policies in the $250-300+/day range - the average cost of care in Connecticut, for example, is $370, according to the 2012 MetLife Market Survey of Long-Term Care Costs. (Actually, Connecticut state law requires Connecticut nursing homes to provide at least a 5% reduction in their private pay rate for Partnership policyholders at no additional premium cost. This discount is not required for non-Partnership policyholders.) Just be careful—if your care costs more than the insurance policy pays in benefits, you will be responsible for paying the additional costs, and don't forget that drugs and medical supplies are usually billed on top of the room and board charge for facility care. Consider carefully how much you can afford to pay out of your income and insure yourself adequately. The Partnership policies require an inflation benefit for appropriate ages so that inflation doesn't erode your benefit.

3. Since you are responsible for paying your premiums, your

discretionary income must be sufficient to pay your long-term care premiums and keep your policy in force, although there is a premium waiver if you have a claim. Individuals with income less than $20,000 or couples with incomes less than $40,000 may not have enough discretionary income to purchase long-term care insurance as premium payments may significantly impact their standard of living. If you fall into these income categories, and if you have assets less than $50,000, not counting your house and car, you probably will qualify for Medicaid in a short period of time, and LTC insurance of any type—standard or Partnership—may not be an appropriate purchase for you.

For many people, however, the Partnership LTCI policies offer a wonderful alternative to transferring assets and relying on the government (Medicaid) to pay for their long-term care expenses.

A few points you may be wondering about with the Partnership policies:

Benefit Choices—Benefit choices are the same as for non-Partnership policies, in that there is a daily or monthly benefit, an elimination (waiting) period, a home health care/adult day care benefit level, an inflation feature, and a benefit period/lifetime maximum. You may be surprised to learn that many California and Connecticut Partnership policyholders have purchased a lifetime (unlimited) benefit period. They did this because they don't intend to access Medicaid, but if for any reason their assets are lowered for reasons beyond their control; i.e. a stock market plunge, they have asset protection provided by their Partnership policy. This is true because at any time benefits paid out equal your assets plus the amount Medicaid (MediCal in California) allows the healthy spouse to keep, the policyholder is allowed to access Medicaid and shelter their assets. For example, if a policy had paid out $250,000, the person receiving care could apply for Medicaid when the couple's assets are spent down to $367,920, which is equal to the $250,000 in benefits plus $115,920 (the 2013 asset maximum for the healthy spouse) plus $2,000 (the asset maximum for the person needing care). (Indiana and New York have total asset protection after benefits paid equal $291,050 for Indiana for 2013 purchasers and after the three or four-year benefit period for New York is exhausted.)

Portability—If you move to another state, the Partnership policy will pay, and the benefits will accumulate toward your asset protection threshold. All states except California practice reciprocity with the asset protection feature of owning a Partnership policy. You are subject to the functional or cognitive eligibility requirements in the state in which you apply for Medicaid. You can see a Partnership reciprocity map at www.dehpg.net/ltcpartnership.

Underwriting—You still must qualify for the Partnership policy medically just as you would for a standard long-term care insurance policy. The younger you are, the better the chance to qualify for a policy, and the lower the premiums. Pre-retirement ages (40's and 50's) are strongly encouraged to apply. In fact, the Connecticut Partnership reports that 95% of purchasers in 2012 were under age seventy, and 58% under age 60. The single largest age group of purchasers was 50-59 with 46% of purchasers falling in that age range. The average age for all Partnership purchasers was 57 with an age range of 20-88![30]

Policy Continuance—If for any reason the Partnership program is discontinued either nationally or in its particular state, all policies in the original four states will be honored and appropriate benefits paid by the insurance company that issued the policy. Post-DRA Partnership states are expected to do the same, but you should read the Partnership literature provided by your financial professional to be certain.

The History of the Original Four Partnership States

The original Partnership states were grandfathered, but the Partnership was halted by the 1993 budget bill ("OBRA" - Omnibus Reconciliation Act of 1993), which said that new states could offer asset protection only during the policyholder's lifetime. At death, the state was required to seek estate recovery for Medicaid's payment. This happened because of concern that the Partnership would cause Medicaid utilization to increase, when in fact, the opposite is true. Since the Partnership for Long-Term Care was implemented in the early 90s, only about 535 policyholders out of almost 350,000 policies sold in all four operational Partnership states as of 12/31/11 have had to turn to Medicaid for help after using their long-term care insurance benefits first![31]

The Partnership Expansion Post-DRA

Partnership policies offered by new states are required to:

- be tax-qualified

- Include specific consumer protection requirements of the 2000 National Association of Insurance Commissioners (NAIC) LTC Insurance Model Act and Regulation.

- provide the inflation benefit as follows:

  ○ compound inflation is required under age 61

- o   some type of inflation benefit must be offered between ages 61 – 76

- o   inflation may be offered past age 76 but is not required

- provide asset protection according to the dollar-for-dollar model, not the total asset protection models like the New York and Indiana Partnerships have. This means the insured may still be subject to estate recovery but only for assets that exceed the amount of benefits received from the Partnership long-term care insurance policy.

The above inflation requirements are just the boiler plate template for states that wish to participate in the Partnership for Long-Term Care. The appropriate inflation protection based on purchase age is an integral part of the whole Partnership concept, which is to expand the LTCI market to middle-income Americans. Without adequate inflation protection, middle-income Americans simply won't be able to make up a really large gap between the daily or monthly benefit at claim time and the cost of care at that time. The good news is that if that does happen, Partnership policyholders generally do not have to exhaust their benefits before turning to Medicaid for help.[32]

Your financial professional can tell you which inflation options meet your state's Partnership inflation requirement. Plus, when you get your policy, it will state clearly that it is intended to be a Long-Term Care Partnership policy. **Do not accept a policy without that language if it is your intention to buy a Long-Term Care Partnership policy.**

Partnership State Contact Information:

California (916) 552-8990 www.dhs.ca.gov/cpltc

Connecticut (860) 418-6318 www.Ctpartnership.org

Indiana (800) 452-4800 ; (317) 233-1470 www.in.gov/fssa/iltcp

New York (518)-474-0662 www.nyspltc.org

Other States http://www.dehpg.net/ltcpartnership/map.aspx

The Laws They Are A-Changin'

The information discussed in this chapter is based on current laws. With the budget-cutting microscope finally swinging toward entitlements, this information is subject to change dramatically in the direction of scarcer benefits and more aggressive estate recovery. A great example of this is Pennsylvania's recent enforcement of its filial responsibility law. In *Health Care & Retirement Corp. of America (HCR) v. Pittas*, Pennsylvania's Superior Court ruled that a son should be responsible for paying his mother's $93,000 nursing home bill after the family moved her to Greece to be with other relatives.[33]

Twenty-nine states have filial support laws that could be used to hold adult children responsible for parents' long-term care bills, but these laws have rarely been enforced.[34] As state budgets continue to shrink, amidst a political climate of shifting the burden for health care financing to higher income individuals, these laws may continue to surface.

Chapter Eight:

THE M & Ms OF MEDICARE

———⊶∞⊷———

This section is for the Doubting Thomases so they will KNOW not to look for LTC benefits from Medicare and its cousins:

    a. Medicare

    b. Medicare supplement, also known as MediGap

    c. Medicare Advantage

    d. Medicare Prescription Drug Program

As you saw in Chapter One, at least a third of the population continues to labor under the gross misunderstanding that Medicare pays for long-term care.[1] The National Institute on Aging collects data about medical out-of-pocket spending every two years. Here's a key finding as reported by *The New York Times* on September 21, 2012:[2]

> *Long-term care expenses in a facility (nursing home, assisted living), which aren't covered by Medicare much to many families' deep surprise, were the No. 1 category of out-of-pocket spending, followed by home health care.*

Does Medicare Have a Role in the Long-Term Care Story?

Rather than listen to me answer this question, let's hear the answer from a very reputable and credible source, the National Health Policy Forum at George Washington University in Washington DC:[3]

> ***Medicare plays no role in financing long-term services and supports (LTSS).*** *Medicare is intended to cover acute and post-acute medical care for people age 65 and older and for younger populations who qualify for Social Security because of disability. The program was not designed to cover LTSS. Medicare covers skilled nursing facility (SNF) care following a hospital stay of at least three consecutive days for those who require daily skilled nursing and/or rehabilitation services for up to 100 days of care. Medicare also pays for medically necessary home health services; part-time or intermittent skilled nursing care; or physical, speech, or occupational therapy for homebound beneficiaries. It does not cover home care services for those who need sustained assistance over time as a result of a physical or cognitive disability, or frailty.*

Has anyone looked at a Social Security benefits statement lately? You know you can go to www.ssa.gov and access that anytime you like. At the top of p. 4 under "Some Facts About Social Security", you will see in the first paragraph:

> *Medicare does not pay for long-term care,*
> *so you may want to consider options for private insurance.*

A number of people are asking me how the upcoming health care reform will affect the long-term care insurance industry. I keep reiterating that it makes it even more important to own long-term care insurance as benefits you thought you would get from Medicare for acute care may not be there as much as you had planned.

Some people think Medicare is sufficient to handle their health care financing needs, but as this section will show, Medicare is designed to pay short-term care, which leaves long-term care as the greatest risk to one's financial plan, according to a well-respected financial columnist.

> *"What's the greatest risk in your financial plan? We've seen how a stock market crash can devastate retirement plans. But the greatest risk is not the longevity of this bear market, or even another bear market. It's the devastating cost of long-term care."* Terry Savage, *financial columnist for The Chicago Sun-Times and author of* **The New Savings Number: How Much Money Do You Need to Retire?** [4]

Dallas Salisbury, President and CEO of the Employee Benefit Research Institute, had this to say about health care costs in retirement:[5]

> *Medicare now pays an average of half with new income-based premiums. Assume it drops over time to pay 25% and that premiums continue to rise. Plus health costs continue at a high rate. At retirement at 65 or older assume you need $300,000 set aside for retiree medical and $300,000 for long-term care if you do not buy a long-term care insurance policy. This is individual not couple. Then customize this to*

your family history, and the like. Better to have over saved and under consumed than the opposite.

Finally, Jack VanDerhei, Research Director at the Employee Benefits Research Institute, drives the point home:

The current set of assumptions - that Mom and Dad were OK because of Medicare - may not be the case for future retirees. When you add in the potential for nursing home costs, for just about every demographic group close to retirement, the chances of having adequate retirement savings was hopeless - unless they had long-term care insurance. If nothing else, I'd love people to realize that even if Medicare continued [to provide the same level of benefits it does today], it's never going to cover you for nursing home care... I see too many retirees who think they're all set, and then one goes into a nursing home. And they next thing you know, there goes all the money.[6]

Now don't counter that one with "But I'm never going to a nursing home". Remember, ten hours of home care can cost the same as a day in a nursing home![7]

Here is a broad overview of the Medicare program as it exists today. All premiums, deductibles and co-pays mentioned are for 2013. These generally increase each January.

In a nutshell, Medicare is Federal health insurance for U.S. citizens:

- age 65 years or older;
- with permanent kidney failure; or
- under 65 with certain disabilities.

Enrolling for Medicare

Most Americans are automatically enrolled for Medicare when they reach age 65. The program is administered by the Centers for Medicare and Medicaid Services (CMS) of the U.S. Department of Health and Human Services. The Social Security Administration provides information about the program and handles enrollment. Those desiring to participate in Medicare should contact their local Social Security office for information at least three months before turning 65. You can also call the Social Security toll-free at 1-800-772-1213 (toll-free TTY number, 1-800-325-0778) between 7 a.m. and 7 p.m. EST Monday through Friday if you want to hear a live voice. Or, you can enroll online at http://www.socialsecurity.gov/medicareonly/.

Four Parts of Medicare

The Medicare program is made up of four parts, A-D:

Part A - Hospital Insurance

Part B - Medical Insurance

Part C - Medicare Advantage Plans

Part D - Medicare Prescription Drug Program

The Original Medicare Program

The original Medicare program is called a "fee-for-service" program, which means it reimburses health care providers for each specific service they provide. It has two separate parts. To oversimplify, **Part A** covers inpatient-type care such as hospitals and skilled nursing facilities and **Part**

B covers doctor bills. For our purposes, it's important for you to know that Part A also covers home health care and hospice and Part B covers home health care when the patient doesn't have Part A.

Most people have Part A because it is free to anyone who has worked at least 40 quarters (or been married to someone who has) as it is financed through part of the Social Security (FICA) tax paid by workers and their employers. If someone doesn't qualify for premium-free Part A benefits, he or she may purchase the coverage at age 65 at up to $441 per month.

If you're under 65, you can get premium-free Part A if:

- You were awarded Social Security or Railroad Retirement Board disability benefits for 24 months.

- You have End-Stage Renal Disease (ESRD) and meet certain requirements.

One is automatically enrolled in Part B when first entitled to Part A unless he or she refuses it. It may also be purchased by most people age 65 or over who do not qualify for premium-free Part A coverage. (Note: If you have to buy Part A, you will be required to buy Part B as well.) Most people will pay $104.90 per month for Part B premium, but if your modified adjusted gross income as reported on your IRS tax return from two years ago is above a certain amount, you may pay more.

If your yearly income in 2011 was:		You pay in 2013
Filed individual tax return	Filed joint tax return	
$85,000 or less	$170,000 or less	$104.90
above $85,000 up to $107,000	above $170,000 up to $214,000	$146.90
above $107,000 up to $160,000	above $214,000 up to $320,000	$209.80
above $160,000 up to $214,000	above $320,000 up to $428,000	$272.70
above $214,000	above $428,000	$335.70

The number of Medicare beneficiaries paying the higher amounts has been small, but the health care reform legislation passed in 2010 froze the above income thresholds through 2019, which is expected to increase the share of beneficiaries paying the higher Part B premium.[8]

The Medicare card shows the coverage the person on Medicare (aka the Medicare beneficiary) has—Hospital Insurance (Part A), Medical Insurance (Part B) or both--and the date that coverage was effective.

Medicare Benefits for Short-Term Care

For purposes of this book, we will discuss the benefits that most affect patients who need long-term care:

- Skilled nursing facility
- Home health care
- Hospice

Skilled Nursing Facility

It's common to think of a skilled nursing facility (SNF) as a nursing home, but it may also be a special wing located in a hospital on which the beds are designated as SNF beds for people who don't meet the definition of an acutely ill patient but who are not well enough to go home. This type of care is called skilled care, but a more understandable definition is that it is short-term care. Benefits for SNF care are paid as long as the patient needs at least one skilled service every day. In other words, skilled care has nothing to do with how sick we are. It is determined by the services we receive and they must be services provided by licensed professionals such as physical, speech, respiratory or occupational therapy.

Prior to October 2012, there was also a requirement that the patient must continue to show improvement in order for the care to be documented as skilled and paid by Medicare. However, a preliminary settlement reached in October, 2012 on a landmark case (*Jimmo vs. Sebelius*) eliminated that requirement.[9] The Settlement Agreement which was finalized on January 24, 2013 provides for a review of all claims that were denied on the basis of the Improvement Standard after January 18, 2011 (the date the *Jimmo* case was filed).[10]

Please do not think this case means that Medicare pays for long-term care. If the requirement to need daily skilled care is met, the original Medicare program will pay the first 20 days in a skilled nursing facility in full if:

1. the stay was preceded by a three day hospital stay, not counting the discharge day;

2. the admission to the skilled nursing facility is for the same diagnosis as the hospital stay and occurs within 30 days after the hospital discharge day; and
3. the stay is in an approved Medicare facility.

As long as all these requirements are met each day, an additional 80 days may be paid after a $148.00 daily patient co-pay. This benefit is payable per benefit period, which means an additional 100 day benefit becomes available if the patient is discharged from the SNF longer than 180 days and all of the above requirements are met again, including the three-day hospital stay.

So what is the impact of this legislation? If the patient meets the requirement to need daily skilled care to maintain health, the maximum benefit in a skilled nursing facility per benefit period is 100 days. Three months isn't long-term care; it's short-term care.

Once a patient's care no longer needs daily skilled care, it becomes chronic, maintenance care, also referred to as custodial care. If you go to the handbook, *Medicare & You, 2013* (http://www.medicare.gov/), you will see this information on p. 117:

> *Long-term care includes medical and non-medical care for people who have a chronic illness or disability. Nonmedical care includes non-skilled personal care assistance, like help with everyday activities, including dressing, bathing, and using the bathroom. At least 70% of people over 65 will need long-term care services at some point. Medicare and most health insurance plans, including Medicare Supplement Insurance (Medigap) policies, don't pay for this*

type of care, also called "custodial care." Longterm care can be provided at home, in the community, in an assisted living facility, or in a nursing home. It's important to start planning for long-term care now to maintain your independence and to make sure you get the care you may need in the future.

Home Health Care

At home, Medicare pays for visits of the appropriate licensed medical professional such as a nurse, home health aide, therapies (physical, speech, occupational) nutritional counseling and care-related supplies at 100%. Durable medical equipment such as wheelchairs, hospital beds, oxygen and walkers are paid at 80% of the Medicare-approved charge. A visit averages an hour, so eight-hour shifts are not covered, and a skilled service must be needed periodically, such as every 60 days.

Sound easy? It's not. Even though the *Jimmo vs. Sebelius* case cited above also applies to home health care, it's important to realize that payment for Medicare home care benefits is based on a prospective payment system. This means that Medicare approves a set amount of money for each episode of care, based on what kind of health care an average person in a similar medical situation would need, adjusted for geographical differences, including local wages of home care workers. It is up to the home health agency to make this system work. They lose money on some patients who require a lot of care, and make money on some who require lesser amounts of care. The incentive is to do as few visits as possible while maintaining an acceptable quality of care level.

Benefit clarifications have occurred over the years such as:

- drawing blood is no longer considered a skilled service in order to meet the periodic skilled care requirement.
- The patient must be homebound (i.e. confined to his/her home), except for special occasions such as graduations, family reunions and funerals.
- The care must be provided by a Medicare-approved home health agency.

In reality, Medicare home care patients usually receive a few weeks of care.

You can read more about the prospective payment system for home care at https://www.cms.gov/Medicare/Medicare-Fee-for-Service-Payment/HomeHealthPPS/index.html.

> *Can you see that since Medicare patients typically receive less than three months of care at home or in a skilled nursing facility that Medicare only pays for short-term care?*

Hospice

Medicare provides hospice services for terminally ill patients with no deductible for:

- physician services
- nursing care
- medical appliances and supplies

- counseling
- home health aide and homemaker services
- short-term care in a hospice-designated bed in a Medicare-approved facility for pain and symptom management that can't be provided at home

Hospice pays all but 5% of the cost of outpatient drugs or $5 per prescription, whichever is lower. Inpatient respite care is limited to five days per stay, and hospice does not pay for ongoing eight-hour shifts of non-skilled home care.

Can you see how a long-term care insurance policy can fill in the gaps left by the Medicare hospice benefit? Here are a few ways:

- Long-term care insurance will pay for as many hours of home care as the daily or monthly benefit will cover.
- Long-term care insurance will pay for as many days as necessary for inpatient respite care.
- The patient does not have to meet the "terminally ill" time definition required by Medicare, which is usually a life expectancy of 180 days.

The Most Common Medicare Gaps

Even though this book is primarily discussing how Medicare pays for services that directly affect long-term care (i.e. skilled nursing facility, home care, and hospice), it will help you with the planning process for health care costs in your retirement if I list the major out-of-pocket expenses you will encounter as a Medicare patient.

When Medicare was created in 1965, Congress determined that the patient should share in paying for the cost of the care he or she received. The underlying concept is simple: If the patient shares in the cost of care, he or she will be more likely to use the benefits wisely. So, the program was designed with deductible and coinsurance amounts for the patient to pay.

In the first years of the Medicare program, these deductible and coinsurance charges were moderate amounts. After almost five decades of annual increases, these charges can add up. For example, you must pay:

- the first $1,184 of your bill for each hospital stay separated by 60 or more days. This is known as the Part A deductible.*
- $148.00 each day for days 21 through 100 in a skilled nursing facility…the first 20 days are paid at 100%.
- the first $147.00 of the Medicare-approved amounts for doctor services, medical supplies and equipment, outpatient services and ambulance. This is known as the Part B deductible.
- 20% of the cost of your bills for doctor services, medical supplies and equipment, outpatient services and ambulance.
- charges above the Medicare-approved amount billed by doctors who do not accept Medicare assignment (up to a 115% cap—see "Medicare-Approved Charges" below).

---

* Many people make the mistake of thinking the hospital deductible occurs once a year like the Part B deductible for physician services and supplies. Not so. The hospital deductible is payable per benefit period, which means each time you have a hospital stay separated by more than 60 days, a new hospital deductible is required. If you were extremely unlucky and were admitted to the hospital every 61 days for a one night stay, you could have five hospital deductibles in a 12-month period! That's not going to happen, of course, but it helps you understand how it works, doesn't it?

- all costs for physical or occupational therapy provided by independent therapists (outside a nursing home or hospital) in excess of Medicare's maximum annual allowance. The annual allowance is $1,900 for physical and speech therapy. A separate maximum of $1,900 applies to occupational therapy. These amounts are in addition to your 20% co-payment.

These are the most common Medicare gaps. In addition to financial gaps caused by the deductible and coinsurance amounts, there are also gaps caused by non-covered expenses like long-term care, prescription drugs, dental care, eyeglasses and hearing aids.

A bright spot, however, is that Medicare now pays for many preventive services to help people stay healthy. You can see a list at http://www. medicare.gov/coverage/preventive-and-screening-services.html or on p. 51 of the booklet, **Medicare and You** that is available at www.medicare. gov/publications or by calling 1-800-633-4227 (1-800-MEDICARE).

Medicare-Approved Charges

One of the most misunderstood aspects of Medicare is the way physician charges are determined.

All of your doctor's charges may not be considered eligible for the 80% Medicare Part B reimbursement. Medicare payment is based on the Medicare-approved amounts, not the actual charges billed by the physician or medical supplier. The Medicare-approved amount is based on a national fee schedule. This schedule assigns a value to each physician service based on the specific service performed, his or her medical practice costs, malpractice insurance costs and a geographical factor. Each time you go to the doctor, the amount Medicare will recognize for that service will be taken from the national fee schedule. Medicare will generally pay 80% of that amount. (Example: The doctor charges $100. Medicare may approve $70 and pay 80%, which means that Medicare would actually pay $56.)

Doctors who take assignment on a Medicare claim agree to accept the Medicare-approved amount as payment in full. They are paid directly by Medicare, and you pay them any deductible or coinsurance amount due. Ask your doctor if he or she accepts Medicare assignment.

Many physicians and suppliers accept assignment on a case-by-case basis. If your physician or supplier does not accept assignment, you are responsible for the bill, and Medicare will reimburse you. However, physicians who do not accept assignment of a Medicare claim are reimbursed at a lower level and are limited by law as to the amount they can charge you for covered services. **The most a non-participating physician can charge you for services covered by Medicare is 115% of the fee schedule amount.**

Regardless of whether physicians accept assignment, they are required to file your Medicare claims for you. If they accept assignment, Medicare pays the physician and sends you a notice, called a Medicare Summary Notice (MSN), to let you know how much was paid. If the doctor does not accept assignment, Medicare pays you and you pay the doctor the amount Medicare paid plus all permissible charges, which may include your $147 calendar year deductible for Part B, your 20% co-payment, and any charge above the Medicare-approved amount up to the 115%

cap. **Only Medicare-approved amounts count toward the $147 Part B deductible, not the actual charges billed by the physician or medical supplier.**

You may contact the insurance company that administers the Medicare Part B program in your area for a list of the doctors in your area who take assignment, or you can access a list at www.medicare.gov. However, it's still a good idea to check with the doctor when you make an appointment because the doctor may have stopped taking assignment since the list was updated.

Appeals

If you don't agree with how Medicare handles a claim or if you think more should have been paid, you have the right to appeal the claim. Best results are obtained if you send a letter from your doctor with your appeal. Just ask the doctor to write a letter that further justifies the services performed. Many times an appeal results in an additional payment. Send the appeal to the Medicare carrier listed on your Medicare Summary Notice.

Get Personalized Medicare Information

If you are an Internet user, you may register at MyMedicare.gov to track your health care claims, including your preventive services, and see all of your Medicare information in one place. Explore www.medicare.gov for the wealth of information and services available at that site, including quality of care surveys on home health agencies, nursing homes, hospitals, doctors and dialysis facilities. You also can see lists of doctors who accept the Medicare-approved amount as full payment.

Medicare Supplement Policies

Before I entered the long-term care insurance field, I believed like many people that a Medicare supplement pays whatever Medicare doesn't, and therefore everyone who has Medicare needs a Medicare supplement. This section will show you why that is an inaccurate assumption.

Medicare supplement policies, sometimes referred to as "Medigap" coverage, are individual policies from private insurance companies that are designed to pay some or all of the above gaps after Medicare benefits have been provided. And that's the caution - Medicare supplements are designed to pay only after Medicare has made a payment. This means that with a few exceptions, **they typically do not pay for services not covered by Medicare.** Medicare supplemental insurance policies can be valuable, however, as Medicare alone will not pay all of a patient's medical expenses. About one in four Medicare beneficiaries have a Medicare supplement.[11]

The Standardization of Medicare Supplements

Medicare supplements have been standardized since 1992. All carriers must offer Plan A which is a very basic plan and does not cover the copayment for skilled nursing facilities. Insurance companies can decide which of the other plans to offer.

Currently there are 11 plans available (Plans A-D, Plan F, High Deductible Plan F, Plan G, and Plans K-N). Plans K, L, M and N were created to give beneficiaries new options for higher beneficiary cost-sharing with a lower premium. With K and L, after you meet an out-of-pocket yearly limit ($4,800-K and $2,400-L) and your yearly Part B deductible, the Medigap plan pays 100% of covered services for the rest of the calendar year. Plan M includes 50% coverage of the Part A deductible and no coverage of the Part B deductible. Plan N includes full 100% coverage of the Part A deductible but no coverage for the Part B deductible. In addition, coverage for the Part B coinsurance (as part of the Basic benefits) is subject to a new copay structure. The copay is up to $20 for office visits and up to $50 for emergency room visits that don't result in an inpatient admission.[12]

❧ MY HEROES ❧

Edgar R. Shelton, 1928-2008

William Joseph Pomakoy, 1927-2013

MEDIGAP PLANS [Extracted from *Choosing a Medigap Policy* (CMS)]

How to read the chart:

If a check mark appears in a column of this chart, the Medigap policy covers 100% of the described benefit. If a row lists a percentage, the policy covers that percentage of the described benefit. If a row is blank, the policy doesn't cover that benefit. Note: The Medigap policy covers coinsurance only after you have paid the deductible (unless the Medigap policy also covers the deductible).

Medigap Benefits	Medigap Plans									
	A	B	C	D	F*	G	K	L	M	N
Medicare Part A Coinsurance and hospital costs up to an additional 365 days after Medicare benefits are used up	✓	✓	✓	✓	✓	✓	✓	✓	✓	✓
Medicare Part B Coinsurance or Copayment	✓	✓	✓	✓	✓	✓	50%	75%	✓	✓
Blood (First 3 Pints)	✓	✓	✓	✓	✓	✓	50%	75%	✓	✓
Part A Hospice Care Coinsurance or Copayment	✓	✓	✓	✓	✓	✓	50%	75%	✓	✓
Skilled Nursing Facility Care Coinsurance			✓	✓	✓	✓	50%	75%	✓	✓
Medicare Part A Deductible		✓	✓	✓	✓	✓	50%	75%	50%	✓
Medicare Part B Deductible			✓		✓					
Medicare Part B Excess Charges					✓	✓				
Foreign Travel Emergency (Up to Plan Limits)			✓	✓	✓	✓			✓	✓
							Out-of-Pocket Limit			
							$4,800	$2,400		

*Plan F also offers a high-deductible plan. If you choose this option, this means you must pay for Medicare-covered costs up to the deductible amount of $2,110 in 2013 before your Medigap plan pays anything.

Skilled Nursing Facility and Home Care Coverage: You can see from the chart that Plans C, D, F, G, M and N pay the $148.00 daily co-payment for days 21-100 in a skilled nursing facility. Plan K pays half of it and Plan L pays 75% of it. All of the plans pay the Part B 20% copayment, which is the only out-of-pocket expense for home care you will have and that is only if you wind up receiving home care visits under Part B. Home care is paid at 100% under Part A at this time although there is discussion about implementing a copayment as part of Medicare reform. Massachusetts, Minnesota and Wisconsin have different benefits as these states standardized Medicare supplement coverage earlier than the national requirement. You can see those benefits in the annual publication "Choosing a Medigap Policy" provided by the Centers for Medicare and Medicaid Services at https://www.cms.gov/Medicare/Health-Plans/Medigap/.

Claims-Since Medicare supplements usually can't pay unless Medicare pays first, the Medicare supplement insurance company needs to see a copy of the Medicare Summary Notice (MSN) before processing the claim.

Hopefully this section has dispelled any myths about Medicare supplements simply covering what Medicare doesn't. They only **supplement** Medicare and therefore if Medicare doesn't approve skilled nursing facility or home care benefits, Medicare supplements can't pay either.

But we won't stop here. Because the world of Medicare can be confusing, let's go a little deeper into Medicare supplements.

Do You Need a Medicare Supplement?

There are five types of people who do **not** need a Medicare supplement:

- Individuals *who are enrolled in a Medicare managed care plan* (see "Medicare Advantage Plans" in the next section). Medicare Advantage plans provide all of the services provided by Medicare Part A and B without the deductibles and co-payments you learned about in the last section, so you don't need a Medicare supplement.

- *Low-income individuals,* also known as "dual eligibles", who can get the Medicare Part A and Part B deductibles and coinsurance payments and the Part B premium paid by their state Medicaid program. You may also hear this referred to as the Medicare Savings Program and formerly as the Qualified Medicare Beneficiary program. Low-income means your annual income is below the national poverty level ($951 individual/$1,251 couple). These amounts, which are higher for Alaska and Hawaii, include an additional $20, which is called "a monthly Supplemental Security Income disregard," which means these are the true amounts of income you can have to qualify for this program. Assets, not counting your home or vehicle, must be less than $6,940 ($10,410 for couples).

  Call your local Medicaid office if you think you might qualify, and to obtain current income amounts which are announced each February. Ask for information about the Medicare Savings Program, formerly called the Qualified Medicare Beneficiary (QMB) program. You can also check the CMS website at http://www.medicare.gov/your-medicare-costs/help-paying-costs/medicare-savings-program/medicare-savings-programs.html.

Note: if your income is too much to qualify for the QMB program, you may still be able to qualify for the Specified Low-Income Medicare Beneficiary (SLMB) program, which will pay your Part B premium. Your assets still have to be low, but your income could be as much as $1,137 for an individual and $1,533 for a couple. (Rates for Alaska and Hawaii are slightly higher.)

- *Individuals who are allowed by their employers to continue group health insurance after retiring* usually do not need a separate Medicare supplement policy. Retiree group insurance usually has better benefits (i.e. prescription drugs, hearing aids, vision aids, etc.) than an individual Medicare supplement. However, some employers just pay the premium for a Medicare supplement rather than offering a unique retiree health insurance program. The number of employers providing any health insurance for retirees has dwindled significantly. Twenty-five percent of large firms (200 or more workers) that offer health benefits to their employees offered retiree coverage in 2012, similar to 26% in 2011. There has been a downward trend in the percentage of firms offering retirees coverage, from 32% in 2005 and 66% in 1988.[13] If you are fortunate enough to have this option when you retire, show great appreciation to your employer but it is wise not to count on it.

- *Individuals or spouses who work past age 65* can be covered by an employer's group health plan if the employer has 20 or more employees and should elect to do so as group plans are normally better than individual Medicare supplement policies. Upon retirement, the individual can purchase a Medicare supplement policy if the employer does not provide group coverage to retirees.

- People who decide to self-insure balances to Medicare.

Types of people who **may** need a Medicare supplement:

- People who don't meet the low income requirements of the Medicare Savings Program;
- People who are not covered by an employer or former employer; or
- People who are not enrolled in a Medicare Advantage plan may consider purchasing an individual Medicare supplement policy, unless they decide to self-insure balances to Medicare.

If you are in this second group, here is some basic education about Medicare supplement insurance.

Characteristics of Medicare Supplement Policies Issued After 1992

Guaranteed Renewable—this means the policy can never be cancelled as long as you pay the premiums and as long as you answered all the questions in the application truthfully. It can't be cancelled even if you have a lot of claims. The premium can be increased on an entire class of policyholders, not just on you.

Free-Look Period—You have 30 days after you receive your policy to send it back and get your money back. You can either return it to the insurance professional who sold it to you or send it back to the insurance company with a letter saying you do not accept the policy and you wish to have your money returned. Call your state's Department of Insurance if you have any problems getting your money back.

Open Enrollment—Federal guidelines guarantee that for six months following enrollment in Part B of Medicare, persons age 65 or older can't be declined or charged more for a Medicare supplement because of health problems. Insurance companies cannot impose a waiting period for pre-existing conditions during the initial open enrollment period if you have had at least six months of health insurance coverage before you apply for the Medicare supplement policy. If you've had less than six months, you get credit for the amount of time you have had health insurance coverage.

Open enrollment for disabled people under age 65: On January 1, 1995, federal law extended open enrollment for six months at age 65 to those persons who were first enrolled in Part B of Medicare prior to age 65 by reason of disability or end stage renal disease. If you purchase a Medicare supplement policy as a disabled person prior to age 65, you may only be able to get Plan A. This law means you can get a better policy (Plans C–N) at age 65 with no health questions and possibly for a lower premium, depending on your state. Some states require insurance companies to offer the best price for under age 65 applicants and some states allow companies to charge more for them. If you have had Medicare at least six months before your open enrollment period at age 65, you won't have a waiting period for pre-existing conditions, because Medicare counts as health insurance to satisfy the open enrollment requirement mentioned above.

Open enrollment for people who work past age 65: If you or your spouse continue to work past age 65 so that you are covered under an employer's group plan, you can delay enrollment in Part B of Medicare until you are no longer covered under the group plan. When you know your group coverage is ending, you can apply for Part B of Medicare with no penalty, and you will have the six-month open enrollment period to obtain an individual Medicare supplement policy regardless of any health problems you have. You will not have a pre-existing waiting period under your new Medicare supplement policy because you will have had health insurance for at least six months prior to the effective date of the Medicare supplement.

Right to Suspend a Medicare Supplement Policy If You Go Back to Work: Thanks to the Ticket to Work and Work Incentives Improvement Act of 1999, if you have a Medicare supplement then go to work for a company that offers a group health plan, you can ask the Medicare supplement carrier to suspend your policy until you notify the insurance company of the date that you are no longer covered under the group health plan. Your premium and your coverage will be reinstated on that date without medical questions.

Pre-existing Conditions—If you pass underwriting to replace your old Medicare supplement policy with a new one, the new policy has to cover you immediately for health problems you already have unless the replacement occurs in the first six months after purchasing your first Medicare supplement policy. This means no waiting period for pre-existing conditions for most replacements. If you are just becoming eligible for Medicare and buying your first Medicare supplement policy, the longest you have to wait for coverage for pre-existing conditions is six months. That will happen only if you have not had at least six months of health insurance coverage before you apply for the Medicare supplement policy.

Underwriting—Unless it is your first policy, Medicare supplement policies you apply for can decline you or charge you more if you have health problems. To get a replacement Medicare supplement policy, you must answer questions about your health and allow the insurance company time to review your answers and get more information from your doctor if necessary.

Multiple Policies—You don't need more than one Medicare supplement policy. The reason some people have purchased more than one is because they think they can get all of their bills paid if they have more than one policy. This is unwise use of your money. Today, federal guidelines don't allow an insurance company to sell you a Medicare supplement policy in addition to one you already have. This means if you buy a new Medicare supplement policy, you agree to cancel the one you already have.

Excess Physician Charges—If your doctor does not accept Medicare assignment, you owe the difference between the actual charge and the amount Medicare approves, unless your state doesn't allow the doctor to charge more. In states that do allow it, the doctor can charge no more than 115 percent of the Medicare-approved amount. Again, you don't need multiple policies to get these excess charges paid. Plans F and G pay 100 percent of the excess charges.

Foreign Travel Emergency—If you become injured or get sick unexpectedly during the first 60 days of a trip outside the United States, the standardized plans C, D, F, G, M and N will pay 80 percent of hospital, physician and medical care, subject to a $250 annual deductible and a lifetime maximum of $50,000, if the care would have been covered by Medicare had it been provided in the United States.

Premiums -- The three most common methods for premium calculation for Medicare supplement policies are 1) community rating— all policyholders pay the same rate regardless of age, 2) issue age rating— premium is based on the age you apply for the policy and 3) attained age rating—age 65 premium is usually lower than Methods 1 and 2 but increases either annually or in age bands such as every five years as you get older.

The following states require community rating: Arkansas, Connecticut, Massachusetts, Minnesota, New York, Vermont and Washington, whereas these states require issue age rating: Arizona, Florida, Georgia, Idaho, Missouri and New Hampshire. Nebraska is an attained age rated state.[14]

Rate Increases – With Methods 1 and 2, premiums generally increase each year to reflect the increase in Medicare deductibles and co-payments which means the policy has to pay out more in benefits. For example, Mutual of Omaha reports the market trend for rate increases on new and existing Medicare supplement policies is about 9% for 2013.[15] Method 3 has rate increases as you get older because premiums are actually rising with your age, in addition to medical inflation.

First-time Medicare supplement purchasers are paying about $120-$130 a month for Plan F, but the average Medicare supplement premium is $177 a month, or about $2,100 a year.[16] It's not unusual for tobacco-users to pay more.

Ways to save money on Medicare supplement premium

- You may be able to save money by paying once or twice a year instead of monthly or quarterly.

- You may receive a discount for having your premium automatically deducted from your bank account.

- Other discounts may be available such as for non-smokers or household discounts

- You may be able to save money by using a certain network of hospitals and possibly doctors for non-emergency care. This is called the "Medicare Select" program. Premiums for Medicare Select plans can be as much as 15% less than standard Medicare supplements but may or may not be available in your state.

- You can select a high deductible Plan F which means no benefits are paid until you have paid $2,110 in out-of-pocket costs. This deductible can increase each year. Also, the $250 deductible for foreign travel emergency still applies.

- You can choose Plans K, L or M as these plans pay a percentage of key gaps in Medicare (see chart of plans on p. 307)

Confused About Plan Selection?

You're probably wondering how you can possibly decide which Medicare supplement plan to choose. You also may be wondering what others have done with this decision. Plan A is the lowest cost plan but the only benefit most people will ever see from Plan A is the 20% copayment for doctors that accept Medicare assignment. These amounts are very small and considering that Plan A can cost almost $100 a month at age 65, I think you can do better with one of the other plans. Plan F has been the most popular plan as it covers all of the deductibles and co-payments charged under the original Medicare program, plus it pays for the excess doctor charges. Plan C has the second-highest share of policyholders as it covers everything Plan F does, except for the excess doctor charges. If you live in a state that won't permit doctors to charge more than the Medicare-approved amount, Plan C may be the best choice.

However, a trend may be changing with plan selection.

Consider that Plan G is exactly the same as Plan F except it doesn't pay for the Part B deductible. Here is the kind of analysis you should do:

Monthly Premium for Male Non-Tobacco Age 65 (Mutual of Omaha)

Plan F: *$134.16*

Plan G: *$110.02*

$24.14 x 12 = $289.68 less $147 Part B deductible
= $142.68 annual savings with Plan G

This makes even more sense for someone who smokes as the tobacco rate carries a higher premium.

Whichever Medicare supplement plan you choose, you also will need to select a Medicare prescription drug plan to cover your prescription drug costs, as Medicare supplements don't cover them.

Can One Self-Insure the Balances to Medicare?

For many years I have been saying that Individuals with significant assets who wish to self-insure balances to Medicare can do so as balances after Medicare's payments are small. Some people elect to self-insure balances to Medicare because they feel the money they have been using for Medicare supplemental insurance is better spent to pay long-term care insurance premiums. They understand that long-term care is a much bigger risk than balances to Medicare. Here is a real life story to support that point:

My cousin's husband, age 70, is battling several major health issues. In 2012, here is the financial picture for his health costs. Take a look at the financial picture for his health care costs in a low charge year and a high charge year.

	2009	2012
Total charges	$56,158	$10,109
Medicare paid	$54,358	$ 7,418
Med supp premium	$ 1,980	$ 2,038
Med supp paid	$ 1,715	$393
Net	$265	- $ 1,645

You can see the result is the same, regardless of the size of the bills, can't you? Balances to Medicare are very small.

The average ANNUAL out-of-pocket for age 65+ is only $4,527 for balances to Medicare AND Part B AND Medicare supplemental premium. [17] **That's less than a MONTH of long-term care which averages about $6500 for daily ten hour shifts of home care or care in a nursing facility!!** [18]

To summarize, if you choose Original Medicare Part A and B, you will pay at age 65:

- Part B premium for a minimum of $104.90 a month and more if you have income above $85,000 individual/$170,000 joint

- Medicare supplement premium of around $120-$130 a month

- Medicare prescription drug plan of about $40 a month[19]

Those three premiums can easily cost you $3,000+ a year and will increase as you get older.

The wild card of course is prescription drugs. Not only are prescription drugs becoming increasingly expensive, but you will pay a 1% premium penalty for each month you wait to apply after the seven month open enrollment period surrounding when you become eligible for Part B of Medicare (see "Medicare Prescription Drug Program" later in this chapter). Therefore you may decide to buy just a Medicare prescription drug plan and skip the Medicare supplement. The disclaimer here is that if you change your mind and apply for a Medicare supplement outside of the open enrollment period, you will have to answer health questions.

If this idea seems too risky for you, there is another great way to handle balances to Medicare and that is to buy a Medicare Advantage plan that includes prescription drug coverage with zero premium instead of going with Original Medicare Part A and B combined with a Medicare supplement and prescription drug plan. You will usually still have to pay the Medicare Part B premium, although some Medicare Advantage plans even pay some or all of that. Either way, you can see the immediate savings of getting rid of the Medicare supplement and prescription drug plan premium. Why wouldn't everybody do this? Because the tradeoff is you have to agree to use the health care providers that participate in the Medicare Advantage plan you select.

At this point, I do have to insert a second disclaimer that my advice about self-insuring balances to Medicare is based on today's Medicare program, when balances are generally small. Health care reform may result in larger balances for Medicare beneficiaries.

Medicare Advantage

Medicare Advantage Defined

Medicare Advantage, sometimes called Part C of Medicare, is an alternative to the government-run original Medicare program as it is made up of Medicare plans operated by the private sector vs. the government. Medicare pays a set amount of money for your health care each year to the Medicare Advantage plan you select. If the plan can provide care for less than the amount, the plan makes money, so the plan is encouraged to control costs as much as possible. These plans contract with specific health care providers (hospitals, doctors, skilled nursing facilities, physical therapists, etc.) **to provide all the services covered by Medicare** and most of them (82%) include prescription drug coverage. [20] This is also known as managed care, a concept that is familiar to most Americans as most health insurance plans for people under age 65 work like this.

More people are enrolled in a Medicare Advantage plan today than in Original Medicare with a Medicare supplement. Twenty-seven percent of the Medicare population (13.1 million people) were enrolled in a Medicare Advantage plan in 2012.[21] People enrolled in these plans don't need a Medicare supplement because instead of being responsible for the Medicare deductibles and co-payments, the patient pays small co-payments (i.e., $5 - $15 per doctor visit) and either zero or a small monthly premium. For those with a premium, the average in 2013 for a Medicare Advantage plan with prescription drug coverage is $51.40 per month. However, 87% of Medicare beneficiaries have access to a Medicare Advantage plan with zero premium.[22] You still must pay the Medicare Part B premium, unless the Medicare Advantage plan in which you are enrolled pays part or all of it.

At first, Medicare Advantage plans sound more flexible since they do not require the normal co-payments and deductibles that are part of the original Medicare program. In some ways they are, because Medicare Advantage plans can deliver the benefits however they want in order to be cost effective yet provide for the care of their members. For example, since 2003, Medicare Advantage plans have been allowed to waive the three-day prior hospital stay requirement for skilled nursing facility care if it is cost-effective. This means a patient could be admitted to a skilled nursing facility after a one or two-day hospital stay or directly from home. On the other hand, a Medicare Advantage plan does not have to provide the skilled nursing facility benefit at all and can send the patient home to recuperate.

Depending on the type of plan, the patient either has to receive all non-emergency services from the health care providers on the list to be covered at all or expect a lower benefit to be paid to providers not on the list. You may hear the second type referred to as a "point-of-service" option, which just means you pay more out of your pocket to go to a provider outside the network. You may be required to select a primary care doctor who controls your access to specialists. Some people don't mind these restrictions, especially if the Medicare Advantage plan pays for additional services not covered by Medicare, such as eye and ear exams, dental care, foot care, routine checkups, or pays part or all of Part B premium.

Another attractive feature of Medicare Advantage plans is that they are required to limit out-of-pocket expenses for each enrollee to $6,700 per year and encouraged to bring that down to $3,400 per year, and almost half of them have done that.[23] There is no out-of-pocket limit for those enrolled in Original Medicare A and B, whether or not they have a Medicare supplement.

What Kind of Choices Will You Have?

Health Maintenance Organizations (HMOs) are the most popular, accounting for 58% of all plans offered nationwide and 65% of Medicare Advantage enrollment.[24]

There are many private plans besides HMOs for you to choose from in addition to the traditional Medicare program. Some of these require you to use a specific list of providers to receive any benefits, but the benefits you receive will be at little or no cost to you. Others with the "point-of-service" option mentioned above will allow you to use providers not on the list if you pay more out of your pocket. They can all charge a premium in addition to the Medicare Part B premium. They can all require deductibles and copayments different than Original Medicare. The insurance company, rather than the Medicare program, decides how much you pay for the services you receive.

Other choices include:

Preferred Provider Organizations—You will be given a list of doctors and hospitals to choose from, but you are allowed to use providers not on the list and simply receive lower benefits. PPOs are less restrictive than HMOs because they don't require you to see a specialist without going through a primary care doctor. There are local and regional PPOs. Regional PPOs provide people who live in rural areas greater access to Medicare Advantage plans by covering entire states or multi-state regions.

Private fee-for-service plans—These plans allowed enrollees to use any doctor or hospital but since 2011 have been required to set up provider networks. Generally, they include additional services not covered by Medicare. They also may provide worldwide coverage for emergency care and urgently needed care, which is something the original Medicare program does not do. "Urgently needed" is defined as care needed due to a sickness or injury of sudden and unexpected onset.

Medicare Special Needs Plans – These are plans that specialize in handling people with

1. chronic or disabling conditions like diabetes or end stage renal disease;
2. people who are in nursing homes; or
3. people who are eligible for both Medicare and Medicaid.

Members of Medicare Special Needs Plans usually are assigned a care coordinator who will develop a personal care plan to help them achieve the best overall health possible for their condition.

Medicare Medical Savings Accounts – Another exciting choice is a Medical Savings Account (MSA), which is similar to a Health Savings Account for people under age 65. An MSA is an intriguing choice because it allows people to take more control over how their Medicare benefits are used. Enrollees can't be required to use a provider network. You can use any provider that accepts a Medicare MSA plan.

A Medicare Medical Savings Account has two parts: a high-deductible health insurance plan **with zero premium** and a Medical Savings Account that can be used to pay for any IRS-approved medical expense, not just Medicare Part A and Part B expenses that count toward the high deductible. After the deductible is met, the health plan pays 100% of all Medicare-covered services other than prescription drugs. The high-deductible plan is a Medicare Advantage plan, like an HMO or PPO, and a bank or other financial institution holds the money in your account. You will likely be given a debit card to use when you pay your health care bills, just as people with Health Savings Accounts have.

The maximum deductible in 2012 was $10,600, indexed to increase annually. However, an MSA provider can offer a lower deductible. For example, Blue Cross and Blue Shield of Western New York is using an annual deductible of $4,750 and a deposit of $3,000 in the 2013 BlueSaver Medical Savings Account.

Here is the "behind the scenes" explanation of how it really works: the Medicare MSA Plan deposits the difference between the amount it thinks it needs to provide your care (the "bid amount") and the amount it receives from Medicare for your care into your Medical Savings Account at the beginning of each calendar year, tax-free. Here's an example using a Medicare allowance of $6,000 a year:

Medicare's annual allowance ($600 x 12):	$6,000
Medicare Advantage Plan's bid amount:	- $3,000
Amount the Medicare Advantage plan deposits into an account for you	$3,000

This deposit will be made in a lump sum in the first month of your enrollment in the program. Neither the initial deposit nor the growth will be taxable income to you, as long as you use the money for "qualified medical expenses," according to the IRS. This means you can use the money for medical expenses beyond what the traditional Medicare program covers such as eyeglasses, hearing aids, etc. You must file Form 1040, US Individual Income Tax Return, along with Form 8853, "Archer MSA and Long-Term Care Insurance Contracts" with the Internal Revenue Service (IRS) for any distributions made from your Medicare MSA account. This is how the IRS knows not to tax you on your MSA account withdrawals. If you use the money for any other reason, you will owe both income taxes and a 50% penalty. Just remember that only expenses covered by Medicare Part A or B count toward your high deductible. You also will still pay Medicare Part B premium.

You aren't allowed to put any of your own money into your MSA and you aren't allowed to purchase a Medicare supplement to cover the expenses that count toward your deductible. The amount that the plan deposits into your account will generally be much lower than your deductible so you will have high out-of-pocket costs to pay until you meet your deductible.

However, if you have relatively few medical expenses and have money left over at the end of the year, the money is yours. It stays in your account and can be used for expenses in the following year. The healthier you are, the more money will accumulate in your Medical Savings Account because once a year, the Medicare Advantage Plan will make another lump sum deposit into your account.

The really exciting news is that tax-qualified long-term care insurance premium is considered an IRS-approved medical expense! Therefore, if you are in good health and don't use all of your MSA for medical expenses, there will be money left over which you may choose to use for the age-based amount of your long-term care insurance premium. Depending on your age and how much your premium is, you might be able to pay all of it out of your MSA. (See Chapter 2 for the allowable premium based on your age in 2013.)

You can check with www.medicare.gov/find-a-plan to see if a Medicare Medical Savings Account plan is available in your area. If so, you can enroll during the regular open enrollment for other Medicare Advantage plans, but you can't disenroll for an entire calendar year, unless you meet one of these exceptions:

- you move out of the plan's service area;
- qualify for Medicaid; or
- qualify for Extra Help with Medicare prescription drug costs.

If you do leave the MSA plan, you don't have to pay anything back. Whatever is left of that year's deposit will be refunded to Medicare.

A note about prescription drugs for MSA holders: Since the high-deductible health plan doesn't cover prescription drugs, you will want to purchase a Medicare Part D prescription drug plan, which is explained in the next section. You can't pay Part D premium out of your MSA; however, you can pay Part D co-payments, coinsurance and deductible from your MSA tax-free. These withdrawals just won't count toward your MSA plan deductible, because only expenses covered by Medicare Part A or B count toward your deductible.

Enrollment and Disenrollment

Medicare Advantage plans are required to accept people when they first become eligible for Medicare at age 65, no questions asked. You can join during the 7-month period that begins 3 months before the month you turn 65, includes the month you turn 65, and ends 3 months after the month you turn 65.

People who qualify for Medicare due to a disability before age 65 can join a Medicare Advantage plan from three months before to three months after their 25th month of Social Security Disability Income payments. The exception to this rule is that end-stage renal disease patients usually can't join a Medicare Advantage plan unless they have a successful kidney transplant. If they are already in a Medicare Advantage plan, they can stay in it or join another plan offered by the same insurance company.

If you don't join one when you are first eligible, you are allowed to join once a year during a fall open enrollment period with coverage effective January 1st. The open enrollment period for 2013 coverage was from

October 15 through December 7th, 2012 and coverage was effective January 1, 2013. If you don't like the Medicare Advantage plan you chose during the open enrollment period, you can't switch to another Medicare Advantage plan, but you can switch to Original Medicare for a short time after the first of the year and also pick up a Medicare Prescription Drug plan during that time with no health questions. See the next section for ways to get a Medicare supplement with no health questions.

What If I'm Afraid to Leave the Original Medicare Program?

There are safety nets to help people try Medicare Advantage plans.

- If you enroll in a Medicare Advantage plan when you are first eligible for Medicare and don't like it, you can switch to the original Medicare program within one year of your enrollment, and you can get a Medicare supplement policy "guaranteed issue." This means you can't be turned down or made to wait for pre-existing conditions.

- If you cancel a Medicare supplement policy to enroll in a Medicare Advantage plan for the first time, you can leave the Medicare Advantage plan within 12 months and get a Medicare supplement with no health questions.

However, just buying a Medicare supplement policy isn't enough. You have to disenroll from your Medicare Advantage plan; otherwise, your Medicare supplement plan won't be allowed to pay any of the Medicare deductibles or co-payments. The Medicare Advantage company will give you an official disenrollment form to include with your Medicare supplement application.

What if My Medicare Advantage Plan Withdraws From My Area or Leaves the Medicare Program Completely?

This can happen. If it does, your Medicare Advantage plan is required to notify you at least 90 days before your coverage ends. You can enroll in another Medicare Advantage plan in your area if there is one available or return to original Medicare. If you return to original Medicare, you will have the right to buy a Medicare Supplement policy with no health questions if you apply within 63 days after your Medicare Advantage coverage ends. Whatever happens, there's a really good chance you can keep your doctor, as most Medicare Advantage doctors participate in original Medicare.

You Do Not Have to Switch At All

Because of the necessity to contain health care costs, 99 percent of employees are in some type of managed health care plan.[25] With the Medicare population, that ratio is only 27% as you learned earlier in this chapter.[26] With such a disproportionate ratio, you can see why Congress is hoping many more people will give the private plans a chance because they promote cost containment of health care costs. That's why they usually have lower premium and pay for more services than the original Medicare program. However, you do not have to switch to any of these private programs. You may remain in traditional Medicare if you like.

Medicare Prescription Drug Program

Next to long-term care, the second largest out-of-pocket expense for older Americans has been prescription drugs. Now all but 10% of the 49 million people on Medicare have drug coverage, thanks to the Medicare Prescription Drug Program (Part D of Medicare) that came along in 2006 which insures 63 percent of them. The others are insured mainly by employer-provided health plans, both for people who are still working as well as those who are covered under retiree health plans, and people who are covered by other government programs such as the Federal Employees Health Plan, TRICARE and the Veterans Administration. [27]

This wide blanket of drug coverage is a wonderful companion for long-term care insurance professionals and policyholders. Before Medicare Part D, it was tricky to establish the right daily or monthly benefit because the unknown factor in the equation was prescription drugs.

It's not unusual to hear about nursing home patients who have upwards of $1,500 per month in drug bills. When the client says he or she is willing to pay a third of the costs, for example, it has been difficult to estimate the cost of prescription drugs in addition to the LTC facility or home care costs in preparation for recommending a daily or monthly benefit that would achieve the client's coinsurance goal. Now, it is much easier. With Medicare paying 95% of drugs that exceed $6,955 annually with no maximum, drug aren't a worry anymore, and the daily or monthly benefit recommendation is much easier. Pre-Part D, most Americans didn't have unlimited drug coverage, if they had drug coverage at all. Now Medicare beneficiaries with Original Medicare Part A and Part B can add a standalone prescription drug plan and Medicare Advantage enrollees can have drug coverage embedded into the MA plan or as an add-on.

The 2010 health care reform act reduced the out-of-pocket for prescription drugs even more by reducing the amount the enrollee has to pay in the "donut hole" (charges between $2,970 and $6,955 in 2013). When Part D was first introduced, there was no coverage in the gap. Today some plans provide some gap coverage but many don't. In 2013, enrollees with no gap coverage only have to pay 47.5% of the total cost of brand-name drugs in the gap and 79% of the cost of generic drugs. This amount will continue to decrease until it is at 25% in 2020.[28]

Enrollment Periods

The initial enrollment period for anyone without creditable coverage was November 15 – May 15, 2006. People who missed that enrollment period have to pay a 1% premium penalty for each month they waited to enroll after May 15, 2006 and they have to pay that additional premium the rest of their lives.

Anyone who applies for the Medicare Prescription Drug program now will have a seven month open enrollment period: three months before the month the person becomes eligible for Medicare Part B, the month of eligibility, and the three months after that month. If the person doesn't purchase a drug plan during that seven month period, the premium penalty will kick in.

A popular trend has been to turn to Canada for lower drug prices. Medicare Part D's catastrophic coverage (see "Part D Premium" below) offers far greater protection than lower foreign prices if the policyholder's drug needs escalate in the future.

Part D Premium

Like Part B of Medicare, the government subsidizes Part D premium heavily, so the drug program is a good deal. Enrollees' premium funds 25.5 percent of the program and the government subsidizes the rest. The chart below shows your estimated prescription drug plan monthly premium based on your income. If your income is above a certain limit, you'll pay an income-related monthly adjustment amount in addition to your plan premium. Monthly premiums range from $15 to $165 but average $40 a month in 2013, as we mentioned earlier.[29]

Yearly income in 2011		You pay (in 2013)
Filed individual tax return	Filed joint tax return	
$85,000 or less	$170,000 or less	Your plan premium
above $85,000 up to $107,000	above $170,000 up to $214,000	$11.60 + your plan premium
above $107,000 up to $160,000	above $214,000 up to $320,000	$29.90 + your plan premium
above $160,000 up to $214,000	above $320,000 up to $428,000	$48.30+ your plan premium
above $214,000	above $428,000	$66.60 + your plan premium

Eighty-two percent of Medicare Advantage plans offer prescription drug coverage. You are required to receive it from the Medicare Advantage plan you select if that plan offers it. Almost half of the MA-PD plans offer some coverage in the "donut hole".[30]

Can you see that having drug coverage also frees up dollars for long-term care insurance premium?

Help for Low-Income/Low-Asset Medicare Beneficiaries

People with limited income and assets don't have to pay premium or a deductible and don't have the coverage gap ("doughnut hole") between $2,970 and $6,955 in charges. Their co-pays are only $1 - $2 for generic drugs and $3 - $5 for brand-name drugs. People in this category have incomes below $16,755 (single) or $22,695 (married) and have assets less than $13,070 (single) or $26,120 (married). The asset calculation doesn't include the primary residence, automobiles or personal possessions such as furniture and jewelry. However, an estimated two million people meet the income and asset criteria and haven't stepped forward to claim this help.[31]

If you aren't receiving any government assistance now but fall within those income and asset guidelines, you can apply for this extra help through the Social Security Administration either by mail, phone,

Internet or in person at a Social Security office. Here is the contact information:

Social Security Administration
Wilkes-Barre Data Operations Center
P. O. Box 1020
Wilkes-Barre, PA 18767-9910
800-772-1213
www.socialsecurity.gov (no signature is required for an online application)

You can also call the State Health Insurance Assistance Program (SHIP) counselor in your area for help (see "It's Not a One-Time Decision" below).

People who are already on Medicaid, including nursing home patients, or receiving government assistance such as Supplemental Security Income (SSI) or are part of a low income program as explained on the preceding page are already approved for this extra help. If they didn't enroll in Part D by December 31, 2005, they were automatically switched to one, as Medicaid stopped paying their drug bills after that date.

Choices, Choices, Choices

Now we get to the really important question. How do you decide which Medicare Advantage plan to join? The most precise way to select the best plan is to collect your medicines and enter them by name into a special program developed just for this purpose on the Medicare website at www.medicare.gov/find-a-plan. If you don't use a computer, perhaps a friend or family member will help you.

Why do you need to have your medicines handy when you consider which plan to join? Because the plans vary as far as which drugs they cover. There's no point in joining a plan that doesn't cover a drug that you really need.

Here is the easy process to select a plan using a computer. Go to www.medicare.gov/find-a-plan and follow the simple instructions. There is even a video to show you step by step how to choose the best plan for you. You will be asked to enter your Medicare ID number along with the date your Medicare coverage was effective. This information is on your Medicare card. Then enter your birthday and zip code. The comparison program will ask you to enter the drugs you are taking and will show the plans in your area that cover those drugs. With drug plans, you can sort them by any of these headings:

- your estimated annual drug cost with that plan for retail or mail order drugs;
- lowest monthly premium;
- lowest annual deductible;
- drug restrictions
- off formulary drugs
- if there is any coverage in the gap (charges between $2,970 and $6,955 in 2013) and if so, is it for generic drugs only or does it include brand name drugs?

You can also sort by overall plan rating to see how other enrollees rank a plan's performance in several areas:

- telephone customer service
- complaints
- appeals
- how well the plan communicates enrollment information to pharmacies
- accuracy of drug pricing information
- managing chronic conditions
- preventive care (screenings, tests, vaccines)

For people who have multiple residences in multiple states, there are some national plans that provide coverage in all states and the comparison will identify those for you. When you've selected a plan, you can enroll online.

The great news is that EVERYONE has the chance to change plans EVERY YEAR during the annual open enrollment period. This is important and necessary because as different medical conditions develop, it is quite likely that your prescriptions especially will change, and the drug plan you choose now may or may not be the best fit anymore.

What About Scams?

Companies marketing Medicare Advantage and Prescription Drug plans are allowed to market by telephone or through the mail, but not door to door. They also have to comply with the Do-Not-Call rules and abide by federal and state calling hours. Marketing representatives are not allowed to ask for Medicare ID numbers, Social Security, bank account or credit card numbers.

It's Not a One-Time Decision

Each year, it is important to examine plan options, premiums, benefits, cost-sharing requirements, provider networks and drug formularies to assess which Medicare Advantage plan or Original Medicare plan + a Medicare Prescription Drug standalone plan will best meet your needs for health care coverage.

A wonderful resource to help you determine the best form of Medicare coverage initially and ongoing is the State Health Insurance Counseling and Assistance Program (SHIP) which is located in all 50 states, the District of Columbia, Guam, Puerto Rico and the Virgin Islands. SHIPs were established in 1990 and are primarily funded by grants from the U.S. Department of Health and Human Services. Over 12,000 staff members and volunteers make up a vast network of support to provide a local community resource. You can find the closest one to you at the Medicare Helpful Contacts page (www.medicare.gov/Contacts). While you're on the Medicare website, you might want to grab "A Quick

Look at Medicare", a simple overview of the four parts of Medicare and the decision tree for finding a plan: https://www.medicare.gov/Pubs/pdf/11514.pdf

Now you know more than 99 percent of the people who are talking about Medicare. To "seal in" the information in your brain, put it to practice immediately by checking for yourself or finding a family member or friend who needs your help. It might not be as much fun as figuring out long-term care insurance but the gratitude of the person you help is PRICELESS.

The Impact of Health Care Reform to Improve Quality of Care

As much as the government has done to make private Medicare plans more attractive, many bright minds agreed that the missing piece has been quality of care. Therefore, the Patient Protection and Affordable Care Act of 2010 (PPACA) and subsequent health care reform legislation has focused significantly on improving the quality of care for all patients. For Medicare patients, this legislation has restructured the way Medicare Advantage plans get paid by the federal government to provide care so that those with higher quality ratings can now receive bonus payments. In essence, the plans that provide the highest quality in the most efficient way will survive.

To reward those plans, Medicare has established a five star rating system, and plans that are awarded five stars (excellent) are allowed to accept new members from December 8, 2012 through November 30, 2013 instead of just during the fall open enrollment period. How does the rating system work? Medicare uses information from member satisfaction surveys, plans, and health care providers to give overall performance star ratings to plans. A plan can get a rating between one and five stars. These ratings help you compare plans based on quality and performance. These ratings are updated each fall and can change each year. This system is very new so here are four things you should know.

- The overall plan ratings are available at www.medicare.gov/find-a-plan.

- You can only join a 5-star Medicare Advantage Plan if one is available in your area.

- You can only use this Special Enrollment Period once during the above timeframe.

- If you switch from a Medicare Advantage plan with drug coverage to a 5-star Medicare Advantage plan without drug coverage, you may lose your drug coverage and not be able to get it again until the next open enrollment period. Then you may have to pay a late enrollment penalty for the drug coverage.

Accountable Care Organizations

An Accountable Care Organization (ACO) is a new model of health care delivery in which providers share responsibility for providing high quality care to Medicare beneficiaries. The financial risks and rewards are also shared among the providers in a network. They operate under a theory of shared accountability with financial incentives to provide high quality low cost care. So where do beneficiaries sign up? Simple, they don't. Hospitals, physicians and insurance companies are the participating partners. Providers are obligated to notify patients that they are part of an

ACO and patients may choose not to be included by opting to keep their records outside of the ACO system.[32]

Medicare Bonuses and Penalties for U.S. Hospitals

In December 2012 Medicare implemented a new payment system to hospitals that gives them bonuses or penalties based on their quality measures. Of particular concern was that too many patients have been returning to the hospital in the same month. Medicare will implement a bonus/penalty payment system for physicians starting in 2015 for groups with over 100 professionals and expanding to all physicians by 2017.[33]

Program of All-Inclusive Care for the Elderly (PACE)

The PACE program is an alternative to the four parts of Medicare we have just discussed for lower income Americans. PACE programs coordinate and provide all needed preventive, primary, acute and long term care services so individuals who are 55 years old or older can continue living in the community. Although all PACE participants must be certified to need nursing home care to enroll in PACE, most PACE participants reside at home. If a PACE enrollee does need nursing home care, the PACE program pays for it and continues to coordinate the enrollee's care. PACE is available only in states that have chosen to offer it under Medicaid, and the enrollee may have to pay a monthly premium.

PACE Providers. PACE programs receive Medicare and Medicaid capitation payments for all enrollees eligible for services. Persons financially ineligible for Medicaid must pay that amount privately (out-of-pocket). PACE programs assume full financial risk for enrollees' care without limits on dollars or duration and are responsible for a full range of needed services, including all

Medicare and Medicaid benefits, including prescription drugs. This means that PACE enrollees don't need to participate in Original Medicare or join a Medicare Advantage plan or enroll in a Medicare Part D Prescription Drug plan as PACE provides all of these benefits.

Philosophy

The Program of All-inclusive Care for the Elderly (PACE) model is centered around the belief that it is better for the well-being of seniors with chronic care needs and their families to be served in the community whenever possible.

Services

Delivering all needed medical and supportive services, the program is able to provide the entire continuum of care and services to seniors with chronic care needs while maintaining their independence in their homes for as long as possible. Care and services include:

- Adult day care that offers nursing; physical, occupational and recreational therapies; meals; nutritional counseling; social work and personal care

- Medical care provided by a PACE physician familiar with the history, needs and preferences of each participant

- Home health care and personal care

- All necessary prescription drugs

- Social services

- Medical specialists such as audiology, dentistry, optometry, podiatry, and speech therapy

- Respite care
- Hospital and nursing home care when necessary

History

The PACE model of care can be traced to the early 1970s, when the Chinatown-North Beach community of San Francisco saw the pressing needs of families whose elders had emigrated from Italy, China and the Philippines for long term care services. Dr. William L. Gee, a public health dentist, headed the committee that hired Marie-Louise Ansak in 1971 to investigate solutions. They, along with other community leaders, formed a nonprofit corporation, On Lok Senior Health Services, to create a community based system of care. On Lok is Cantonese for "peaceful, happy abode."

In 1990, the PACE program received the first official payment recognition from Medicare and Medicaid and final regulation to recognize PACE as a permanently recognized provider type under Medicare and Medicaid was passed in November 2006. In 2011, there were 82 PACE programs operational in 29 states.

For more information and a list of PACE service areas, go to the National PACE Association at www.npaonline.org or on the www.Medicare.gov website.

The Silver Lining in the Medicare Plans

OK - We've finished going over all four parts of Medicare as they relate to the services typically needed by long-term care patients; i.e. home care and nursing facility care. (Assisted living facility and adult day care simply aren't covered by Medicare.) We have even discussed the PACE program utilized primarily for low income people in the geographical areas in which it is available. As you wade through the maze of Medicare changes in the next few years, please bear one thing in mind. **The real risk today is long-term care.**

Just remember that the cost of long-term care will triple in the next 20 years and quadruple in the next 30 years if the average historical growth rate of 5-6% continues.[34]

In this era of reigning in health care costs, legislators are thinking more cost-sharing in Medicare and supplemental coverage to Medicare will cause Medicare beneficiaries to use less services.[35] Let me reiterate:

Health care reform makes long-term care insurance even more important as an increasing amount of health dollars is required to pay for acute care through new cost-sharing provisions.

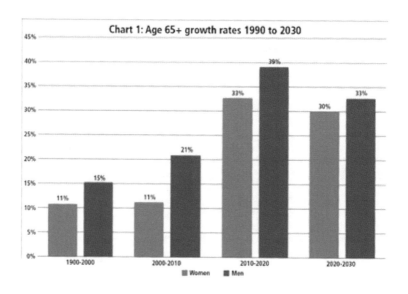

Chart 1: Age 65+ growth rates 1990 to 2030

CONCLUSION

Where Do You Go From Here?

You don't know me. But Ed Carter, Martha Routh, Russell Polston, C. Vernon Duckett, Randy Keith, Pat Bonnett, Susan Bell, Toni Bean, Harold Clemmons, Anne Arney, Kenton Dickerson, and Nathan Horner Jr. all know me. What do they have in common? Because of me, they had money to provide the best care possible for the people they loved…

…people they promised to never let down

…people they promised to take care of forever

…people who loved them and trusted them to be there until they drew their last breath.

Because of long-term care insurance, they had the money to keep every one of those promises.

I said on the first page of this book that it likely will have a short shelf life because of all the changes happening in the long-term care insurance market. That means the advice in it is for you and the people you love TODAY.

Please don't wait. Please RUN, don't walk, to call your financial professional and take of yourself and your family with long-term care insurance. If you don't have a financial professional who can help you, call me. The most important thing is to take action now. Don't wait. Life is too precious and the people you love are depending on you.

Taking Care of You

All of these memories wouldn't mean a thing to me if we hadn't made them together,

and with so many more to make, you can bet that I will take good care of you forever.

Now that say life together is give and take and I've come to see how that's true,

'cause it gives me heart knowing I do my part to always take of you.

Now on the road just beyond the bend we never know quite where or when a curve will turn up unexpected.

But as long as you are by my side, you can just enjoy the ride and rest assured you'll always be protected.

They say life's highway can be a rocky road with so many miles to get through.

As the years disappear I will be right here taking care of you.

When the cold wind blows and this old world shows no mercy as it puts you to the test,

I will be your shelter, always here to help you because taking care of you is what I do best.

Taking care of you is what I do best.

Lyrics by Tanya Savory and Phyllis Shelton, © 1998

ADDITIONAL RESOURCES

Assisted Living and Nursing Home Resources

Leading Age (formerly known as American Association of Homes and Services for the Aging) http://leadingage.org (202) 783-2242

American Health Care Association: www.ahcancal.org (202)842-4444
(Facts and Trends: www.ahcancal.org/research_data/trends_statistics)

Assisted Living Facilities for Seniors: http://helpguide.org/elder/assisted_living_facilities.htm

Assisted Living Federation of America: www.alfa.org (703)894-1805

Assisted Living Info: www.assistedlivinginfo.com (866)342-4297

Consumer Consortium on Assisted Living: www.ccal.org

National Academy for State Health Policy (state assisted living practices): (207)874-6524 www.nashp.org

National Center for Assisted Living: www.ncal.org (202) 842-4444

Nursing Home Compare: www.medicare.gov 1-(800)-MEDICARE Nursing Home Info, Nationwide

Nursing Home Directory: www.nursinghomeinfo.com (888)340-7817

Caregiving Resources

Alzheimer's Association: www.alz.org (800)272-3900

Caregiver information: www.caregiver.com (800)829-2734

Family Caregiver Alliance: www.caregiver.org (800)445-8106

National Alliance for Caregiving: www.caregiving.org

National Family Caregivers Association: www.nfcacares.org (800)896-3650

Well Spouse Association: www.wellspouse.org

Caregiver Information: http://helpguide.org/topics/caregiving.htm

Elder Law Resources

ElderLaw: www.elderlawanswers.com (866)267-0947

Tim Takacs, Elder Law Attorney – publishes monthly "Elder Law Fax Blog" www.tn-elderlaw.com (866) 222-3127

National Association of Elder Law Attorneys: www.naela.org
(703)942-5711
National Senior Citizen's Law Center: www.nsclc.org (202)289-6976

Financial Planning with LTC Insurance Emphasis

Suze Orman: **The Money Class**, www.suzeorman.com http://www.oprah.com/
money/Suze-Orman-Financial-Plans-for-All-Ages
Terry Savage: **The Savage Truth About Money**, www.terrysavage.com

Geriatric Care Management and Social Service Resources

National Association of Professional Geriatric Care Managers:
www.caremanager.org (520)881-8008
National Association of Social Workers: www.socialworkers.org (202)408-8600

Government Websites and Statistics

Centers for Medicare and Medicaid Services (formerly Health Care Financing
Administration) www.cms.gov 800-633-4227 Medicare and Medicaid
information …also www.medicare.gov
Federal LTC insurance program: www.LTCFEDS.com and
www.opm.gov/insure/ltc (800)582-3337
Choosing a Medigap Policy, www.medicare.gov (800) MEDICAR
Health Affairs (health policy journal): www.healthaffairs.org
(301)656-7401
Medicare and You, www.medicare.gov (800) MEDICARE
The Medicare Handbook and Medicare: 85 Commonly Asked Questions, available
from the Social Security Administration or AARP (800)424-3410
National Center for Health Statistics (national nursing home, home care and
hospice surveys) CENTERS FOR DISEASE CONTROL:
www.cdc.gov/nchs (800)232-4636
National Clearinghouse for Long-Term Care Information:
www.longtermcare.gov (202)619-0724
National Conference of State Legislators: www.ncsl.org/programs/health/
forum/caregiversupport.htm
"Own Your Future" Federal Long-Term Care Consumer website
www.longtermcare.gov
Thomas Library of Congress (legislation website): http://thomas.loc.gov

Urban Institute (long-term care government research):
    www.urban.org/health/index.cfm (202)833-7200
U.S. Administration on Aging: www.aoa.gov (202)619-0724
U.S. Census Bureau: www.census.gov
U.S. Government Accountability Office: www.gao.gov (202)512-3000. Report
    Order Line (202)512-6000

Health Care
Agency for Health Care Research and Quality: www.ahrq.gov (301)427-1104
American Psychological Association: www.apa.org (800)374-2721
Kaiser Family Foundation: www.kff.org

Health Insurance and Benefits
America's Health Insurance Plans: www.ahip.net (202)778-3200
Benefits Checkup–The National Council on the Aging:
    www.benefitscheckup.org
National Association of Health Underwriters: www.nahu.org

Home Care and Hospice Resources
Administration on Aging - Adult Day Care Resources:
http://www.eldercare.gov/Eldercare.NET/Public/Index.aspx
    (800)677-1116
American Senior Services, Inc., True Freedom Home Care Service Plans (not
    insurance) www.truefreedomhomecare.com, 888-245-9001
Home Care Compare: http://www.medicare.gov/homehealthcompare/search.aspx
HOMECARE Online: www.nahc.org (website for the National Assoc. for
    Home Care)
Pace Program (Program for All Inclusive Care for the Elderly) www.
    NPAOnline.org (703)535-1565
Right at Home: www.rightathome.net (877) 697-7537
Visiting Nurse Associations of America: www.vnaa.org (202)384-1420

Life Settlements
Life and Viatical Settlements: Asset Servicing Group – www.theasg.net
    (405)753-9100
Life Insurance Settlement Association: www.lisassociation.org (407)894-3797
Life Settlements: Ashar Group, LLC- www.ashargroupllc.com (800)384-8080
Magna Life Settlements: www.magnalifesettlements.com

Long-Term Care

AARP's Public Policy Institute Questions & Answers on Medicaid Estate
Recovery for Long-Term Care Under OBRA '93, 888-OUR-AARP
or online at www.aarp.org/health/medicare-insurance/info-1996/
aresearch-import-629-D16443.html

3in4 Need More – Long-Term Care Planning for Seniors:
www.3in4needmore.com

A New Purpose: Redefining Money, Family, Work, Retirement, and Success. 2009.
Authored by Kenneth Dychtwald, PhD. Major (bookstores/Internet.)
http://www.agewave.com/media/publication_books.php

MetLife Mature Market Institute: www.maturemarketinstitute.com annual
cost of LTC care surveys

The Notebook, Nicholas Sparks (a long-term care love story—major
bookstores, internet)

Long-Term Care Insurance

The ABC's of Long-Term Care Insurance, Author, Phyllis Shelton, www.
ltcconsultants.com, (888)400-1118

LTC Consultants: LTCI Sales and Marketing Tools for Financial Professionals
www.ltcconsultants.com

American Association for Long-Term Care Insurance:
www.aaltci.org/consumer

American Council of Life Insurance - "Passing the Trust to Private Long-Term
Care Insurance", January 2003, www.acli.com,
202-624-2000 (There are other important reports at this site.)

Center for Long-Term Care Reform: www.centerltc.com

Life Foundation: http://www.lifehappens.org/long-term-care-insurance-
introduction/

Prescription Drug Information and Assistance

Medicare Part D Information: www.medicare.gov (800) MEDICARE

The Medicine Program: www.themedicineprogram.com

Prescription Assistance Programs: www.disabilityresources.org/RX.html

Reverse Mortgage Resources

Department of Housing and Urban Development: http://www.hud.gov
(202) 708-1112

National Reverse Mortgage Lenders Association: www.reversemortgage.org

Reverse Mortgage Information: www.reversemortgage.com
Reverse Mortgage information: www.reversemortgagenation.com

Senior/Elder Care Information

AARP Public Policy Institute: www.aarp.org/research or
    www.research.aarp.org/ppi (888)687-2277
Elder HelpLine: (800)262-2243
Eldercare Facilities: www.eldercarelink.com
Eldercare Locator: www.eldercare.gov (800)677-1116
ElderCare Online: www.ec-online.net
ElderWeb Online Eldercare Sourcebook: www.eldercareweb.com or
    www.elderweb.com
Gerontological Society of America: www.geron.org (202)842-1275
National Council on Aging: www.ncoa.org (202)479-1200
PACE (Program for All Inclusive Care for the Elderly):
    http://www.cms.hhs.gov/pace/

SOURCES

Preface

1. Alonzo-Zaldivar, Ricardo. "Demise of Obama Plan Leaves Gap", *The Washington Times*, October 24, 2011
2. Based on an average 6% compound growth rate between $56 daily cost in 1987 compared to $222 in 2012. Source for 1987 costs: Medical Expenditure Panel Survey (MEPS) Chartbook #6 "Nursing Home Expenses 1987-1996", Agency for Health Care Research and Quality, p. 6. Source for 2012 cost of care: *Market Survey of Long-Term Care Costs*, MetLife, November 2012, p.4.
3. Kaye, H. Stephen, Charlene Harrington, and Mitchell P. LaPlante. "Long-Term Care: Who Gets It, Who Provides It, Who Pays, And How Much?" *Health Affairs,* January 2010 29:11-21 (Less than 15% of LTC is in a nursing home and 42% of people who need LTC are under 65)
4. National Center for Health Statistics. *Health, United States, 2011: With Special Feature on Socioeconomic Status and Health*. Hyattsville, MD. 2012, Table 145, p. 412.
5. *The 2012-2013 Sourcebook for Long-Term Care Insurance Information*, American Association for Long-Term Care Insurance, pp. 22, 34.

Chapter One: It's Not All About You

1. Kaye, H. Stephen, Charlene Harrington, and Mitchell P. LaPlante. "Long-Term Care: Who Gets It, Who Provides It, Who Pays, and How Much?" *Health Affairs,* January 2010 29:1, p. 13.
2. Maker, Scott. "Protecting the Earning Power of American Workers", *Benefits Selling*, June 2012, p. 84
3. Centers for Disease Control and Prevention Stroke Facts, updated 12/9/11
4. Marchione, Marilynn. *"Strokes are Rising Fast Among Young, Middle-Aged"*, American Stroke Association conference, February 10, 2011, www.strokeconference.org
5. *Ibid*
6. Hellmich, Nanci. "Percentage of Severely Obese Adults Skyrockets", *USA Today,* 10/1/12
7. Begley, Sharon. "Fat and Getting Fatter: U.S. Obesity Rates to Soar by 2030", Reuters, 9/18/12.
8. Behan, Donald F. and Samuel Cox. "Obesity and Its Relation to Mortality and Morbidity Costs", Society of Actuaries, December 2010, pp. 52 and 59.
9. *Ibid*, abstract.
10. 2010 LTCI Sourcebook, American Association of Long-Term Care Insurance, p. 25

11. Morgan, Chris. Genworth LTCi Claims Experience Data, December 2009 Update, 2010, pp. 2, 3, 5

12. *MetLife Market Study of Long-Term Care Costs*, November, 2012.

13. Based on an average 6% compound growth rate between $56 daily cost in 1987 compared to $222 in 2012. Source for 1987 costs: Medical Expenditure Panel Survey (MEPS) Chartbook #6 "Nursing Home Expenses 1987-1996", Agency for Health Care Research and Quality, p. 6. Source for 2012 cost of care: *MetLife Market Study of Long-Term Care Costs*, November, 2012.

14. Rix, Sara E. "Recovering from the Great Recession: Long Struggle Ahead for Older Americans", Insight on the Issues 50, AARP Public Policy Institute, May 2011, p. 7

15. The 3% is based on about 8 million long-term care insurance policies in force (2011 National Association of Insurance Commissioners Long-Term Care Experience Reporting, Form 1, plus 2012 sales vs. 230 million people in the United States over age 18 (Census Bureau).

16. Rix, Sara E. "Recovering from the Great Recession: Long Struggle Ahead for Older Americans", Insight on the Issues 50, AARP Public Policy Institute, May 2011, p. 11

17. "Long-Term Care Insurance: A Piece of the Retirement & Estate Planning Puzzle", The Prudential Insurance Company of America, 0193261-00001-00, 2011, p. 6

18. Table 6.8 - Number and Distribution of Covered Admissions for Medicare Beneficiaries Admitted to Skilled Nursing Facilities (SNF), by the Leading Principal Diagnoses: Calendar Years 1998, 2003, 2010, Center for Medicare and Medicaid Services, 2011 Statistical Supplement, www.CMS.gov

19. "National Spending for Long-Term Services and Supports", National Health Policy Forum, The George Washington University, Washington DC, February 2012, p. 3

20. "The Fiscal Survey of States", National Association of State Budget Officers, Spring, 2012, p. 53

21. "The Medicaid Program at a Glance", Kaiser Commission on Medicaid and the Uninsured, September 2012 (30% today); "Medicaid Long-Term Care: The Ticking Time Bomb", Deloitte Center for Health Solutions, June 21, 2010 (50% by 2030)

22. Oliff, Phil, Chris Mai, Vincent Palacios. "States Continue to Feel Recession's Impact", Centers on Budget and Policy Priorities", June 2012, p. 1

23. *Ibid,* p. 6

24. *Ibid*

25. "The Employment Situation – September 2012", Bureau of Labor Statistics News Release, 10/5/12

26. "5 Key Questions About Medicaid and Its Role in State/Federal Budgets & Health Reform", Kaiser Commission on Medicaid and the Uninsured, May 2012, p. 2

27. "Medicaid and CHIP in 2014: Eligibility Final Rule Wrap Up", Center for Medicaid and CHIP Services, May 10, 2012, p. 1

28. Vicini, James. "States Oppose Obama Healthcare Law", Reuters Business and Financial News, January 10, 2012. (Supreme Court cases were National Federation of Independent Business v. Sebelius, No. 11-393; U.S. Department of Health and Human Services v. Florida, No. 11-398; and Florida v. Department of Health and Human Services, No. 11-400)

29. NATIONAL FEDERATION OF INDEPENDENT BUSINESS ET AL. *v.* SEBELIUS, SECRETARY OF HEALTH AND HUMAN SERVICES, ET AL. No. 11–393. CERTIORARI TO THE UNITED STATES COURT OF APPEALS FOR THE ELEVENTH CIRCUIT, Argued March 26, 27, 28, 2012—Decided June 28, 2012 http://www.supremecourt.gov/opinions/11pdf/11-393c3a2.pdf

30. "Who Buys Long-Term Care Insurance in 2010/2011?" (Washington, DC: AHIP, March 2012), Figure 17, p. 41.

31. Valdez, Linda. "Caregivers are Bracing for Baby Boomer Tsunami", *The Arizona Republic*, June 5, 2010.

32. *Caregiving in America*, International Longevity Center – USA and Schmieding Center for Senior Health and Education, p. 1

33. Francese, Peter. "Baby Boomers Will Transform This (Late) American Life", *Aging Today*, July-August, 2012, p. 15

34. Korn, Donald Jay. "Stuck in the Middle: Boomers Delaying Retirement to Help Kids, Parents", *Financial Planning*, May 29, 2012

35. Adams, Susan. "The Prophet of the Coming Age Boom", *Forbes,* May 19, 2011

36. Social Security Administration life expectancy calculator http://www.ssa.gov/planners/lifeexpectancy.htm

37. Francese, Peter. "Baby Boomers Will Transform This (Late) American Life", *Aging Today*, July-August, 2012, p. 7

38. Census Bureau 100+ projections

39. *Smiler* magazine (Rod Stewart quote)

40. Mature Services, Inc. http://matureservices.org/

41. "Manhattan Project Chemist Helped Build the A Bomb", *Los-Angeles Times,* July 30, 2005.

42. Nola Ochs, Wikopedia entry and Ft. Hayes State University Department of History newsletter, November 18, 2011.

43. Blumenthal, Ralph. "She Knows a Thing or Two About Aging", *The New York Times,* July 7, 2009.

44. "Table 1. Civilian labor force, by age, sex, race, and ethnicity, 1990, 2000, 2010, and projected 2020", Bureau of Labor Statistics

45. Cheryl Matheis, Senior Vice President, AARP, NPR Interview, May 1, 2012

46. "Caregiving in the U.S. 2009", National Alliance for Caregiving/AARP, November 2009, p. 14

47. "Table 1. Civilian labor force by age, sex, race, and Hispanic origin, 1998, 2008, 2010 and projected 2020", Bureau of Labor Statistics

48. Long-Term Care Insurance Carriers Cost of Care Surveys, 2012.

49. Shelton, Phyllis. **The ABCs of Long-Term Care Insurance,** LTCi Publishing, 2013, p. 6

50. *Ibid,* p. 7

51. Samson, Richard. "The LTC Benefit Battle", *Employee Benefit Advisor,* July 1, 2012

52. "America Talks: Protecting Our Families' Financial Futures", a national survey conducted by Age Wave/Harris Interactive, sponsored by Genworth Financial, March 2010.

Chapter Two: So You Think You Can Self-Insure For LTC?

1. Based on an average 6% compound growth rate between $56 daily cost in 1987 compared to $222 in 2012. Source for 1987 costs: Medical Expenditure Panel Survey (MEPS) Chartbook #6 "Nursing Home Expenses 1987-1996", Agency for Health Care Research and Quality, p. 6. Source for 2012 cost of care: *Market Survey of Long-Term Care Costs,* MetLife, November 2012, p.4.

2. "Health Care Costs in Retirement Consumer Study", Nationwide Financial February, 2012, p. 6

3. "About Social Security and Medicare", Social Security benefits statement available at www.ssa.gov, p. 4.

4. "Study: Nearly Half of Soon-to-be-Retired, High-Net-Worth Americans 'Terrified' of Health Care Costs in Retirement", Nationwide Financial Press Release, May 7, 2012.

5. *Ibid*

6. Society of Actuaries LTC Experience Intercompany Study, 1984-2007, Appendix E-1, June 2011. http://www.soa.org/Research/Experience-Study/ltc/research-ltc-study-1984-report.aspx

7. Calculated with LTC Economic Impact Planning Model™ Patent 7,328,183

8. Public Law 104-191, Title III, Subtitle C, Section 321(C)

9. Pension Protection Act of 2006, Public Law 109-280, Section 844(a) and (b)

10. Based on an average 6% compound growth rate between $56 daily cost in 1987 compared to $222 in 2012. Source for 1987 costs: Medical Expenditure Panel Survey (MEPS) Chartbook #6 "Nursing Home Expenses 1987-1996", Agency for Health Care Research and Quality, p. 6. Source for 2012 cost of care: *Market Survey of Long-Term Care Costs,* MetLife, November 2012, p.4.

11. Pension Protection Act of 2006, Public Law 109-280, Section 844(a) and (b)

12. Society of Actuaries LTCI Experience Committee Intercompany Study, 1984-2007, Appendix E-1, 2011

13. "Combination Life Insurance Product Sales Rise at 'Remarkable Rate'", *Insurance & Financial Advisor,* May 23, 2012

Chapter Three: The Ins and Outs of LTC Insurance

1. Ujvari, Kathleen. "Long-Term Care Insurance 2012 Update", AARP Public Policy Institute, 2012, p. 1, and Current Population Reports, Census Bureau.
2. Based on an average 6% compound growth rate between $56 daily cost in 1987 compared to $222 in 2012. Source for 1987 costs: Medical Expenditure Panel Survey (MEPS) Chartbook #6 "Nursing Home Expenses 1987-1996", Agency for Health Care Research and Quality, p. 6. Source for 2012 cost of care: *Market Survey of Long-Term Care Costs*, MetLife, November 2012, p.4.
3. *Ibid*
4. U.S. Department Of Labor, Bureau of Labor Statistics, Consumer Price Index, All Urban Consumers - (CPI-U), U. S. City Average, All Items, 1913-2011 (accessed December 31, 2012)
5. Premium study conducted by *LTC Consultants*, Fall, 2012.
6. Society of Actuaries LTC Experience Intercompany Study, 1984-2007, Appendix E-1, June 2011. http://www.soa.org/Research/Experience-Study/ltc/research-ltc-study-1984-report.aspx
7. Alzheimer's Association www.alz.org

Chapter Four: Where the Rubber Hits the Road

1. Thau, Claude, Dawn Helwig and Allen Schmitz. "2012 Long-Term Care Insurance Survey", *Broker World*, pp. 8-9 (of the article).
2. *LTC Consultants'* worksite enrollments, including the State of Tennessee, a 143,000 employee group
3. "Who Buys Long-Term Care Insurance in 2010-2011?" America's Health Insurance Plans (AHIP), March 22, 2012 (Reports/Research/White Papers: www.ahip.org), p. 11
4. *LTC Consultants* rate survey, September 2012.
5. *Ibid*
6. Thau, Claude, Dawn Helwig and Allen Schmitz. "2012 Long-Term Care Insurance Survey", *Broker World*, p. 13 (of the article) and "The 2012-2013 Sourcebook for Long-Term Care Insurance Information", American Association of Long-Term Care Insurance, p. 2
7. Kaiser Foundation Medicare Primer, 2010
8. Orman, Suze. **The Money Class: Learn to Create Your New American Dream",** Spiegel & Grau, New York, 2011, p. 235
9. Orman, Suze. "Suze Orman Reflects on a Missed Investment", *Chicago Sun-Times,* August 20, 2012.
10. Ujvari, Kathleen. "Long-Term Care Insurance 2012 Update", AARP Public Policy Institute, 2012, p. 2
11. Sisk, Richard. "Census: A Half Million Centenarians by 2050", New York Daily News, April 25, 2011
12. Bell, Allison. "NAIC Panel Calls for LTCI Model Rate Stability Updates", *LifeHealthPro,* August 14, 2012

13. Florida SB2290/HB1329, 2006
14. California AB 999 http://legiscan.com/CA/text/AB999/id/663337
15. South Carolina proposal to amend State Regulation 69-44 as published in the South Carolina *State Register* on May 25, 2012 and at www.scstatehouse.gov/regnsrch.pdp
16. 2010 LTCI Sourcebook, American Association of Long-Term Care Insurance
17. "Diabetes Statistics", American Diabetes Association, accessed January 2, 2013.
18. "A1C" Lab Tests Online http://labtestsonline.org/understanding/analytes/a1c/tab/test
19. Stallard, Eric. "The Impact of Obesity and Diabetes on LTC Disability and Mortality", *Long-Term Care News*, September 2011, pp. 10, 12.
20. "Diabetes Statistics", American Diabetes Association, accessed January 2, 2013.
21. Cawley, John and Chad Cawley, John and Chad Meyerhoefer. "The Medical Care Costs of Obesity: An instrumental variables approach" *Journal of Health Economics,* Volume 31, Issue 1, January 2012, Pages 219-230
22. "Fact Sheet: The Genetic Information Nondiscrimination Act (GINA)", National Institutes of Health, updated October 2010, p. 2
23. Thau, Claude, Dawn Helwig and Allen Schmitz. "2012 Long Term Care Insurance Survey", Broker World, July 2012
24. National Association of Insurance Commissioners LTCI Experience Report, 2012
25. 2012-2013 LTCI Sourcebook, American Association of Long-Term Care Insurance and NAIC 2011 Long-Term Care Insurance Experience Reporting – Form 1
26. 2010 LTCI Sourcebook, American Association of Long-Term Care Insurance
27. Personal client story used with permission of Randall Keith, son of Ella and Fred Keith
28. "Lifetime Chance of Using Policy Benefits", *The 2012-2013 Sourcebook for Long-Term Care Insurance Information*, American Association for Long-Term Care Insurance, p. 31.

Chapter Five: Employers: Why You Have to Lead, Not Follow

1. industry sales statistics based on the sum of multi-life and true group sales divided by total sales
2. "Caregiving in the U.S. 2009", National Alliance for Caregiving/AARP, November 2009, p. 4
3. *Ibid*, p. 14
4. *Ibid*, p. 20
5. *Ibid*, p. 11
6. *Ibid*, p. 50
7. "The MetLife Study of Caregiving Costs to Working Caregivers", MetLife Mature Market Institute, June 2011, p. 2

8. *Ibid*, p. 7
9. Inskeep, Steve interview with Cheryl Matheis, SVP AARP. "Workers Turned Caregivers Lose More Than Wages", NPR, May 1, 2012
10. "Table 1. Civilian labor force, by age, sex, race, and ethnicity, 1990, 2000, 2010, and projected 2020", Bureau of Labor Statistics
11. "The MetLife Study of Caregiving Costs to Working Caregivers", MetLife Mature Market Institute, June 2011, p. 4
12. "Table 1. Civilian labor force, by age, sex, race, and ethnicity, 1990, 2000, 2010, and projected 2020", Bureau of Labor Statistics
13. "Caregiving in the U.S. 2009", National Alliance for Caregiving/AARP, November 2009, p. 14
14. "Online Alzheimer's Course Offers Relief for Caregivers", *Aging Today*, July-August 2012, p. 15
15. "Caregiving in the U.S. 2009", National Alliance for Caregiving/AARP, November 2009
16. *Ibid*, p. 54
17. "The MetLife Study of Caregiving Costs to Working Caregivers", MetLife Mature Market Institute, June 2011, p. 10
18. "Caregiving in the U.S. 2009", National Alliance for Caregiving/AARP, November 2009, p. 23
19. "The MetLife Study of Caregiving Costs to Working Caregivers", MetLife Mature Market Institute, June 2011, p. 10
20. "Caregiving in the U.S. 2009", National Alliance for Caregiving/AARP, November 2009, p. 17
21. *Ibid*, p. 21
22. *Ibid*, pp. 28,29
23. *Ibid*, pp. 52,53
24. *Ibid*, p. 54
25. *Ibid*, p. 55
26. *Ibid*, p. 28
27. *Ibid*, p. 15
28. "Who Buys LTCI and Why", AALTCI 9th Long-Term Care Insurance Producers Summit, Session LTC-944, April 4, 2011 (LifePlans, Inc.)
29. Shelton, Phyllis. **The ABCs of Long Term Care Insurance**, LTCi Publishing, 2013, p. 14
30. "The Growth in Employer-Sponsored LTCI", Center for Insurance Education, America's Health Insurance Plans, July 30, 2008, p. 7
31. "The MetLife Study of Caregiving Costs to Working Caregivers", MetLife Mature Market Institute, June 2011, p. 3
32. "The MetLife Study of Working Caregivers and Employer Health Care Costs", MetLife Mature Market Institute, February 2010, p. 4

33. "8th and 9th Annual Study of Employee Benefit Trends", MetLife, 3/10, p. 8 and 3/11, p. 10

34. "6th Annual Study of Employee Benefit Trends", MetLife, March 2008, p. 25

35. "America Talks: Protecting Our Families' Financial Futures", a national survey conducted by Age Wave/Harris Interactive, sponsored by Genworth Financial, March 2010

36. "The Employment Situation – September 2012", Bureau of Labor Statistics News Release, October 5, 2012..

37. "Table 42. Health-related benefits: Access, civilian workers, National Compensation Survey, March 2012", Bureau of Labor Statistics.

38. "Number of Firms, Number of Establishments, Employment, and Annual Payroll by Enterprise Employment Size for the United States and States, Totals: 2010", U.S. Census Bureau.

39. 2011 industry sales statistics

40. "Who Buys LTCI and Why", AALTCI 9th Long-Term Care Insurance Producers Summit, Session LTC-944, April 4, 2011 (LifePlans, Inc.)

41. Mulvey, Janemarie and Kim Colello. "Community Living Assistance Services and Supports (CLASS) Provisions in the Patient Protection and Affordable Care Act (PPACA)", Congressional Research Service, May 13, 2011, p. 14

42. *Market Survey of Long-Term Care Costs*, MetLife, November 2012, p.4.

43. Medical Expenditure Panel Survey (MEPS) Chartbook #6 "Nursing Home Expenses 1987-1996", Agency for Research and Quality, p. 6

44. American Association for Long-Term Care Insurance, 2011 LTCi Sourcebook, (www.aaltci.org), p. 16

45. Kaye, H. Stephen, Charlene Harrington, and Mitchell P. LaPlante. "Long-Term Care: Who Gets It, Who Provides It, Who Pays, and How Much?" *Health Affairs,* January 2010 29:1, p. 13.

46. Orman, Suze. **The Money Class**, Spiegel & Grau, a div of Random House, Inc., NY, NY, 2011, p. 235

47. Kaye, H. Stephen, Charlene Harrington, and Mitchell P. LaPlante. "Long-Term Care: Who Gets It, Who Provides It, Who Pays, and How Much?" *Health Affairs,* January 2010 29:1, p. 13.

48. Maker, Scott. "Protecting the Earning Power of American Workers", *Benefits Selling,* June 2012

49. *Ibid*

50. "Critical Findings in Long Term Care Insurance Buyer and Non-Buyer Behavior", The 11th Annual Intercompany LTCI Conference, March 8, 2011, slide 10 (LifePlans, Inc.)

51. "Who Buys Long-Term Care Insurance in 2010-2011?" America's Health Insurance Plans (AHIP), March 22, 2012 (Reports/Research/White Papers: www.ahip.org),

52. "2012-2013 LTCI Sourcebook", American Association of Long-Term Care Insurance and NAIC 2011 Long-Term Care Insurance Experience Reporting – Form 1

53. Sammer, Joanne. "Financial Education – Stress = Improved Productivity", *HR Magazine*, 6/1/12, p. 72

54. "Healthcare Costs in Retirement – Consumer Study February 2012", Nationwide/Harris Interactive

Chapter Six: Alternatives to LTC Insurance

1. Case study provided by Asset Servicing Group (theasg.net)

2. Alzheimer's Association. 2012 Alzheimer's disease facts and figures. *Alzheimer's and Dementia: The Journal of the Alzheimer's Association*. March 2012; p. 142

3. Geffner, Marcie. "Real Estate: Reverse Mortgages Become Affordable", bankrate.com, January 6, 2011.

4. Tergesen, Anne. "The Reverse Mortgage Gets a Makeover", *Wall St. Journal*, January 8, 2011

5. Interview with Barb Stucki, CEO of NestCare FPA and formerly the reverse mortgage authority for the National Council on Aging, January 25, 2013.

6. Department of Housing and Urban Development Mortgagee Letter 2012-26, December 6, 2012

7. Interview with Barb Stucki, CEO of NestCare FPA and formerly the reverse mortgage authority for the National Council on Aging, January 25, 2013.

8. Bernard, Tara Siegel. "Two Big Banks Exit Reverse Mortgage Business", *Bloomberg News*, New York edition, June 18, 2011, p. B1.

9. Silver-Greenberg, Jessica. "A Risky Lifeline for the Elderly is Costing Some Their Homes", *The New York Times,* October 14, 2012

10. *Ibid*

11. Lieber, Ron. "A Red Flag on Reverse Mortgages", *The New York Times,* March 11, 2011

12. "HUD Targeted in Suit for Illegal Reverse Mortgage Foreclosure Actions", AARP Press Release, March 8, 2011.

13. Interview with Barb Stucki, CEO of NestCare FPA and formerly the reverse mortgage authority for the National Council on Aging, June 4, 2011

14. Lieber, Ron. "A Red Flag on Reverse Mortgages", *The New York Times,* March 11, 2011

15. "AARP Lawsuit: Reverse Mortgages Cause Foreclosures", *Reuters Wealth*, March 11, 2011.

16. Tergesen, Anne. "The Reverse Mortgage Gets a Makeover", *Wall St. Journal,* January 8, 2011

17. Peter Bell, President and CEO of the Reverse Mortgage Lenders Association, December 8, 2012
18. The Housing Economic and Recovery Act of 2008, Section 2122 Home Equity Conversion Mortgages
19. "Just the FAQs: Answers to Common Questions about Reverse Mortgages", National Reverse Mortgage Lenders Association, 2011, p. 11.
20. http://www.reversemortgage.org/YourRoadmap/Counseling.aspx
21. "Continuing Care Retirement Communities: Risks to Seniors", U.S. Senate Special Committee on Aging, July 21, 2010 http://aging.senate.gov/events/hr224cr.pdf
22. 2010 National Health Expenditures, Centers for Medicare and Medicaid Services, published January, 2012
23. Long-Term Care Insurance Carrier Cost of Care Surveys, 2012

Chapter Seven: People Who Do Not Qualify for Long-Term Care Insurance

1. "National Spending for Long-Term Services and Supports", National Health Policy Forum, The George Washington University, Washington DC, February 2012, p. 3
2. *Ibid*
3. "Medicaid Home and Community Based Services Program: Data Update", Kaiser Commission on Medicaid and the Uninsured, December 2011, p. 2.
4. The Deficit Reduction Act of 2005, Public Law 109-171, enacted February 8, 2006, Section 6014 (substantial home equity)
5. The Deficit Reduction Act of 2005, Public Law 109-171, enacted February 8, 2006, Section 6013 (income first rule)
6. *Wisconsin Dept. of Health and Family Services v. Blumer,* Supreme Court of the United States, 00-952, February 20, 2002.
7. Tennessee Supreme Court, (M2009-02107-SC-R11-CV 5/30/12.
8. Interview with Barb Stucki, CEO of NestCare, FPC (formerly reverse mortgage authority for the National Council on Aging), January 25, 2013
9. "Most Frequently Asked Questions-Social Security and Medicare", National Reverse Mortgage Lenders Association, www.reversemortgage.org
10. Interview with Barb Stucki, CEO of NestCare, FPC (formerly reverse mortgage authority for the National Council on Aging), December 9, 2012.
11. *Ibid*
12. The Deficit Reduction Act of 2005, Public Law 109-171, enacted February 8, 2006, Section 6014 (substantial home equity)
13. Ohlemacher, Stephen. "Social Security Now Pays Out Less Than People Pay In", *The Tennessean*, pp. 1,7A
14. The Deficit Reduction Act of 2005, Public Law 109-171, enacted February 8, 2006, Section 6011 (lengthening look-back period; change in beginning date for period of ineligibility)
15. *Ibid*

16. The Deficit Reduction Act of 2005, Public Law 109-171, enacted February 8, 2006, Section 6016d (life estates)

17. The Deficit Reduction Act of 2005, Public Law 109-171, enacted February 8, 2006, Section 6012c (balloon annuities)

18. The Deficit Reduction Act of 2005, Public Law 109-171, enacted February 8, 2006, Section 6012b (requirement for state to be named as remainder beneficiary)

19. Macgillivray, Mark. "A Closer Look at the Medicaid SPIA Marketplace", *LifeHealthPro*, September 24, 2012

20. Tax Relief and Health Care Act of 2006, H.R. 6111, enacted December 20, 2006, Section 405, CERTAIN MEDICAID DRA TECHNICAL CORRECTIONS, "Clarifying Treatment of Certain Annuities (Section 6012)".

21. "National Spending for Long-Term Services and Supports", National Health Policy Forum, The George Washington University, Washington DC, February 2012, p. 3

22. *Ibid*, p. 4

23. "Medicaid and Long-Term Care Services and Supports", Kaiser Commission on Medicaid and the Uninsured, Medicaid Facts, March 2011, p. 2

24. "Weathering the Storm: The Impact of the Great Recession on Long-Term Services and Supports", AARP Public Policy Institute in conjunction with Health Management Associates and National Association of States United for Aging and Disabilities", January 2011, pp. 23-24

25. Houser, Ari. Kathleen Ujvari and Wendy Fox-Grage. "Across the States 2012: Profiles of Long-Term Services and Supports", AARP Public Policy Institute, p. 12

26. "Weathering the Storm: The Impact of the Great Recession on Long-Term Services and Supports", AARP Public Policy Institute in conjunction with Health Management Associates and National Association of States United for Aging and Disabilities", January 2011, p. 26

27. "Medicaid Home and Community-Based Services Programs", Kaiser Commission on Medicaid and the Uninsured, December 2012, p. 3.

28. Kaye, H. Stephen, Charlene Harrington, and Mitchell P. LaPlante. "Long-Term Care: Who Gets It, Who Provides It, Who Pays, and How Much?" *Health Affairs*, January 2010 29:1, p. 13.

29. Ujvari, Kathleen. "Long-Term Care Insurance 2012 Update", AARP Public Policy Institute, 2012, pp. 1-2.

30. Guttchen, David J. "Quarterly Statistics for the Connecticut Partnership for Long-Term Care", January 24, 2013, p. 1.

31. California, Connecticut, Indiana and New York Long-Term Care Partnership websites plus personal correspondence with Partnership directors in November 2012

32. Research the author did for LTCiTraining.com

33. Pearson, Katherine C., "Filial Support Laws in the Modern Era: Domestic and International Comparison of Enforcement Practices for Laws Requiring Adult Children to Support Indigent Parents" (2012), p. 21. *Scholarly Works*. Paper 35. http://elibrary.law.psu.edu/fac_works/35

34. Greene, Kelly. "Are You on the Hook for Mom's Nursing Home Bill?" *Wall St. Journal*, June 22, 2012.

Chapter Eight – The M & Ms of Medicare

1. "Long-Term Care Insurance: A Piece of the Retirement & Estate Planning Puzzle", The Prudential Insurance Company of America, 0193261-00001-00, 2011, p. 6

2. Graham, Judith. "The High Cost of Out-of-Pocket Expenses", *The New York Times,* September 21, 2012, p. 1.

3. The George Washington University, National Health Policy Forum, "National Spending for Long-Term Services and Supports (LTSS)" (Washington, DC: The George Washington University, February 2012), p. 3

4. Terry Savage, Syndicated Financial Columnist and author of **The New Savage Number: How Much Money Do You Need to Retire?** John Wiley & Sons, Inc, 2009 and **The Savage Truth on Money**, John Wiley & Sons, Inc., 2011.

5. Powell, Robert. "Get Ready for Social Security, Medicare Meltdowns", *MarketWatch*, May 19, 2011

6. Buckner, Gail. "A Harsh Retirement Reality Check", *Fox Business* reporting on the Employee Benefits Research Institute's 2010 Retirement Confidence Survey, www.ebri.org.

7. LTCI Carriers Cost of Care Surveys, 2012

8. "Medicare Spending and Financing", Kaiser Family Foundation Medicare Policy Fact Sheet, November 2012, p. 2.

9. *Jimmo vs. Sebelius,* CA, No. 5:11-CV-17-CR (D. VT, filed January 18, 2011; proposed settlement agreement filed 10/16/2012)

10. *Jimmo vs. Sebelius*, Center for Medicare Advocacy, 11/20/12 (www.medicareadvocacy.org).

11. "Medicare At A Glance", Kaiser Family Foundation Fact Sheet, November 2012, p. 2.

12. "2012 Choosing a MediGap Policy", Centers for Medicare and Medicaid Services, p. 11

13. "Employer Health Benefits: 2012 Annual Survey", Kaiser Family Foundation, p. 11, Exhibit 11.1

14. Vice President, Product Management, Bankers Life and Casualty, January 4, 2013.

15. *Mutual of Omaha Express* (agent newsletter) December 17, 2012

16. Graham, Judith. "The High Cost of Out-of-Pocket Expenses", *The New York Times,* September 21, 2012, p. 2.

17. "Medicare At A Glance", Kaiser Family Foundation Fact Sheet, November 2012, p. 2

18. LTC insurance carriers cost of care surveys, 2012

19. "The Medicare Prescription Drug Benefit", Kaiser Family Foundation, November 2012

20. Medicare Advantage Fact Sheet, Kaiser Family Foundation, December 2012, p. 2

21. *Ibid*, p. 1

22. Gold, Marsha, et al. "Medicare Advantage 2013 Spotlight: Plan Availability and Premiums", December 2012, p. 1

23. *Ibid*, p. 7

24. *Ibid*, p. 2 and Medicare Advantage Fact Sheet, Kaiser Family Foundation, December 2012, p. 1

25. "Employer Health Benefits: 2012 Annual Survey, Exhibit 5.1", The Kaiser Family Foundation and Health Research and Educational Trust, September 2012, p. 72

26. "Medicare at a Glance", Kaiser Family Foundation, December 2012, p. 1

27. "The Medicare Prescription Drug Benefit", Kaiser Family Foundation, November 2012, p.2

28. *Ibid*, p. 1

29. *Ibid*, p. 1

30. Medicare Advantage Fact Sheet, Kaiser Family Foundation, December 2012, p. 2

31. "The Medicare Prescription Drug Benefit", Kaiser Family Foundation, November 2012, p.2

32. Takacs, Tim. *The Elder Law Fax*, November 2012 www.tn-elderlaw.com/Publication/Elder_Law_Fax

33. Rau, Jordan. "Medicare Discloses Hospitals' Bonuses, Penalties Based on Quality", *Kaiser Health News,* December 20, 2012

34. Based on an average 6% compound growth rate between $56 daily cost in 1987 compared to $222 in 2012. Source for 1987 costs: Medical Expenditure Panel Survey (MEPS) Chartbook #6 "Nursing Home Expenses 1987-1996", Agency for Health Care Research and Quality, p. 6. Source for 2012 cost of care: *Market Survey of Long-Term Care Costs*, MetLife, November 2012, p.4.

35. Jaffe, Susan. "MediGap Policies Get Scrutiny from Officials Looking to Reduce Medicare Spending", *The Washington Post*, November 21, 2011